101 KRUGER TALES

D0807249

101 KRUGER TALES

EXTRAORDINARY STORIES FROM ORDINARY VISITORS TO THE KRUGER NATIONAL PARK

Compiled & Edited by
JEFF GORDON

LEADWOOD
Publishing

I would like to acknowledge all the Kruger National Park visitors who granted me permission to publish their true stories *(continued on page 352)*.

First published in South Africa by Leadwood Publishing in 2014.

5 7 9 10 8 6 4

Distributed by Struik Nature (an imprint of Penguin Random House South Africa (Pty) Ltd)
Reg. No. 1953/000441/07
The Estuaries No. 4, Oxbow Crescent, Century City, 7441 South Africa
PO Box 1144, Cape Town, 8000 South Africa
www.randomstruik.co.za

Printed and bound by Paarl Media, Western Cape, South Africa.

Copyright © in published edition, 2014: Jeff Gordon
Copyright © in introduction & other peripheral text, 2014: Jeff Gordon
Copyright © in stories, 2014: as credited on page 352
Copyright © in photographs, 2014: as credited on page 358

The permissions and picture credits at the back of the book constitute an extension of this copyright page.

The right of Jeff Gordon to be identified as the author of this Work has been asserted in accordance with the Copyright Act 98 of 1978.

No part of this publication may be reproduced, stored or introduced in a retrieval system, or transmitted, in any form, or by any means (electronic, mechanical, photocopying or otherwise) without the prior permission of the publisher.

Cover design by Kit Foster
Layout and typesetting by Grzegorz Laszczyk
Map design by Vlad Popon

ISBN 978-0-620-61132-9

Every effort has been taken to ensure that the vital contents of all the submitted stories included in this book are accurate, fair and truthful. I apologise for any errors, omissions, infringements or unintended statements possibly of a harmful nature within any of the stories or other parts of the book, including photographs. In the event of the above please notify corrections@krugertales.co.za and these will be rectified in future editions and listed at *www.krugertales.co.za/corrections*.

Got an extraordinary Kruger story of your own? Submit it for the next edition.
www.krugertales.co.za

To that dying breed of Kruger visitor: the one who still drives slowly, still raises a finger of greeting to every oncoming car and still stops to share, with barely concealed delight, what you may find in the shade of an umbrella thorn just a few kilometres down the road

CONTENTS

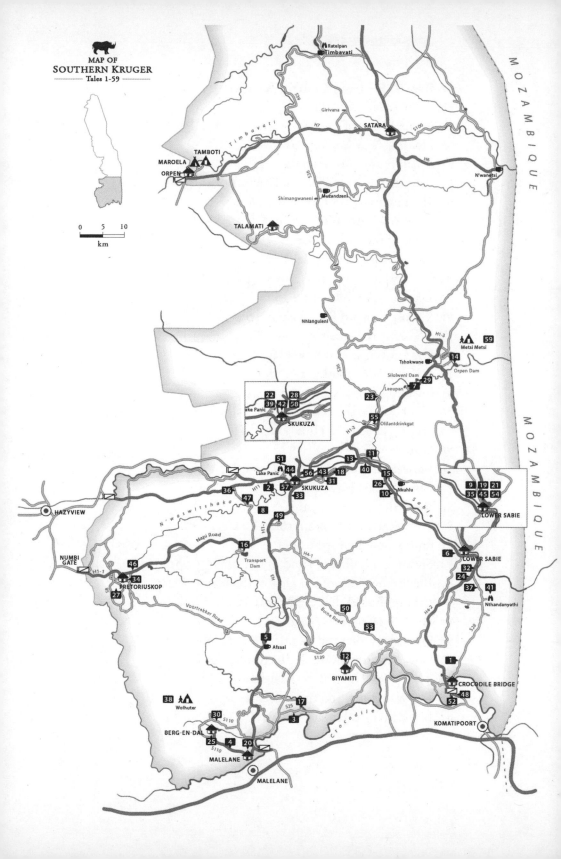

MAP OF SOUTHERN KRUGER
Tales 1-59

km
0   5   10

MOZAMBIQUE

Ratelpan
Timbavati

Girivana

SATARA

S100

H7

Timbavati

599

S95

H6

N'wanetsi

TAMBOTI
MAROELA
ORPEN

Shimangwaneni   Muzandzeni

TALAMATI

Nhlanguleni

H1-3

Metsi Metsi **59**

S125

Tshokwane **14**
Orpen Dam

Silolweni Dam
Leeupan **7** **29**

23

55 Olifantdrinkgat
H1-2

Lake Panic
22 **28**
39 **42** **50**
SKUKUZA

51
Lake Panic **44**
13 **11**
56 **43** **18**
40
15
26 Nkuhlu
10

9 **19** **21**
35 **45** **54**
LOWER SABIE

36
47 H1-1
2 **57**
8 SKUKUZA
33
31

HAZYVIEW

49

Napi Road

16
Transport
Dam

H4-1

6 LOWER SABIE

Sabie

NUMBI
GATE
H1-7

46
34
PRETORIUSKOP
27

32
24
37 **41**
Nthandanyathi

Voortrekker Road

Biene Road
50

53

H4-2

S28

5
Afsaal

S139

12
BIYAMITI

1

38
Wolhuter

30

S110

17

3

CROCODILE BRIDGE
48
52

BERG-EN-DAL
25 **4** **20**
MALELANE
S110

S25

Crocodile

KOMATIPOORT

MALELANE

Part Two: Tales from Central Kruger

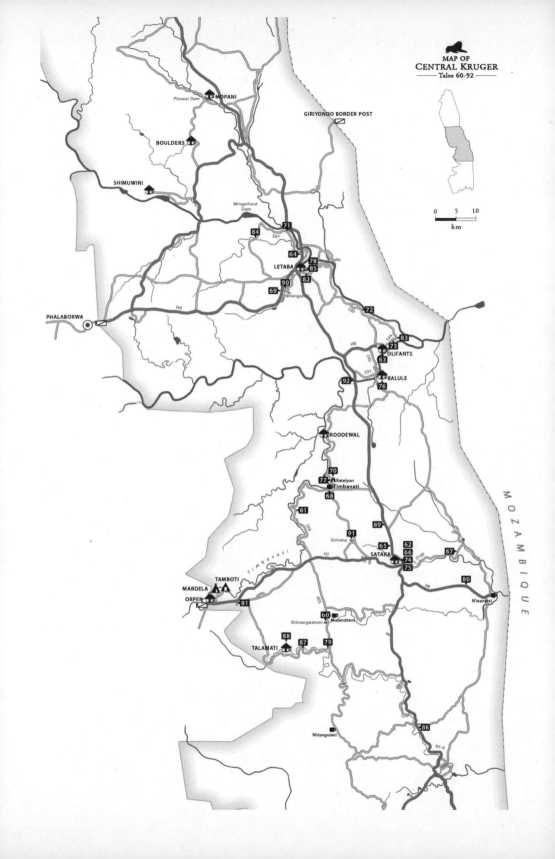

Part Three: Tales from Northern Kruger

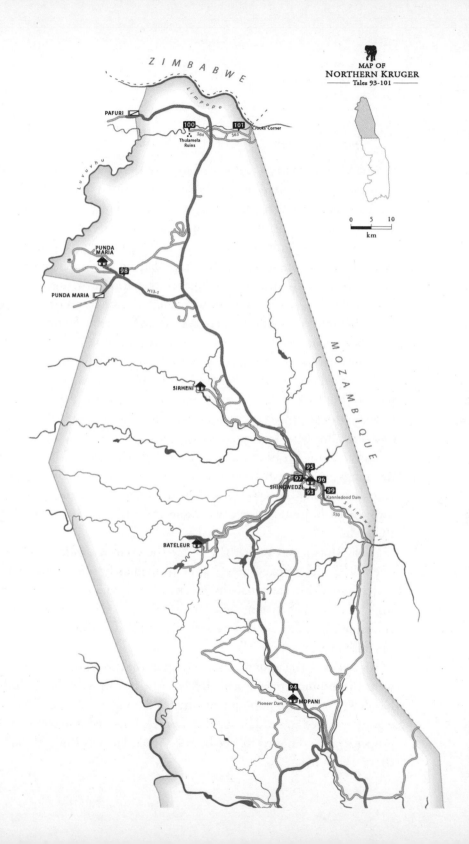

ZIMBABWE

Limpopo

PAFURI

100   101   Crooks Corner

S64   S63

Thulamela
Ruins

Luvuvhu

PUNDA
MARIA

98

PUNDA MARIA

H13-1

SIRHENI

MOZAMBIQUE

95

97   96

SHINGWEDZI   93   99

Kanniedood Dam

S50

Shingwedzi

BATELEUR

94

Pioneer Dam   MOPANI

0   5   10

km

FOREWORD

WE IN SOUTH AFRICA are blessed to have the Kruger National Park. It is, and always will be, one of my favourite destinations. Anyone who has been lucky enough to have visited this special place will have a story or two to tell. Well, I am no different.

About a year before my final tour to England, I met a man, Frik Rossouw, who changed my life – not that he ever intended to. He heads up the anti-poaching intelligence operation in Kruger and was instrumental in steering me towards the cause of rhino conservation following my retirement from cricket. Albie Morkel, a fellow cricketer, was good friends with his son, Jean, who lives in Skukuza, and together they organised a tiger fishing trip to the lower Sabie River.

The expedition, which would take us far from the publicly accessible parts of the Park, included Albie and his brother (the formidable fast bowler, Morne), my team mate Jacques Rudolph, as well as Jean and two other brothers, Ludwig and Jaco Sevenster.

It was going to be a three or four-day trip, with fishing in the mornings and game drives in the evenings. We slept in tents and made camp every night – it was bliss. On the final day we pushed deeper into the Park, found a large waterhole and made camp around it for the night.

Albie Morkel was to be the chef for the evening. When he opened one of the cooler boxes, however, he immediately smelled something rotten and discovered that the chicken we were going to *braai* that night had completely gone off. He did his level best to clean out the cooler, but in doing so, he unwisely discarded the rotten chicken into the bush nearby.

It wasn't as dangerous for the Morkels or the other guys because they were all sleeping in army tents made of thick canvas. I, on the other hand, was in a small pop-up tent which I'd bought in Cape Town and was more suited to a kiddies birthday party. I pitched it in between the proper tents and hoped for the best. Poor old Jacques Rudolph had to share it with me.

It had been a superb day. We had seen seven or eight rhino, and we could hear the elephants drinking at the waterhole and the lions roaring in the distance. But the smell of that discarded chicken in the bush seemed to be making the hyaenas go crazy. We had a couple of mugs of red wine to celebrate the day and help us get to sleep.

At about one o'clock in the morning, long after we'd got to sleep, the fire was going down and the hyaenas were, we thought, at a safe distance. I was abruptly woken by quite a commotion and, moments later, heard a voice yelling: 'F— off, f— off, *voetsak*!' Jacques and I were suddenly very aware that our tent was about as thick as GladWrap.

We looked nervously out of the entrance and there was Albie, standing up and shining a torch about frantically. When I asked what the problem was, he said something had just tried to bite his head through the tent. I thought he was joking, but he insisted that something really had just tried to bite his head. Taking the torch, we went round the back of the tent, and there in the darkness stood a clan of about 15 hyaenas, just staring at us. We clapped and shouted '*voetsak*', before they reluctantly turned and ran away.

With the hyaenas gone, we inspected the tent to see what had happened. Albie had been lying with his head right up against the back of the tent, but fortunately the canvas was pulled just tight enough to prevent the hyaena getting a proper grip on his skull. We still weren't sure whether to believe him – until we saw all the fang marks and the slobber and saliva on the canvas. The sports headlines the following day would certainly have made for interesting reading if that tent had been made of a thinner fabric. Needless to say we didn't get much sleep for the rest of the night. We woke Frik – who had the rifle – and lit the fire again, then stayed up chatting until dawn. It was an incredible experience.

On that trip we were privileged to explore parts of the Park inaccessible to regular tourists. But countless Kruger visitors have had remarkable experiences on the Park's roads, in the rest camps and even on foot – and they are well documented in this book. Some are funny, many are hair-raising and others genuinely scary. I particularly enjoyed the story of the leopard stealing the bacon off a *skottel* at Afsaal picnic spot – I've eaten breakfast there on quite a few occasions…

That's what nature enraptures us with: the right to be extremely unpredictable in its own environment. And that is perhaps what keeps us all returning to Kruger time after time – you never quite know what you might encounter around the next bend.

People will know I have been heavily involved in the war against rhino poaching. I have been witness to a few crime scenes in Kruger, and it is not a pretty sight. It is the sad truth of how human greed can get the better of us. I do, however, have hope for our rhinos, among other struggling species. There are plenty of unsung heroes out there doing awesome work for conservation. It is because of these people that I believe I will one day have the pleasure and privilege of bringing my children to this special place, to continue to add to the amazing encounters in this book.

MARK BOUCHER

Mark Boucher is a former South African cricketer. Widely regarded as one of the greatest wicketkeepers of all time, he still holds the record for the most dismissals by a wicketkeeper in Test cricket. Forced to retire in 2012 following an horrific eye injury, he has thrown himself into conservation, particularly the fight against rhino poaching, and spearheads SAB Boucher Conservation – a non-profit fundraising organisation aimed at saving South Africa's threatened rhino population.

PREFACE

THE IDEA FOR THIS COLLECTION OF 101 extraordinary tales from the Kruger National Park arose purely from envy. I have never considered myself particularly lucky in the Park – but then nor have I had the misadventure of a breakdown, a close shave or an animal attack. I am, however, always flabbergasted by the tales of other visitors, recounted – with perhaps a smattering of exaggeration – in rest camps in the evenings, or shared through open car windows when I've asked, 'Seen anything interesting today?' Surely, I thought, others would be as interested as I am in the tales of those for whom Kruger has dealt a more thrilling hand?

When I first set about collecting stories for the book four years ago, I never anticipated the sheer wealth of incredible tales, accounts and anecdotes I would receive. I certainly never anticipated that the spectrum of stories would extend so much further than just animal sightings. The book this has become is an entirely different beast from my first humble imaginings. Much like the Park itself, the whole somehow feels greater than the sum of its parts: there are stories of heartbreak, tragedy, high jinks, disappointment and astonishing luck; there are stories from the rest camps, the dirt and tarred roads, the watering holes, the picnic spots and the walking trails; and there are funny stories, curious stories, sad stories, creepy stories and stories that you'll find almost impossible to believe. But each one, I hope, captures and shares a little of the wonder and the thrill we all feel when we pass through the gates, full of anticipation of what lies ahead, into the great expanse of one of Africa's greatest treasures.

Hundreds and hundreds of people of all ages and backgrounds, from across South Africa and the world, took the time and effort to open their memory vaults, pen their Kruger experiences and submit them for consideration. Although I couldn't possibly use everything, I was overwhelmed by the generosity of spirit of every contributor and would like to humbly thank each and every one of them. There was not a single story I did not delight in reading. The criteria for selecting the stories were simple: they should all be extraordinary in one way or another; they should all take place in the Kruger National Park itself, not one of the adjoining reserves of Greater Kruger; they should only take place on any of the publicly accessible tourist roads, rest camps, picnic sites or walking trails; and importantly, they should primarily be the tales of ordinary Park visitors like you and me – not game rangers, field guides or any of the other lucky people who work and live in the Park.

The result, I hope, is a celebration of Kruger and what makes it so special amongst all the national parks in Africa. That an extraordinary encounter could just as easily happen to a family in a two-door hatchback on their first sojourn into the Park as a hardened Park veteran in a dusty 4x4, or a wealthy foreign tourist on the back of an open safari vehicle, is evidence of Kruger's unique egalitarian streak. Yes, Kruger is the great safari leveller, and this book is the proof of that. Whether you dip in and out of it, or read it from cover to cover, you'll find yourself excitedly optimistic (or justifiably terrified) that the next time you're in the Park, it could be you...

CAPE TOWN, SOUTH AFRICA
APRIL 2014

ACKNOWLEDGEMENTS

THIS BOOK TOOK THE BEST PART of four years to source, compile, edit and bring to publication. It was a labour of love – but it was by no means a solo effort. I would like to thank the following people for their various contributions, without which the book would simply not exist:

Each of the 100 or so people who so kindly granted me permission to edit and publish their remarkable stories, and for the photographers amongst them – and in addition to them – who allowed their pictures and video stills to be used. Their patience, kindness and good humour as I bugged them incessantly for clarifications, elaborations and other minutiae was almost saintly.

Those contributors who so graciously responded to my individual requests to write up and submit their stories, then endured months, and sometimes years, of correspondence as the finer details and other particulars were nailed down.

Every one of the hundreds upon hundreds of individuals who took the time and energy to write down and submit a Kruger story, anecdote or memory for consideration. While I couldn't possibly include every story received, I was honoured not only to receive, but to read each one. Without such a wealth of varied contributions to choose from, this book would have no sizzle.

Isabelle King for her patient, conscientious copy editing in the earlier phases of the book, as well as her sagacious and quietly diplomatic contributions to many sticky editorial quandaries.

Georgia Stephens for her tireless efforts copy editing and scrutinising the manuscript, admirably fighting her corner about what is grammatically correct and patiently offering almost boundless amounts of invaluable editorial insight and advice.

Dr Peter Rattray for his generous legal advice and guidance.

Dr Werner Barnard, Andries Combrinck, Linda Groenewald, Enrico Liebenberg, Anel Pretorius Duvenhage and Sheenaugh-Lee Thompson for their kind assistance with translations from Afrikaans to English, and vice versa.

My ever supportive family for their gentle encouragement throughout the seemingly never-ending process of bringing the book together.

And the following people who contributed in other important ways: Dana Atkinson, John Baldwin, Mark Boucher, James Clark and the Clark family for ensuring the inclusion of Andrew Clark's story following his untimely death prior to publication, Kate Collins at Wild Magazine for always going the extra mile to raise awareness of the project, Donné Commins, Esther Erasmus, Cameron Ewart-Smith, Craig Fyvie from EcoTravel Africa (www.ecotravel.co.za) for providing a reference source for the book's maps, John Griffin, Piet Grobler, John Guy, Monica Guy, Naomi Havemann, Laura Heslop, Penny and Bobby Legg, Ludi Lochner, Rudi Lorist, Albie Morkel, Grant Nicol, Katie O'Shea, Nadav Ossendryver, Grant Pearson, Martie Pelser, Roxanne Reid, Kim Rose, Paula Rutherford, Dolores Shea, Joep Stevens, Johan van der Merwe, Frank Watts (safari guide and author of *The Other Animals of the Kruger National Park* – www.theotheranimals.co.za), Andrea Weiss, Alison Westwood, the teams at Go Magazine and Getaway Magazine, and all the thoughtful people who alerted me to interesting Kruger stories they had stumbled across.

With the multi-tentacled nature of a book like this, it is likely I have inadvertently left out the names of some of the people who helped, guided and supported me throughout the process. For this I am sorry, but remain inexpressibly grateful to every single person who contributed, in any way, towards making the publication possible. I hope you'll be rewarded on your next trip to the Park with sightings to rival the best in this book.

Finally, I would like to thank the rangers, the staff and the administrators of the Kruger National Park for their tireless and conscientious stewardship of the Park, often against tremendous odds. Without their contribution towards maintaining and protecting – sometimes with their lives – this cherished corner of South Africa, there would be no stories to tell – nor any hunger to read them.

INTRODUCTION

STRETCHING ALMOST 400 KILOMETRES along the low-lying north-eastern border of South Africa, and covering an enormous two-million hectares – larger than many small countries – the Kruger National Park is one of the greatest game reserves on earth. No park in Africa can boast quite as many mammal species: an astonishing 147 in total, including all the usual safari suspects. The birding tick-list exceeds 500 species, ranging from the world's largest to one of the world's smallest. An embarrassment of botanical riches, throbbing with insect life, cover the Park's 14 distinct ecozones. There are well over 100 types of reptile, more than half of which are snakes. And with the so-called Big Five – lion, leopard, elephant, rhino and buffalo – in such abundance throughout much of the Park, even a first-time visitor could, with a bit of blind luck, tick them off before lunchtime.

Perhaps less well known internationally than its northern cousins like the Maasai Mara and the Serengeti, the Kruger National Park has been attracting South Africans (and increasingly, foreign tourists) from as far back as 1926, when it was first declared a national park. Since then, Kruger visitors – now numbering over a million a year and largely using their own cars – have traversed and explored the 2500 kilometres of gravel, dirt and tarred road criss-crossing the park like a capillary system, racking up enough extraordinary sightings, close encounters and gobsmacking stories to fill a mountain of postcards home.

This is perhaps what makes Kruger unique amongst its game reserve counterparts in Africa. Whereas the safari experience north of the Limpopo is overwhelmingly confined to those with the thickest wallets and a Big Five checklist, Kruger allows anyone to experience true African wilderness for themselves – in the comfort of their own cars, at their own pace and choosing their own routes. And all of this at a fraction of the cost of a private safari. That is not to say the top-end market is not catered for; it most certainly is. Open-topped guided safaris and luxurious lodges straight off the pages of a glossy magazine are a part of Kruger too – they just don't take precedent over the time-honoured do-it-yourself method of enjoying the Park.

But Kruger is no theme-park or tourist trap. Yes, a good 850 kilo-metres of the Park's roads are tarred; some rest camps in season can feel overwhelmingly busy; and big cat sightings – particularly in the busier southern sections – can cause 'traffic jams'. But it shouldn't be forgotten that Kruger is first and foremost a conservation area of world renown at the forefront of global ecological and scientific research steered by an army of dedicated and skilled personnel. Tourism is the handy by-product that keeps much of it ticking along. If there is any doubt, consider this astonishing statistic: if you drove every kilometre of accessible tourist road in Kruger, and were able to see for 100 metres on either side the entire way, at the end of it all you would have only seen just over two-and-a-half percent of the entire Park.

Yet in that two-and-a-half percent of largely untouched Africa, incredible things happen. A long and twisty food chain, from microbes to elephants, plays out in front of your eyes – and you need not be an expert, game ranger or safari guide to find it. With a bit of luck (sometimes good, sometimes bad) and a sprinkling of common sense (or lack of it), the extraordinary behaviours of wild animals, the hair-raising adventures, the close shaves and the nature-documentary sightings are there for the average visitor to savour, to shriek about, to wonder over and to share.

That is what this book is all about.

UNDERSTANDING KRUGER

FOR MANY SOUTH AFRICANS, the Kruger National Park is an institution. Indeed, some of the contributors in this book have been visiting the Park since the 1930s, others since they were babies, and one even whilst still in the womb. For those people, Kruger needs no explanation – the lore of the Park is imprinted in their DNA.

But for those who have never visited, the accounts in this book may, at times, seem baffling. In the 101 Kruger tales that follow, you will, from time to time, come across reference to a number of elements and principles peculiar to the Park, as well as numerous colourful colloquialisms and local words sprinkled throughout the text.

If you are familiar with Kruger, you can comfortably skip this section and jump straight to the main course. But for those who aren't, a rough understanding of these details will be helpful in grasping the thrust of many of the stories, and will almost certainly add to your enjoyment of them. So here are a few Kruger fundamentals worth getting your head around before tucking into the tales.

The Big Five

The loose grouping of lion, leopard, elephant, rhino and buffalo – the Big Five – is without doubt Kruger's major drawcard, given their abundance throughout much of the Park and, consequently, the relative ease with which they can be found. Lions can be seen in every corner of Kruger, often right on the roads, and it is an unlucky visitor who exits the Park after a few days without a single lion sighting. With the elusive leopard, even the casual visitor has a decent chance of spotting one, not least in the area along the Sabie River between Skukuza and Lower Sabie rest camps, which is said to harbour the densest leopard population on earth. Kruger's southern section remains the best place in Africa to see the endangered black and white rhino, despite a staggering onslaught by poachers. The Park can barely handle any more elephants, and buffalo herds, large and small, can be found lazily chewing the cud, wallowing in mud or lumbering through the bush across the length and breadth of the Park.

The term Big Five derives from big-game hunting vernacular. These five species were considered the most dangerous for a hunter to bring down. From a game spotting perspective, however, the term is largely arbitrary, fuelled more by its own hype than by any real significance. After all, what about cheetah, wild dog, hippopotamus, giraffe or any of the other iconic African species you may find in the Park? And what of the rarer species? Does a buffalo sighting really trump even a fleeting glimpse of a handsome sable antelope?

Nevertheless, while seasoned veterans roll their eyes at first-timers with 'Big Five fever', it is unlikely that even the most hardened Kruger visitor doesn't at least perform a secret Big Five count in their heads as they drive around the Park.

Gates

With the Park entirely ring-fenced (with the exception of some portions of the Park's eastern border with Mozambique) visitors must enter Kruger through one of nine main gates.

All of Kruger's gates comprise a reception building (some include a shop, petrol station and other facilities), and guards closely control who enters and exits the Park.

Some gates double as rest camps too, as in the case of Crocodile Bridge in the south and Orpen in the west.

Rest Camps

There are currently 24 fenced rest camps (excluding the 17-odd private safari lodges) dotted around Kruger, providing accommodation for visitors overnighting in the Park. Accommodation varies from the basic – camping spots for tents and caravans, simple thatched huts with communal ablution and kitchen facilities, and permanent safari tents – up to fully-contained and quite luxurious, air-conditioned bungalows and guest cottages.

While some of the newer camps remain rustic, many of the larger camps have all the facilities of a resort, with a restaurant, petrol station, laundry facilities and a shop. Skukuza rest camp, the Park's 'capital', is more like a small town, boasting a bank, a post office, a museum, a library, a doctor's rooms, a plant nursery, a police station, a small airport and even a nine-hole golf course. Behind the scenes, the camp is the Park's administrative, maintenance and research hub, and many visitors would be astonished to see the industrial-scale workshops, the abattoir and cannery, the church, the primary school, the sports complex and the neat suburban-like streets of the staff village.

The Park's rest camps are all surrounded by electric fences, and entry and exit is through a camp gate, which in the bigger camps is usually manned. The gates are opened just before dawn and closed again at dusk. Visitors must remain in the camps at night.

Gate Opening and Closing Times

As tourists are not permitted to drive around the Park at night, all rest camps and gates have strict gate opening and closing times. Failing to get back to camp or to the exit before the gates close – even by just a few minutes – results in a heavy fine or a stern ticking off.

Rest camp gates open slightly earlier than the Park's entrance gates, giving overnight visitors a head start in fanning out into the Park.

Early mornings – particularly in summer when the sun rises early – can feel like the starting line at a Grand Prix, with visitors all jockeying to be the first out of the gate as it is swung open by a bleary-eyed guard.

Picnic Spots

Unfenced and usually within an hour or two's drive from many of the camps, Kruger's picnic spots provide a welcome respite for tired-eyed game-spotters.

Often positioned alongside a river or near a water source, and usually shaded by large trees, Kruger's pleasant picnic spots are famous for their gas-fired *skottel braais*, which can be hired at a reasonable rate and allow visitors to cook a full fried breakfast.

The constant human activity around the picnic spots is usually enough to keep predators away, but conversely it attracts opportunistic monkeys, baboons, the odd brave antelope, and squadrons of remarkably fearless birds eager to snap up an easy meal from inattentive tourists.

Tarred (or Paved) Roads

Of the 2 500 kilometres of tourist road in the Park, almost 850 kilometres of it is tarred. While tarred roads may initially seem out of keeping with a safari experience, many Kruger visitors soon come to prefer them – if not for practicality and a smoother drive, then for the fact that animals seem to prefer them too. Lions are often seen slumped on the warm tar in the early mornings, while grazers and browsers – which in turn attract predators – prefer the sweeter grass and foliage that grows on the verges of the road, fed by the run-off of rainwater and untainted by the dust that covers much of the vegetation that lines the gravel roads.

Gravel (or Dirt) Roads

The majority of Kruger's roads are graded gravel or dirt roads, and are generally less busy than the tarred roads. In the dry winter months, the corrugations become particularly bone-rattling, and no matter how fast or slow you drive, if your tyre pressure is high you're almost guaranteed to lose your dentures. In the rainy months, some of these roads can become dangerous and, as a result, may be closed off for days until they dry out.

Signposts, Maps and Navigation

Tell anyone who has never been to Kruger that you simply drive around the Park on your own, and you're bound to see a flash of panic in their eyes. 'How do you know where to go?' 'What if you get lost?' 'In a Fiat Punto – are you crazy?'

But with all vehicles strictly prohibited from straying off-road anywhere in the Park, and with the admirably well-maintained road network peppered with detailed stone-block signposts (often stating exact distances) at every junction, it would be hard – some would say impossible – to get lost in Kruger. Detailed maps, with accurate estimated driving times between points, are all available for a small fee at all entrance gates and Park shops.

Park Rules

Allowing over a million visitors a year free reign through an African wilderness the size of Kruger requires a contract of understanding between the Park's administrators and the tourists. Mercifully, the rules are few – but they are strictly enforced and, for the most part, are dutifully adhered to by the vast majority of visitors. Do not speed, do not litter, stay on the designated roads, stay within your vehicle (that includes not leaning out of windows or sun roofs), do not feed or disturb the animals and ensure you return camp on time are the basic cornerstones of Kruger's regulations.

Unfortunately, there are always a few who flout the rules, and a number of stories in this book include reference to such rule breaking – either as *mea culpas* or as observations of rule breaking, and usually with the consequences one would expect. These stories have been included not to glorify bad behaviour, but to demonstrate the need for such rules – and to serve as cautionary tales of what happens when rules are bent.

Game Drive

A game drive, in the context of this book, is the term used by most Kruger visitors to describe driving around the Park looking for animals.

Most Park visitors will split their day by heading out in their car on a morning game drive, then returning to camp for lunch and a siesta before going out for another late afternoon game drive when the animals start moving around again as dusk approaches.

In the general sense, game drives can also refer to organised excursions in a safari vehicle, driven by an experienced guide.

Night Drive

Night drives in Kruger are organised game drives in open safari vehicles that set out from the main rest camps in the early evening to allow visitors the chance to spot nocturnal wildlife. They are led by a professional guide, employed by the Park, and the vehicles are equipped with powerful handheld spotlights.

Visitors in their own cars are not permitted out of the camps at night, so night drives in Kruger are always exclusively operated by Park employees, using official game viewing vehicles.

Walking in the Park

While Kruger visitors are strictly not permitted to get out of their vehicles (except in rest camps, picnic spots, at hides and a few other designated viewpoints), walking on foot in the Park is, however, possible under the leadership of experienced, armed guides as part of either a short guided walk or as part of longer multi-day 'walking trails'.

For both, the possibility of bumping into small – and even big – game is real, despite the relatively small distances covered. But the walks are not simply an exercise in searching for animals. They are a chance to learn about the intricacies of the bush: the geology, the plant life, the folklore, the insects, the subtle tracks and signs of the complex mesh of creatures in an environment unsullied by human encroachment. On a deeper level, they offer a unique chance to appreciate what it was like for our ancestors who roamed the African plains long before civilisation, ever mindful of what may be lurking in the long grass.

Despite the fact that a small number of stories in this book – three in total – revolve around disastrous incidents on foot in the Park, it cannot be overstated that these incidents are singularly exceptional and so overwhelmingly rare that they are but statistical blips. The safety record over the three-and-half decades since the inception of guide-led walks in the Park is exemplary. The primary, secondary and tertiary concern of the guides – all of whom are highly trained, many with years of experience under the belt – is the safety of the walking group coupled with a deep respect for the great and small of the bush. So situations which may be risky to the group or distressing to the wildlife are stringently avoided, and participants must at all times follow a series of unwaveringly strict rules to ensure their safety.

Guided Walks or Morning Walks

On guided or morning walks, a small group of paying guests are led through the bush for several hours by two experienced armed guides. These popular excursions often take place early in the morning, which is why you may see them referred to as morning walks. Setting out from camp long before the sun rises, the guides drive the group to an area some distance from camp, from where the walk begins. There are no set trails and only very loosely designated walking areas – the precise location and route is determined by weather conditions, the time of year and the guides' intuition on the day.

Walking Trails

Like guided walks, walking trails in Kruger allow visitors to explore little-seen parts of the Park on foot under the guidance of highly knowledgeable, armed trail guides. Initiated in 1978, the walking trails do not follow set routes (with the exception of the Mphongolo and the Olifants River Backpack Trails, both of which follow an approximate route over the course of four days). Instead, participants stay for a number of days in simple bush camps far from the tourist roads and camps, and explore the surrounding area on a series of guided morning and afternoon walks.

Hides

Dotted variously around the Park, and overlooking a waterhole or dam, hides (sometimes called bird hides or animal hides) are wooden shelters that allow visitors to observe birds and wildlife at close quarters. Kruger's hides are simple structures, built of dark wood, often on stilts and covered with a neatly thatched roof. Crucially, they include an open horizontal viewing slot – big enough to see out of, but not big enough for the hide's occupants to distract or alert the animals – as well as a basic bench to sit on.

Open Safari Vehicles

The majority of visitors to Kruger do so in their own cars, and are governed by the rules prohibiting standing up through sunroofs, leaning out of windows, sitting in the back of open *bakkies* or putting the top down on a convertible. Licensed private operators, however, are permitted to guide tourists around the Park in open safari vehicles.

Even for these operators, rules are strict: they must stay on the roads just like everyone else, the vehicle must have a canopy, and the driver and their guests must adhere to all the same rules that apply to any other visitor. While becoming increasingly common, owing in part to the blossoming of the tourism industry outside of the Park, open safari vehicles in Kruger are still not nearly as numerous as ordinary private vehicles.

What on Earth is a *Bakkie*, a *Braai*, a *Rondavel* and a *Skottel*?
Some of the stories in this book may include the odd word that will
be unfamiliar to non-South Africans. While context should hopefully
provide meaning most of the time, a full glossary of the unfamiliar
terms used in the stories can be found at the back of the book.

But to get you started, here are perhaps the four most frequently used
words you are likely to come across in the stories that follow:

Bakkie – A popular type of vehicle with an open (or sometimes
canopied) rear cargo area. Beloved by South Africans, they come
in all shapes and sizes, the most common these days being the
four-wheel drive, double-cab variety. Americans will know them as
'pickups', and Australians as 'utility vehicles' or 'utes'.

Braai – The South African word for barbecue, derived from the
Afrikaans word *braaivleis*, meaning literally 'grilled meat'.

Rondavel – A circular, thatched hut. The majority of accommodation
units in Kruger are rondavels, continuing a tradition from the very
first overnight huts built in the Park.

Skottel – A waist-high, gas-fired griddle used as an alternative to a
wood or coal *braai*.

PART ONE

TALES FROM SOUTHERN KRUGER

SOMETIMES UNFAIRLY MALIGNED for its high density of visitors and buzzing main rest camps, the popular southern section of Kruger – which, for the purposes of this book, stretches from the lush banks of the Crocodile River in the south to around Tshokwane picnic spot in the north – is also arguably one the most productive game viewing regions in Africa, particularly for the Big Five. So it is no coincidence that such a large number of the stories in this book take place in this part of the Park, particularly in the areas around Skukuza and Lower Sabie rest camps, and not least inside the camps themselves.

In the stories that follow, you will get a flavour of southern Kruger's staggering variety of wildlife and a feel for the remarkably varied landscapes of the region, from the granite *koppies* and tall *suurveld* grass around Pretoriuskop rest camp in the west, via the riverine vegetation along the Sabie River so beloved of leopards and elephants, to the rich savannah plains teeming with game on the foothills of the Lebombo Mountains in the east.

1

THE LEOPARD THAT KILLED THE CHEETAH
THAT KILLED THE IMPALA
Brian Gardiner

IF YOU VISIT THE KRUGER NATIONAL PARK enough times, the law of averages rules that at some point you will get to see a sighting exciting enough to dine out on for many years to come. If you're very lucky, you may see something that very few people ever get to see. And maybe, if the stars align just right and the bones land in perfect sequence, you'll be lucky enough to see something so extraordinary – barely believable almost – that it becomes Kruger folklore.

Next time you drive the gravel s28 from Crocodile Bridge towards Lower Sabie, look out for a large fever tree on your left, about seven kilometres along the road. Apart from its size, the tree is undistinguished and, with the exception of some large birds' nests in its branches, it is unlikely you'd ever give it more than a passing glance as you trundle past. But this is the tree, back in the late winter of 2009, that formed the centrepiece to this most bizarre episode.

My family and I were on an afternoon game drive in an open safari vehicle when the guide stopped to listen to a feverish VHF radio discussion of a sighting that was taking place nearby. When the transmission crackled off, our guide turned to us, visibly shocked. The information he had just gleaned must have been truly amazing, as he had to sit for a few seconds to gather himself before telling us what had apparently just transpired.

He struggled to find his words at first, but began thoughtfully, saying that in his entire life he had never heard of such an occurrence. From his tone alone, we knew that whatever had just happened must really be of some significance. As he explained in detail what the other guides had just reported, there were audible gasps from many of us in the back.

When he asked whether we all wanted to go and take a look, the voracious response nearly knocked him backwards. We would have run there if we had to.

The cluster of cars and other safari vehicles all parked alongside the fever tree gave the position away before we had even arrived. As we pulled up, we caught a brief glimpse of the leopard that had caused all the fuss, just as it slunk away into the bush to seek some solitude from the growing audience of shocked onlookers.

There, in the boughs of that fever tree, we could clearly see the impala draped over one of the larger branches a metre or so from the fork where the branch meets the trunk. And lying prone over the same branch, closer to the fork, was the limp carcass of the cheetah.

In my 20 years of being involved with the private safari industry in East and Southern Africa, while having once heard rumours of something vaguely similar, I had never seen anything quite like this.

The guide who had earlier reported the sighting over the radio had, incredibly, seen the entire episode unfold in front of him and his guests. They had watched the cheetah successfully hunt and capture the impala ewe. Having taken it down and suffocated it, the cheetah did not take too much time to rest and immediately began to eat from the rear end of the impala. In the next instant a leopard appeared, drawn to the commotion of the kill. Being the perennial opportunist, it ambushed, caught and killed the cheetah.

Remarkably, the leopard first dragged the impala up into the branches of the fever tree. Then, once safely slung over a large limb away from other potential competitors, it returned to the ground for the cheetah and hauled that up into the branches as well, stowing it alongside – but not on top of – the already-stored booty.

Looking at the two lifeless carcasses hanging from the tree, it was interesting to note that the leopard had lodged the impala specifically in a place that would allow room for the easy placement of the cheetah straight afterwards. Given the considerable amount of energy a leopard expends hauling a carcass into a tree to prevent it being stolen by scavengers, it would not be far-fetched to deduce that this leopard may well have intended to eat the cheetah in addition to the impala.

We returned to the sighting early the following morning. To our great surprise the leopard was in the tree, repositioning and eating the impala carcass. Only the impala seemed to have been fed on. The cheetah, at least from our viewpoint, appeared to have been untouched – although others have reported seeing some exposed flesh on the side of the cheetah's torso, most likely from the plucking of fluff off the skin that is so typical of leopard behaviour.

A little later that morning, I am told, the leopard simply tipped the cheetah from the tree onto the ground below, where it no doubt became hyaena fodder.

Of course, we were far from the sole witnesses to this extraordinary sighting. Being in one of the busiest sections in the Park, and playing out over multiple days, many visitors were able to say that they too got to see the famous cheetah and impala in the tree episode.

One such visitor – a well-known South African cricket commentator – still laments that the only time she ever saw a cheetah in Kruger was when it was hanging lifeless from the fork of a tree!

We were incalculably fortunate to have seen something like this; something so extraordinary and so implausible that, were it not for the photographs as evidence, few would believe it ever happened. It just emphasises the undeniable importance of places like the Kruger National Park that provide a stage for the continuance of the natural dramas – like the leopard that killed the cheetah that killed the impala – that make up the rich and unpredictable tapestry of life in the bush.

2

THE OTHER KRUGER MILLIONS
Louis von Broembsen

IN 1978, MY NEPHEW and fellow student friends were pacing themselves to reach Skukuza rest camp before the gate's evening closing time when they came upon a small pride of lions lying just off the road.

They had no more time than to slow down and catch a quick glimpse of the cats as they passed by. However, as the car drew level with the lions, my nephew's girlfriend exclaimed: 'Look! There's a wad of banknotes lying between the paws of that male!' They screeched to a stop; students are not known to miss such an opportunity.

Sure enough, right there on the ground, below the chin of the big male and lying within a few inches of its paws, was a thick roll of banknotes. But time was not on their side and the lions did not look like moving on. For a few confused moments they discussed their options, before deciding the best thing to do would be to mark the spot and return the following day to relocate the money.

And so followed a restless night of repeating dreams about whether the money would still be there the next day and, if so, how much it could amount to. That was a thick wad of notes, after all.

They were first out of camp at dawn – an impressive feat for a bunch of students – and made for the marked spot. Such was their excitement at the thought of retrieving the cash that they would not even have noticed a leopard leaping onto the bonnet of their car. But things seldom look the same in the morning as they do in the evening. The intensity and the angle of the sun is different, and shadows that weren't there before can completely alter the landscape. At the spot where they were sure the lion had been lying the previous evening, there appeared to be nothing but sand.

Anguished, the group drove slowly forwards and backwards searching intently for the wad, but it seemed to have disappeared. Driving back and forth slowly in Kruger is always going to attract attention, and soon a car stopped behind them, interested in what they had seen. Not a moment later, my nephew spotted the money. It was lying exactly where it had been the night before and had simply been obscured by a shadow. But with the money located, the car behind had suddenly become a threat. What if they also spotted the cache?

Everyone held their breath and pretended to not look interested. After a few tense moments, the car behind moved on, and my nephew's girlfriend leant out of the passenger door and picked up the treasure. It was tightly rolled up, with the outermost notes badly weathered and faded. Once counted, it amounted to over a thousand rand – which, in those days, was worth something.

Where such a sum of money came from, and how it landed up between the paws of a lion on the side of a road in the middle of the Kruger National Park, remained a mystery. What became of it after it was found, though, is a lot clearer. Civilised protocol was, understandably, not followed. Instead, part of the bounty was used to finance that evening's celebration at the camp, and the rest happily divided between them.

3

ANGRY ELEPHANT'S ROAD RAGE RAMPAGE
Sander Hofman

IF ONLY THE AMERICAN HAD REVERSED. The terrifying chain of events that followed – one car damaged, another almost totally destroyed, a newly-engaged couple shocked and injured, and headlines around the world – may well have been avoided.

It all began on a Monday morning in early November 2012 along the winding gravel road that follows the banks of the Crocodile River across a good part of the far southern section of the Park. It was nine o'clock, and my wife and I were heading back towards Berg-en-Dal rest camp when, around a bend, we came across an enormous bull elephant trudging along the road in front of us. Stopping some distance behind it, I reached for my binoculars and checked for any signs that it was in musth. While there were no leaky tear ducts or dripping urine, the elephant's demeanour looked suspect, and it showed no signs of wanting to move from the road. I wasn't about to take any chances with a bull of that size, so kept a safe distance and rumbled along slowly behind it.

The bull was not eating, not really pausing either, and kept up its march westwards along the road – the same direction as us. Keeping a safe 50-metre gap between the bull and our car, we followed it for a while. In the meantime, three other cars had fallen in line behind us and they too rolled along slowly, respecting the fact that, for now, the elephant ruled the road.

After about a quarter of an hour, the inevitable happened: a car approached from the other direction. The oncoming car was about 20 metres away from the bull when they saw each other. Instead of doing the one sensible thing in a situation like this – reverse and give the bull the space it requires – the driver instead turned off his engine, rolled down his window and began taking photos. As the elephant lumbered closer and closer, dwarfing the car, the driver of the tiny Chevrolet Spark quickly pulled his camera back through the open window. This elephant was not one to be challenged, and we held our breaths as it loomed to within a whisker of the obstructing car. We only exhaled again when the elephant turned to the left and appeared to walk into the bush. But our relief lasted no more than a second. In a flash, the elephant spun around and mock charged the car, stopping just centimetres short of the driver's side. That should have been all the man needed to know about this elephant, but he decided to hang around.

The bull walked off into the bush again a few metres behind the parked car. Having seen its mock charge once, we didn't dare take our eyes off it. When it puffed itself up, standing tall and raising its head and flapping its ears out to make itself look bigger, we inhaled again. But still, the driver did not get the message and would not move. That was enough for the bull. It came crashing out of the bush from behind – and this time it did not stop. It stabbed one of its tusks straight through the car's boot. We could not hear the crunch through our gasps, but we could see plainly enough the elephant lifting the back of the man's car clear off the ground, then shaking it up and down, before dropping it.

We expected to see those wheels spinning as soon as they hit the ground again, but I suspect the driver was too scared to get his car started. It was only when the bull had turned and began walking away that the driver finally got his engine running and drove on towards us.

It was hard to believe what we had just seen. Had that elephant really just lifted a one-tonne car off the ground with its tusk and given it a shaking? The driver, who appeared to be an American chap on his own, had clearly had quite a scare. Pulling up alongside us, he asked whether we would check the rear of his car. When I told him that he had a great big tusk-hole next to the licence plate, he mumbled that the people at the car rental firm would not be happy. I imagine he was right. We gave him some advice about reversing next time, and with that, he drove off.

Suddenly we realised that while we had been talking to the driver, we had lost track of the elephant. I reversed to the *bakkie* behind us, where the friendly South African couple driving it explained that the bull had continued along the road and disappeared around the bend.

With us being in a small Fiat Punto barely waist-high to that elephant, they asked whether we were afraid to drive further. I told them no, but we would certainly drive slowly and be observant. The bull could be anywhere and was clearly in the mood for a fight.

Slowly we moved on, with the convoy behind us. As we rounded the bend in the road where the elephant was last seen, we were met with a shocking sight: not 50 metres further down the road, a small white car lay on its roof. There was no movement, no human, no elephant bull – just an overturned car lying on the grass verge. I stopped and reached for my binoculars again to see if anyone was still inside the car, but with the morning shadows so stark, it was impossible to be sure. Again, we discussed the situation with the South African couple behind us. We were all equally flabbergasted. Had the elephant just done this? We had to go and check; there could be someone in that car. Our fellow rescuers cleverly suggested we both reverse to the scene to allow a swift getaway should the bull be lurking in the thick bush nearby. Just as we began turning our cars around to prepare for our rearguard approach, the overturned car began hooting. So there was someone inside it. Having seen us evidently turning around, they must have thought that we were bailing out and leaving the scene.

The elephant bull was nowhere to be seen when we reversed up to them. Inside the cabin of the small Hyundai Atos, a British couple sat strapped in upside down, unable to get out. Keeping a keen eye out for the elephant, we got out, and the South African guy wrenched open their driver's side door and helped the couple out.

Apart from shock, the only obvious injury was to the man's knee. It turned out that they were in the Park celebrating their engagement and were heading towards Lower Sabie rest camp when they came across the angry bull just beyond a bend in the road. The elephant was so close that the only thing the driver could do was pull the car over next to the road. But it was already too late – the bull pierced the passenger door of their rental car, lifted it with its tusk and flipped it on its roof, before walking off.

While the man remained quiet, sipping on some Coca-Cola my wife had given him to help with the shock, his fiancée showed remarkable good humour under the circumstances, quipping that she was grateful that they had fully insured their rental car. There would certainly be no deposit returned on this one.

I was only vaguely aware of it at the time, but with the injured man down on one knee, clutching his shoulder, and the rest of us standing in the road in front of the upturned car, a driver in a vehicle further back was snapping away at this remarkable scene. Within days the photographs had found themselves splashed across newspapers and on websites all over the world with headlines like 'Hellephant', 'No Entry – This is a Trunk Road' and 'Jumbo Takes Tourists to Tusk'. I am told the photos are also now hung prominently on notice boards in a number of the Park's rest camps as a reminder of how dangerous elephants in Kruger can be.

We had barely been in the road more than a minute or two when another car, driven by some American tourists, slowed down alongside us and, rather hysterically, told us to get back in our cars as there were probably lions around. I suppose that they felt they were somehow being useful, but our concern at that point was less for the vague threat of lions in the daytime than for the wellbeing of the couple who had just been on the receiving end of a rampaging bull elephant.

With the emergency number called, the couple were ushered into the back seat of the South Africans' large double-cab *bakkie* where they waited in safety for the Park's rescue team to arrive. We wished them well and headed on nervously back to Berg-en-Dal, keeping our eyes peeled for elephants.

What became of the bull? The rumour mill went into overdrive after the incident, and word spread that it went on to attack a family sedan a bit further north some weeks later and had to be shot. Thankfully, this was nonsense. In reality, the elephant unknowingly saved its hide by promptly joining a breeding herd, where it could no longer be easily identified, and now continues to roam southern Kruger. Whether or not it has forgiven and forgotten the American who should have reversed is anyone's guess – but we all know what they say about an elephant's memory...

4

A SMALL KNIFE AND A BIG DILEMMA
Henk & Hilda Maree

ALL REGULAR VISITORS TO KRUGER will no doubt have had at least one extraordinary experience that they would wish to one day share with their grandchildren. Having visited the Park over a period of well over 25 years, we have several stories to tell, but one in particular stands out starkly above the rest.

It happened one morning in the early nineties, not long after we entered the Park at Malelane Gate. It was the impala rutting season, so it wasn't long before we encountered the first rams challenging one another for dominance over a nearby herd of females. As is usual during this time of the year, we came across several fascinating episodes of loud snorting, clashing horns, grunting and furious pursuits through the trees.

On the tarred road leading to Berg-en-Dal rest camp, we stopped to watch a particular pair having a very serious go at one another, kicking up dust and stones as they locked horns. It was fascinating to watch, and after some minutes the weaker of the two eventually capitulated, turned and ran away, with the victor in hot pursuit. We pulled off again slowly and had barely gone a few metres when the pair reappeared again suddenly from the thick bush. The one in front dashed across the road immediately in front of us, missing the minibus by a fraction. The victor, very close behind, veered sharply to the left to miss us, but its hooves slipped on the hard tar surface and it fell heavily and slid under the vehicle. There was a sickening thump as the left rear wheel then ran over it.

We stopped immediately and, rules or no rules, got out of the car. It was an appalling sight. The ram, in the prime of its life, was lying in the road kicking furiously and bleating loudly, with what was obviously a severely broken back. We had to make a decision: do we simply ignore it and drive away leaving it to die a long and painful death, we asked, or do we put it out of its misery? The latter was the only humane thing to do. But how?

The only method at our disposal, we came to realise, was to cut its throat. But dare we even try? In the Kruger National Park of all places. Not just that, but the only knife at our disposal was a tiny Joseph Rodgers pen knife – with a blade not much bigger than you'd find on a pair of nail scissors.

By that point other visitors had pulled up and were watching wide-eyed with astonishment at what we were about to do.

After some more brief debate, we reluctantly jumped into action. One of us held down the flying hooves – not without some difficulty – while the other turned and pulled the head back to expose the neck, the little knife at the ready. Having grown up within the hunting culture I knew exactly where to make the initial cut, but the remainder of the grisly deed was easier said than done. With such a small knife, it required what felt like an endless series of agonising, and at times forceful, cuts and thrusts to get to and eventually sever the spine, with the impala still bleating and kicking out viciously.

With the deed done, there was silence again and we sat back with bloodied hands and arms and shirts, exhausted from the exertion and shocked by what we had just been impelled to do. Goodness knows what went through the minds of the gawking onlookers.

We pulled the carcass some distance into the bush, marked the crime scene by tying knots in the tall grass, and drove on to Berg-en-Dal where we nervously reported the incident. Our by now well-rehearsed story, far-fetched as we thought it was, was simply accepted in good faith and noted. The section ranger was radioed, and one of us was asked to explain what happened and where the incident took place. That was it.

The next day we paid a courtesy visit to the ranger to more fully explain what had happened and apologise for the incident. He listened quietly, nodding understandingly, and then, unbelievably, thanked us for the fresh meat we had provided to his staff.

We still have the little knife – in fact, I have carried it around in my pocket every day since. But I can thankfully say that it has no additional notches on its handle marking the slaughter of any other antelope.

5

LEOPARD RAIDS THE BRAAI
Gretha van Huyssteen

THE FLYING GANGS of glossy starlings and hornbills at Kruger's picnic spots are a menace. Drop your guard for a minute and they'll descend onto the hot *skottel braai* like gannets, and before you know it your bacon is flying away. It's all part of the experience of a traditional mid-morning brunch in the Park. But on my first ever visit to Kruger, the *skottel braai* raider didn't have wings and a beak – it had spots and fangs.

I was just nine years old at the time. But if I live to 100, I will still never forget that sunny morning in March. We had entered at Malelane Gate and everywhere I looked I saw impalas. While they may be boring to many, as a young first-timer I was captivated, gazing out the window as they rutted and grazed beside the road all the way up to Afsaal picnic spot.

Afsaal, like all picnic spots in Kruger, is unfenced. It is carved into the bush about half an hour's drive from Malelane Gate on the tarred road up to Skukuza, right on the junction with the old Voortrekker Road that heads west to Pretoriuskop. Being roughly equidistant from both camps, and sitting in one of the most game-rich areas of southern Kruger, it is a popular stopping point. By mid-morning, the *skottel braais* in the shade of the tamboti trees are usually hissing away, and children are scampering around the tables and benches. But when we arrived that morning, it was still relatively quiet; a handful of families and couples were enjoying a late breakfast, while a group of people near the wooded edge of the picnic spot piled strips of bacon onto their *skottel*.

Several years back, a pair of scops owls made their home in one of the trees in the middle of the picnic spot and have remained there ever since. It was there where my family and I were standing, peering up into the branches, when I turned to see a leopard wander out of the bush just metres behind me. For a second, it felt like a dream. Before I could even gasp, one of the women in the group near the edge of the picnic spot saw it too and screamed, 'Leopard! Leopard!'

Everybody spun around to see the group backing away slowly from their table and a leopard padding casually towards it. One of the men in the group turned and ran to get help, while the others continued to retreat cautiously. The leopard was not interested in the people, though – it could smell the bacon and made a beeline for the *braai*. With the gas hissing away, the leopard stared at us for a moment, before it jumped up on its hind legs, placed its two front paws on the edge of the *braai* and began tucking into the bacon.

The game ranger, alerted by the man who had run for help, came running and yelled at everyone to stay back. He moved forward a little and shouted at the leopard to scare it off, but the leopard had bacon on its mind – and in its mouth – and simply ignored the racket. It didn't even glance over. A few people laughed nervously, but the rest of us stood silently, watching in disbelief.

I had been barely 10 metres from the leopard when I first saw it emerge from the bush, but I slowly backed away behind the crowds and watched it instead from just outside the doors of the small shop near the picnic spot's entrance. Word spread quickly, and people inside the shop filtered out to see what the fuss was about, almost falling over backwards as they saw the leopard casually propped up against the *braai*.

The rangers eventually gave up trying to scare it off and stood back and watched it with the rest of us. For almost half an hour, the leopard remained up on its hind legs, slowly eating the slices of bacon while the *skottel* continued to hiss away. I have no idea how its paws did not get burnt, but if the bacon was underdone when the leopard arrived, it must have been very crispy by the time the last strip was polished off. With nothing left on the *braai*, the leopard hopped down and, without even a glance in our direction, sidled off into the bush and disappeared.

For a short while nobody said a word. Then, when it was clear the leopard was gone, there was a sudden outpouring of relief as the crowd erupted with laughter and nervous chatter. Nobody dared go near the edge of the picnic spot for quite some time. Eventually, the victims of the smash-and-grab returned to their table, but they had clearly lost their appetite – they abandoned their picnic plans, packed up their belongings and left.

For us, it was a good half an hour before we felt safe enough to sit down and eat our sandwiches, but we made sure it was nowhere near the edge of the site. I'm pretty sure we didn't even taste the food as we wolfed it down; we weren't going to risk that leopard coming back for second helpings.

6

THE HIPPO, THE IMPALA
AND THE NATURAL ORDER OF THINGS
Sylvester 'Silvo' Motaln

HIPPOS HAVE A FEARSOME REPUTATION. Grumpy, short-tempered and indiscriminately belligerent, they are said to be responsible for more deaths in Africa than any other large animal. But in the early summer of 2011, in the midst of a remarkable and gut-wrenching plight of an unlucky impala, we got to see another side to the hippopotamus – a scarcely believable altruism that flies in the face of their cantankerous reputation.

We were sitting in our car at Sunset Dam, just a stone's throw from Lower Sabie rest camp, admiring the hippos, crocodiles and birds when suddenly the dense bush to our right exploded into action. An impala ewe burst out of the thicket, pursued by a brute of a hyaena, and fled past us straight down towards the water's edge.

It was a tragic blunder for the impala; with trees overhanging the water to its right, and a steep bank to its left, it was trapped on the shoreline. Its fate was sealed, and the hyaena moved in for the kill.

But this impala seemed malcontent with the natural order of the food chain. With no way out on the land, it realised that there was still one possible, albeit unlikely, escape route: straight into the water. Why it didn't just swim around the overhanging trees and get out the other side was beyond us all. Instead, it plunged into the water and began swimming towards the middle of the croc-infested dam.

'You've got to be joking,' exclaimed someone from one of the other cars as the impala paddled furiously, its head straining upwards, barely above the surface. We watched in horror as the crocodiles sunning themselves on the banks raised their bellies off the mud and slipped into the water in the way you only ever seem to see on television. The outcome was inevitable.

From the bank, the hyaena watched with interest.

As the impala reached the middle, so did a large crocodile. There was a splash and the impala seemed to rise up out of the water, exposing much of its upper torso, before the croc readjusted, grabbed the ewe's neck and began to pull it under. It was an awfully cruel thing to witness; the impala had escaped the jaws of a hyaena only to land up in the jaws of a crocodile.

A semi-circle of hippos, submerged up to their eyes barely metres from the frothing attack, looked on dispassionately. It all seemed over for the impala, when suddenly something extraordinary happened. An enormous hippo – possibly the dominant male – broke ranks, surged through the water and viciously attacked the crocodile.

Realising that it had bigger problems on its hands than trying to drown its lunch, the crocodile let go of the impala, which immediately began swimming back towards the bank. There was a loud cheer from the growing crowd of incredulous onlookers parked up on the edge of the dam.

However, the hippo's work was not done. It had stopped the attack and seen off the crocodile, but what followed was so unexpected and so utterly extraordinary, if it were fiction it would stretch credibility to breaking point. The hippo swam quietly up behind the impala and began gently nudging it along through the water, lifting it from below whenever the impala floundered or began to sink, patiently escorting it all the way to the safety of the shallows. It was a display of altruism that was as touching as it was baffling. What possible benefit could a hippo reap from such an act of apparent kindness? And this from the most grouchy and ill-tempered animal in Africa.

With the impala safely on its legs again, waist-deep in the water, the hippo waited a moment and seemed to take a bow as it received its thanks from a grateful audience. Then it turned around and swam back to the middle of the dam.

Meanwhile, the impala staggered forward a little, to within four or five metres from dry land. With the water barely reaching its knees, it stood for a while, rebuilding its strength. Incredibly, there was not a spot of blood on its neck or torso. It appeared to have emerged from its encounter with the crocodile unscathed.

But, like something from the Book of Job, the biblical misfortune continued to rain down on the poor impala. We hadn't been the only ones watching the remarkable rescue: the hyaena that had chased the impala into the water in the first place had been keeping a keen eye on proceedings too, and had scuttled around the side of the dam to greet the impala head-on.

An uneasy standoff ensued. For what seemed like an eternity, the impala stood bolt upright, frozen in the shallows, and stared across the few metres of water at the waiting hyaena. As time passed we could only speculate how this would play out. The hyaena was clearly unwilling to enter the shallows and get its feet wet – even when the impala edged forward to within a body's length from the shore. The impala was not so foolish as to make a dash for it. Would it come down to which animal was most patient? Would we return tomorrow and find them exactly as we left them, still locked in a stalemate?

The urge to somehow place myself between the two and allow the impala to scamper out of the water and away into the bush was so strong, but this was nature at its most raw. All we could do was watch sadly and wait in hope that perhaps the impala would get one final chance – but it never came. The impala's fate was sealed by another crocodile emerging unexpectedly from the depths. It grabbed the impala violently from the rear, before dragging it into deeper water.

Earlier, the dominant hippo had given the impala a second chance at life, but there was no third chance this time – and no altruistic intervention. The hippos barely noticed, and the water birds didn't even glance up. Scrambling for my camera, I managed to capture one last photo of the impala's muzzle, gasping its final breath, before it slipped beneath the surface.

The extraordinary spectacle was over and the natural order of things resumed. The hyaena skulked off into the bush to find a less plucky meal, the hippos grunted and grumbled in the depths, and the water birds huddled down as the afternoon faded. But for maybe an hour afterwards, the successful crocodile paraded around the dam with the dead impala, holding aloft its trophy, as if declaring its victory over disorder.

7

A SHORT STROLL THROUGH LION COUNTRY
Anrie Botha

I WAS ALREADY IN MY THIRD WEEK of working as a tourism intern at Skukuza reception, and despite spending every moment of my spare time trawling the roads in my little red Corolla looking for game, I was frustrated that I had still not seen any lions.

This was particularly frustrating given that the Skukuza area is considered a real hotbed of lion activity – a fact reinforced by the frequent reports of lion sightings I endured daily from just about everyone I spoke to in camp.

So, late one January, after yet another visitor had told me that he'd seen a pride of lions at Leeupan waterhole up near Tshokwane picnic spot, I decided to take a drive up that way, as I had the afternoon off. Armed with determination, a bottle of water, my cellphone and a pair of binoculars, I jumped into my car and headed off to track down those lions.

It was a beautiful summer afternoon, and the impala in particular were out in force all the way up there, at some points lining the road in such numbers it felt like a parade crowd cheering me on.

Leeupan is a large pan – as big as five rugby fields – lying at the end of a curved dirt track about a kilometre or so off the main HI-2 tarred road. Completely dry in the winter, it comes alive in the summer months when it is full of water and attracts game in abundance – not least lions, after which it is named.

I followed the Leeupan turnoff and bumped all the way along the narrow dirt road before pulling up alongside the pan and switching off the engine. Being the only car there, all was very quiet. I waited patiently for the lions to reveal themselves, but I soon realised that a herd of grazing impalas nearby were far too relaxed for any predators to be in the area. Befitting my luck in this department, the lions had no doubt moved on to any part of the Park where I wasn't.

It was after four o'clock and the sun was starting to wane, so I cut my losses and decided to start driving slowly back to Skukuza. There was one small problem, though: when I turned the ignition, the engine just went *click!*

I tried again – *click!*

What do I do now? I waited a few minutes and gave it another go – *click!* This was not good; I had been in such a rush to head out and find these lions, I hadn't told anyone where I was going. I reached for my phone to call for help, but I could pick up no reception whatsoever. What a perfect time to discover that in Kruger there is just a small radius of cell phone reception around the camps, after which you need to either get yourself to a very high point or use a two-way radio. Neither of these options were possible for me at low-lying Leeupan, some 30 kilometres from Skukuza, and in a car boasting technical specs that barely stretched beyond the cigarette lighter.

I began weighing up my options: I could stay in the car and hope someone would take the turnoff to the waterhole at this late hour, or perhaps if I waited a while, the car would miraculously start again before it got dark. But it was getting late, and with gate closing time approaching, the odds of a car having the time to take the Leeupan turnoff and still make it back to camp were narrowing.

I started to panic; I couldn't see myself sleeping in the car in the middle of the bush with tyre-eating hyaenas around, or, even worse, the elusive lion pride eventually showing themselves – and an interest in me!

After much philosophical pondering, I settled on what many would agree was a most reckless decision, and one that, I admit, still makes my blood run a little cold when I think about it today: I decided to walk.

Leaving the safety of my car, I set off along the dirt track I had previously driven in on. I walked in the middle of the sandy road, flanked on either side by the high grass and thick bush harbouring a scary chorus of hidden crackles, rustles and chirps. My only comfort came from the small groups of grazing impala here and there which acted as my canaries in the mine, so to speak. The distance between my car and the tarred road was only about one kilometre, but I can honestly say that it was the longest 20-minute walk of my life.

Of course, tar is no safer than sand to a person on foot in Kruger, but when I eventually stepped onto the H1-2 with the dirt road now behind me, I felt like I could breathe again. I was back on a main road, and a final straggler would surely pass by soon on their way to Skukuza before the gates closed. I just had to not be dead before that happened. So I climbed onto the waist-high stone-block signpost, assuming, probably incorrectly, that I at least had the advantage of a bit of height over anything wanting to eat me. And I waited.

Luckily I didn't have to wait long; a white car sped past and almost instantaneously lit its brake lights and slowed to a halt. The car idled there for what felt like an age before finally reversing back to me. I still wonder what they must have thought when they saw me sitting on the signpost and imagine the conversation that followed in those moments before they reversed. The woman in the passenger seat rolled down her window and, without irony, asked, 'Do you need help, young lady?'

Arriving at Skukuza I quickly arranged a lift back to Leeupan with a man from roadside assistance to either try and fix the car or else tow it back to camp. At Leeupan I tried the ignition again to illustrate the clicking sound, but to my embarrassment, and the amusement of the mechanic, the engine turned and the car started without a stutter. Murphy apparently applies his law even in the bushveld.

Oh, did I mention that I did see lions that day? On my way back to Skukuza, with the car now running smoothly and just a few minutes down the road from where I had been sitting on the signpost earlier, I came across a pride of six lions lying in the road. I stopped alongside them, but my lesson had been learnt: this time I kept the engine running!

8

'LOCAL BUTCHER GORED BY ELEPHANT'
John Anslow

WHEN MY MOTHER-IN-LAW, out shopping in the town of Stafford in England, saw the newspaper placard on the pavement outside the corner shop declaring 'LOCAL BUTCHER GORED BY ELEPHANT', she didn't have to perform any mental gymnastics to conclude that something on our South African safari holiday had gone terribly, terribly wrong.

I had booked a tour of South Africa for my wife's 50th birthday and had invited our son along with us. The highlight of the tour was the few days we'd be spending in Kruger, and my son and I had been particularly keen on the idea of joining one of the guided morning walks we'd heard about. Although we had been on safari before – in Kenya, some years before – we'd never walked in the wild, and the idea of getting up close and personal with the great and small of the African bush seemed thrilling.

I suppose one should be careful what one wishes for. And I suppose one should be thankful for small mercies too, as it was only by a small twist of fate that my wife hadn't come with us on the walk that morning; there had been only two places remaining, and with me and my son being the keenest, we had filled the slots while she stayed safely back in camp.

Long before it got light, we were piled into the back of the game drive vehicle along with a group of South Africans and Americans and set off out through the gates of Skukuza. I suppose for the armed guides driving us out to the walking spot that March morning, it was just another day in the Park with just another group of wide-eyed tourists in khakis and walking boots. I hazard to suggest that today they probably still remember each and every one of that tender-footed group.

The vehicle pulled up at the start of our walking area, not far from the N'waswitshaka River, just as it was getting light. We all stood around as the guides talked us through the ins and outs and dos and don'ts of walking in the bush. This walk in the Park was clearly no walk in the park given the seriousness with which we were briefed and the frighteningly large calibre of the rifles slung over the shoulders of the guides. Outside of the vehicle and on foot we were, after all, now on a humblingly low rung of the food chain.

And so the walk began. As silently as we could, we tramped single file through the open bushveld so characteristic of that area around Skukuza. About three quarters of an hour later we crossed a dry river bed, and then, a little further on, the guides stopped us and, in an excited whisper, pointed out through the bush far ahead of us the unmistakable grey shapes of elephants. Quietly, and keeping a close eye on the wind direction, they steered us closer. I remember a palpable excitement in the group as we emerged into a clearing, and there, not more than 200 metres away, was the herd of five or six elephants with some youngsters among them.

Being downwind, the elephants were impervious to our clunking presence. Through a series of whispers and elaborate hand gestures, the guides indicated that by circling around and keeping the wind in our faces, we could safely get a little closer without disturbing the herd.

We didn't get far.

There was a sudden heavy rustling, an urgent shout of 'Elephant!' and then, from out of the bushes barely 25 metres to our right, with ears flared and trumpeting loudly, an elephant stormed straight towards us.

I am told an elephant at full tilt can reach speeds of 40 kilometres per hour. Considering it had burst out of the bushes from nowhere and now had just the length of a tennis court to cover, you can perhaps appreciate the crazed panic that followed as the guides shouted at us to get behind the trees, their voices drowned by the shrill trumpeting of the four-tonne juggernaut bearing down on us. Unfortunately, there weren't all that many trees to get behind – just some scrawny acacias that, in my brief calculations, I estimated wouldn't offer much resistance to a charging warthog, let alone a raging elephant.

The group split in two. One lot, including my son, scattered in one direction, while I and a few others clamoured in the other direction towards a cluster of small trees.

That was when I tripped on a root.

I recall the sensation of twisting in the air, gliding in slow motion to the ground and, before I'd even hit the dust, letting out some of my choicest Anglo Saxon. For a second, there I lay: flat on my back in sand and thorns with the horrible metal taste of adrenaline in my mouth. And this, I thought, was how I was to die. In moments the elephant would be on top of me, crushing me flat into the *veld* with its feet.

I just had time to bring my knees up in a defensive position before the elephant surged down on me and began pushing down on my legs with the hard bridge of its trunk. It was a weight and strength like nothing I had ever felt before in my life. I pushed back as hard as I could, but what chance does a butcher from Staffordshire have against an elephant from Kruger? And so it seemed I wasn't going to die by being trampled by an elephant as I had first feared; I was going to die being slowly crushed into the ground by the front end of its rock-solid trunk instead.

It must have been a helpless and sickening sight – a man on his back, knees up, desperately pushing back with every ounce of strength in his body against the weight of a furious elephant hell-bent on pulverising him into a mush.

It felt like an eternity before the shot rang out, although it was probably only seconds. The guides had swung around and managed to position themselves where they could get a clear shot of the elephant without inadvertently taking out any of the dispersed group with a stray bullet.

I don't recall the sound of the bullet entering the elephant's skull, but I remember its trunk relaxing before it slowly collapsed forward onto its knees. Suddenly, the terror of being crushed into the ground by an angry elephant was replaced by the terror of being crushed into the ground by a collapsing one. But instead the stricken beast toppled over to the side and crashed to the ground. As it slumped, its body rolled over in the dust and trapped one of my fellow walkers – a South African girl who'd been running ahead of me when I tripped – under the weight of one of its legs.

She was pulled free by one of the others, and the rangers shouted at us to get up and move away from the fallen elephant. I was surprised to find that despite my ravaging, I was able to stand up and stumble over to the rest of the group, dusty and grazed and with a dull throbbing in my shoulder, but alive and mobile. I owed my life to the quick thinking and the professionalism of those rangers who – in protecting our lives – had been forced to do something I imagine they'd hoped they'd never, ever have to do: shoot an elephant.

Meanwhile, my son – who had watched horrified from behind the bushes – hadn't realised it was his father who'd been battling the elephant. His eyes widened as it dawned on him that it was me now standing up and making my way over to him.

I don't recall much about the long walk back to the game drive vehicle except that it was done in near silence, broken only occasionally by a nervous joke from one person or another, to which we'd all respond with equally nervous laughter.

Back at Skukuza I was taken to the clinic in the camp. There, the doctor sat wide-eyed as I explained what had just happened. He jumped up and rushed out of the surgery to call his twin brother in to come and hear my story for himself.

'By all accounts, we should been collecting you from the bush in a body bag,' one of them said. People who find themselves attacked by elephants, he explained, invariably land up as flesh and bones in the *veld*.

I returned home to England a few days later to discover that word had somehow reached the British press, and I had become somewhat of a cause célèbre in my home town of Stafford. In war, they say, the first casualty is the truth. This apparently applies equally to elephant attacks. According to some of the local reports, I'd been gored by the elephant's tusks and suffered a grisly open wound to my leg. In truth, the only injuries I sustained were torn ligaments in my shoulder from where I had pushed back so hard against the elephant. But I suppose torn ligaments don't sell papers.

I often get asked how I feel about elephants now. To their surprise, I am at pains to explain that I hold no animosity towards elephants whatsoever, and despite a few jangled nerves when I next encountered them on a safari in Kenya a year or two later, no longer hold anything other than a very healthy respect for those giants of Africa.

And the rest of the holiday? Despite my unfortunate brush with the local fauna – and its achingly tragic outcome – my friends are always surprised to hear me tell them that it was probably one of the best holidays I've ever had.

9

ONE WILD MORNING IN LOWER SABIE
Penny Legg

ONE OFTEN HEARS STORIES of first-time visitors to Kruger stumbling across the most remarkable sightings barely through the entrance gates, or ticking off a list of animals in a single day that some people never see in years of visits to the Park – and you imagine they must think that that is what Kruger is like all the time.

In 1998 we had the privilege of introducing three friends to the magic of Kruger, and on account of what happened in a very short space of time one morning in Lower Sabie, it is difficult to imagine how their perception of rest camps in the Park wasn't dramatically skewed forever.

It was early in the morning when one of our newbies burst into our bungalow with the news that there was an elephant in camp. He had heard what, to him, sounded like somebody slapping their shoes together and had gone out to investigate. He discovered a camp worker frantically clapping his hands and an extremely large elephant plodding around in the middle of the camping area.

We all dashed out of the bungalow just in time to see the elephant simply heft itself back over the fence and continue browsing on the other side. One of the occupants of a tiny dome tent was regaling all and sundry with the tale of her harrowing night – the elephant literally right outside the tent flap. Every time she unzipped the flap to check if the coast was clear, all she could see was a very large, grey body blocking the view, so promptly zipped it up again. Eventually the camp worker had persuaded the elephant, which had by that point consumed a large proportion of the camp's aloe plants, to climb back over the fence at the same spot where it had flattened the wire on its way in.

We had all just returned to our bungalow when our same guest, looking quite ashen-faced now, came tearing back into the lounge and declared, 'There's a f-f-f-f-f-ing lion in camp!' He was so flabbergasted and distraught that even the swearing did not quite come out right.

Once again, we all hot-footed it to the edge of the camping area and arrived just in time to see a great big, black-maned lion disappear behind one of the bungalows. We prudently decided that it would probably be unwise to investigate this on foot, so we all jumped into the car instead.

Now, at this time of morning, campers were getting going, and folk who were staying in accommodation without ablution facilities were all making their way to the shower blocks. So when the lion decided that this was the right time to vocalise its frustration at the situation it found itself in, what ensued was total chaos. We will never forget the look on one man's face as he walked out onto his veranda yawning, only to find a big male lion roaring virtually right on his doorstep.

With hubby driving, the videoing of the chaos was delegated to yours truly. We now have the most unreal footage of the lion running between the bungalows along with extended sessions where, in my excitement, I filmed the ceiling, the floor and the dashboard of the car, all the while assuring my husband that I was indeed capturing this for posterity.

By then the whole camp, it seemed, had been alerted to what was happening, and there were disbelieving people running hither and thither. But only when they either caught sight of the lion or heard it roar did it seem to hit home that this was no fairground ride; there was a lion on the loose in one of Kruger's busiest camps. We tried to warn as many people as possible to stay indoors, and I'll never forget the various reactions we received, which ranged from disbelieving laughter to blind terror.

An official Park's vehicle arrived, but they could do little about the situation, as apparently the only dart gun was in Skukuza and they would have to wait for it to arrive, along with the person qualified to use it. In the meantime, they eventually managed to corral the lion into the fenced garden of one of the staff houses on the boundary fence. And with that, we left for our morning drive with our senses tingling like crazy. On our return we were told that there had been no need for a dart gun, or mercifully any other kind of gun, as they had eventually persuaded the lion to return to the other side of the fence – through a gate, no less.

To say that we were on a high after that morning was putting it mildly. Everywhere we went that day, and the ensuing days, the story was told over and over by our enthusiastic guest. And in each telling, his imitation of how the lion roared became louder and ever more convincing. It became our mission to try and film him whenever he was regaling someone with the tale, and my husband and I would have to stifle our giggles as we waited for the punchline and the roar.

Sadly, two of our three friends are no longer with us, but I still smile when I think back to their extraordinary introduction to Kruger, and how they must have left the Park believing that its rest camps were some of the wildest places on earth.

10

BLESSED IMPALA'S FLYING LEAP OF FAITH
Samantha Pittendrigh

WHEN LEGENDARY AMERICAN talk show host Jay Leno based one of his *Tonight Show*'s opening monologue sketches on the cellphone footage I had recorded in Kruger just a few days earlier, I understood what it meant for something to go viral. Here was a live studio audience on America's longest-running late night talk show watching my strangled squeals of 'The cheetah, the cheetah, the cheeeeetah!' and the barely believable moment when the fleeing impala leapt straight through the open window of a car full of tourists.

And I owe it all to the birds of prey that bless their food.

It had started like any other day trip to the Park with my three closest girl friends. But after six hours of dusty driving and rising temperatures we decided to head towards the shade of Nkuhlu picnic spot, on the banks of the Sabie River midway between Lower Sabie and Skukuza rest camps, where the allure of an ice cream from the small kiosk there proved too hard to resist.

It is always when you are in a hurry to get somewhere that Mr Murphy decides to completely disrupt your plans, but I don't think even Murphy anticipated all of what was about to come next. A fellow tourist caught our attention when he signalled us to slow down.

'There are five cheetahs in the area,' he said as we pulled up alongside him, 'so be on the lookout.'

My senses were piqued: in all my years of visiting the Park, I had never seen a cheetah with even a single mate, let alone another four. We scoured the bush as we drove, before eventually reaching a cluster of about six cars parked up in the middle of the road. Had we found the cheetahs? With no gaps to get past, and no obvious sign of what they were looking at, we waited patiently.

That is when I saw the birds of prey. I'll always remember the way my mother explained the reason birds of prey circle in the sky before a kill. I had imagined that they were arguing over who landed first, but she told me they do it because they were like us: before they ate, they had to bless their food. For an 11-year-old, it seemed a reasonable explanation, so I went with it. Nine years later, boxed in by a cluster of cars on a road in Kruger, I looked up for some reason – perhaps to get a sense of how high the sun was – and circling in the sky above were birds: birds blessing their food. I reached for my phone and immediately started recording. It was as though they waited for me to realise what was about to happen, because seconds later, it started.

Like a shoal of flying fish, a herd of uneasy impala broke from the thorn trees on our left and leapt across the road immediately in front of our car. Sailing two metres in the air and clearing the entire width of the road in a single bound, it was safe to say they were running from something. And just as we were about to ask the question, we got our answer.

'The cheetah, the cheetah, the cheeeeetah!' I shrieked as I filmed through my open window, the excitement constricting my airway until my voice reached a high-pitched squeal.

A cheetah, its tail bobbing in the air, shot across the road, just metres behind the final impala in the herd, and for a second they disappeared into the thicket on the right. But, deep in the bush, the impala must have swung around sharply, because suddenly, through the stems and branches of the thorn trees on the side of the road 10 metres in front of us, the blur of two figures – one chasing, one being chased – hurtled back towards the road at a breathtaking pace, with just a hair's breadth between them.

Breaking free from the bush and onto the dusty verge, the impala, in its hunger for survival, did something unheard of, something barely even plausible: it launched itself off the ground and leapt head-first for safety into the only available refuge – the inside of a Toyota Prado. There was a heavy thud, a series of gasps from my friends, and the man leaning out of the Toyota's passenger window on the other side almost dropped his camera in fright at what had just landed on the seat inside. The pursuing cheetah skidded across the verge and slid under the car, while its hunting partner, which had just cantered in from the left, panicked and shot off into the bush. In the commotion, it was difficult to assimilate what had just happened, but when men in other cars began desperately bellowing 'Open your door! Open your door!' we realised the impala was *inside* the tourists' car.

What the scene was like inside that car's cabin is anyone's guess, but the passenger hanging out of the opposite window dropped back in, and in a blink his door opened, and the impala was bundled over his lap and out onto the road, safely separated from the cheetahs. The door was quickly pulled closed again, and the impala tottered uneasily through the cars – a little dazed – and hobbled off into the safety of the bush on the side of the road.

With that, it was over. A few cars hung around for a while, hoping to catch more action, but with the impalas long since dispersed and the cheetahs nowhere to be seen, the cars slowly filed away and that little stretch of road returned to normal. Anyone passing it even five minutes later would never know that they had just missed one of Kruger's most gobsmacking episodes.

A couple of days later, my photos of the impala's daring escape – grabbed from the stills of my cellphone footage – decorated the front pages of a number of South African newspapers, and for the next few days my life became a whirlwind, as rumours spread that there weren't just photos of the incident, but video too. Eventually, after passing it through a profanity filter a couple of times, the video was released and the world went bananas. In less than 24 hours, over one-and-a-half million people had viewed the clip online, and it continued to go through the roof. Three days later it had topped five-million views, and by then the story, pictures and video clip had been lapped up by newspapers and media houses all over the world, topping viral video charts and occupying the 'And finally...' slot on countless television news programmes in who knows how many languages. Toyota even approached me to possibly use the clip in an advert. Strangely, I am yet to hear from the makers of the Chevrolet Impala. In Jay Leno's sketch on *The Tonight Show*, he purported to show the 'extended clip' of the incident, which ended with an hilarious recreation of the impala, sitting upright in the driver's seat, hooves on the steering wheel, driving the car away while the two defeated cheetahs trailed off behind it – although it probably would have been funnier if they hadn't mistakenly used a prosthetic springbok to play the part of the impala.

And what of the real stars? The cheetahs didn't go hungry. We passed them a little while later, a few kilometres up the road, dragging a fresh kill into the long grass. And as for the lucky impala, whether or not it lived to see another sunrise over the Lebombos, I don't know, but one thing is certain: it can be thankful for the birds of prey that bless their food.

11

AN ASTONISHING CONFLUENCE OF KILLERS
Hennie van Deventer

ONE MORNING IN 1973 on the Salitje Road, the old gravel road that skirts the much quieter northern bank of the Sabie River between Skukuza and Lower Sabie, my wife and I learned an important lesson about wildlife. From that day onwards, nobody would ever be able to sway us from our belief that it is always better to find a quiet spot to sit, relax and wait, rather than drive around endlessly.

It was that morning that we experienced what an erstwhile Bloemfontein neighbour would tease my wife about for many years after, tirelessly imploring her: 'Tell me again about the lion and the leopard, wild dogs and hyaenas and elephants and hippos and impalas and the crocodile…' He was exaggerating, of course; wild dogs, hyaenas, elephants and hippos do not figure in the story. Lions do, though. And a leopard. And impalas. And an enormous crocodile. Certainly enough ingredients for a wildlife drama of the highest order.

The previous day, my wife and I had sat for hours in our blue 1970 Fiat 125 under the dense canopy at a viewpoint beside the Sabie River. Some eagle-eyed visitors in another car had indicated that they had seen the wriggle of a leopard's tail in one of the far-off trees. We strained our eyes until they watered, but we saw nothing.

The next day – the day the drama played out – our two-year-old son had tired of us driving around in the heat. So we navigated towards the inviting shade of that same viewpoint just off the Salitje Road, which we had so enjoyed the day before.

Parked up under the ancient Natal mahogany trees with four or five other cars to keep us company, we whiled away the morning watching the antics of a troop of vervet monkeys. An hour passed and, with the exception of the monkeys, we hadn't seen a thing. It seemed the heat was as oppressive for the animals as it was for us humans. Just then, a herd of impalas appeared behind the car and headed down towards the water to drink. They moved slowly and cautiously past the left-hand side of our car, jumping with fright at the slightest crack of a twig. Quite why they were so skittish I didn't know; an hour of careful scanning had revealed the area to be free of anything but monkeys – and flies.

Suddenly, the monkeys emitted a panicked chorus and they dispersed into the trees, chattering loudly. This was enough for the jittery impalas, which snorted and scattered in a flurry of dust.

'Look!' cried my wife, motioning to the leopard storming towards us from the right.

'Look!' I cried, motioning to the two lions running towards us from behind the high embankment on our left.

The impalas were in disarray – with the lions bearing down on them from the left, and oblivious to the leopard on the right, the herd stampeded past us. One of them leapt cleanly over the car's bonnet and sailed across to the other side, while another kicked out wildly and – *bang!* – knocked a dent into the car door. Hot on their heels came the lions. Next to us, a guy sitting on the roof of his car with his big, clumsy camera froze as the lions flashed narrowly past him.

We hadn't even exhaled when we heard a frantic splashing from the water in front of us. We swung our heads around in time to see the jaws of a huge old crocodile slam shut into a death grip around the torso of one of the impalas that had fled towards the water. And – can you believe it? – behind us, there were the lions again. Their mouths hanging open as they skulked back in the direction from which they had come, growling under their breaths in frustration at their lack of success – with the daredevil still sitting terrified on the roof of his car.

After a few moments, the crocodile disappeared under the water with its prey. The lions disappeared back behind the embankment. The leopard was nowhere to be seen. The monkeys sat in the branches in silence and the flies buzzed around as before. It was all as if nothing had happened. There and then, my wife and I made a decision which we were to stick to over some 450-odd further visits to the Park: we will always drive around less and spend a whole lot more time sitting in a good spot, waiting for the action to find us instead.

12

THE BIYAMITI STOWAWAY
Gordon Parratt

I HAVE NO IDEA why nature had it in for us on that trip. Looking back now, the series of unfortunate events on our final day in the Park were little more than warning shots across our bow. The final assault wouldn't be unleashed until the next day.

It was the late February of 2009 and my wife, Ilda, and I had decided to do one final game drive before packing up later that night. We were a few kilometres along the N'watimhiri Road when we came across a young bull elephant enjoying the rich pickings of fallen fruit beneath a marula tree, and making it very clear that we were not to pass. Each time we tried to edge past, it became very aggressive and charged the vehicle, stopping just short each time. Our efforts to retreat were thwarted by a small jam of cars behind us and, before we knew it, a whole hour had passed and gate closing time was approaching. Eventually, we made a dash for it, and the great beast had the cheek to chase the car just as we passed it.

About five or six kilometres further on, we came across a small elephant herd with several calves. As I attempted to pass, a calf bellowed out. With that, a very large bull ran at us, and I was forced to accelerate and wheel-spin my Hyundai Terracan madly to get away. To top it all, just before we got back to Biyamiti Bush Camp, we reached the Biyamiti weir only to find it had been washed away earlier that day. We were beginning to get the distinct feeling that nature was holding a noticeable grudge towards us.

We eventually made our way back to camp via the Crocodile Bridge road, arrived late and accepted a mild scolding from the 'camp captain'. We didn't know it then, but nature's grudge was far from over. On the contrary, what lay in store was to land us on the pages of newspapers around the world and send shivers down the spines of hundreds of thousands – perhaps millions – of people who'd go on to read about our escapade.

I unpacked the car that evening to make ready for our return home to Pretoria in the morning. I placed boxes, a cooler box and all the clutter that seems to fill the car on Kruger trips onto the ground behind my beloved 4x4, tidied everything up, then repacked it all again. With that, we were good to go at first light.

I drove that day, with Ilda in the passenger seat beside me. We left the Park at Numbi Gate just after 10 AM and headed for home. I hadn't been driving long when I felt what I thought was a bug fluttering around my left leg and ankle. I tried to brush it away, but it persisted. With my eyes on the road, I leaned down again to shoo it away, only to feel something much larger than an insect against my hand. Looking down, I saw the head, and about 10 or 15 centimetres, of a snake. We had somehow picked up a passenger.

In that brief and not-so-comfortable moment (and despite being nothing of an expert on snakes) I determined two things: one, this was not a small snake, and two, it was one of the cobra species – either a Mozambique spitting cobra or a snouted cobra; both deadly and neither of which you'd care to have slithering around your bare feet.

I pondered my next move. I didn't want to alarm Ilda, nor did I want to cause a situation where the snake would bite – neither scenario being mutually exclusive! Leaning over to her and simultaneously developing chameleon-type eyes looking all over the place, I gingerly broke the news.

To be fair to Ilda, she could have reacted worse. That doesn't mean she didn't immediately become a contortionist, though, placing her feet up onto the dashboard and somehow lifting her bum high off the seat, as rigid as a plank, and remaining that way for several kilometres. And my stress levels? Luckily for me, at times of great stress I am not the panicky type. I figured that the snake had, up to this point, been undisturbed by the movement of my feet on the car's pedals, so saw no reason why continuing in the same vein until we could get some help would do anything to provoke a bite. I appreciate that this wouldn't necessarily be everyone's first choice of action.

Thinking back, the snake must have sneaked into the boxes that I had rested on the ground whilst tidying up the car in Biyamiti the previous evening. Frighteningly, the wetness that I had felt on my cheek as I was packing, which I had assumed was Ilda emptying the teapot next to me – something she insists she never did – was more than likely a spray of venom from the frightened cobra. Clearly, it was nature's final grudge attack of the previous day's mischief.

Soon we entered the area just before the Hazyview turn-off where dozens of hawkers and taxis operate from the gravel verge on the side of the road. We stopped amongst the hawkers and both rapidly piled out of the car, attracting some odd looks from the traders more accustomed to seeing tourists in holiday-mode disembark in a more orderly fashion.

We tried to do a search from a respectable distance, but the snake had disappeared into one of the dark recesses of the car's cabin and neither of us were inclined to go poking our heads around inside.

This was no place to abandon my beloved vehicle, I thought, so was left with the rather unenviable task of either sacrificing my hubcaps, my wheels, or indeed the entire 4x4 – or getting back in and driving on.

I do love my car. So, very gingerly, we drove on to Hazyview to get some advice from the tourist information bureau there. It was a sensible decision, as they contacted the local reptile park and a really enthusiastic and helpful young man asked me to drive to the site where he worked. Soon after, under the watchful eye of our new accomplice, we unloaded everything from the car. But the snake had hunkered down and was in no mood to reveal its position. So we repacked the car once again and all drove on to a local panel beater, who assisted in very carefully removing as many of the car's interior panels and covers as possible.

A good three hours passed and still the snake had not shown itself. Perhaps it had slithered out as secretly as it had found its way in, so I decided there was not much more we could do except continue home. Our enthusiastic snake man gave me a briefing as to how to apply a tight elasticated crepe bandage, and other sobering advice, should I be bitten.

Shortly after leaving Hazyview the snake announced that it had not disembarked as I had hoped, and reappeared several times around my feet and legs. Bearing in mind I was wearing shorts and was barefoot, I could feel each touch of its cold body with frightening clarity. Nevertheless we pressed on to Sabie, nestled on the Escarpment overlooking the Lowveld, enduring many snake reappearances around my feet.

In Sabie we must have looked like lunatics to the locals – rapidly stopping and getting out, discussing the situation, before getting back in and driving off. If only people knew what was going on inside the car.

Traffic up and down Long Tom Pass to Lydenberg was very fast and dangerous on those hairy hillside curves. Impatient drivers were tailgating us and adding generously to the somewhat elevated blood pressures in the car. There is no internationally recognised hand signal for 'snake in car', though, so there was not much we could do except continue on to Lydenberg and hope not to get bitten.

I was extremely grateful to Ilda for bearing with it all – and thankful that the snake was on my side only. It had been six hours since we first discovered our stowaway, and still with so far yet to go, I was starting to have my doubts that we'd survive the trip all the way back to Pretoria without finding one of us on the business end of its fangs.

About 15 kilometres before Lydenburg – perhaps sensing the altitude change, or perhaps having heard what Lydenburg is like – the snake became very active. It started to move up my leg and became more visible, inching its way up to just below my knee. Only then was I more certain that this was indeed a Mozambique spitting cobra, and it looked to be about a metre long.

With very heavy rain, windows misting up, visibility not good and perilous traffic, what was I to do but drive on? At the top end of Long Tom, we saw three people bird-watching and hastily stopped alongside them. All were very helpful, and plied us with hot, sweet coffee to help settle our nerves. They managed to contact a local snake expert, who very kindly drove out and escorted us into Lydenberg to a guesthouse for the night.

With Ilda safely holed up in the guesthouse, the snake expert drove with me to his home, where we again removed everything from the car and stripped out every panel. But, once again, the snake remained hidden. I knew it was in there somewhere, though, so I very carefully put my hands under the rear seat to release the catch and flip it forward. But just as my fingers touched the lever, a red-brown tail appeared from under the seat cover. Luckily for me the seat had not yet flipped, otherwise I may well have been left staring eyeball to eyeball with a spitting cobra.

The snake quickly moved back under the seat cover, but its hideout was revealed now. When we lifted the cover to expose it, it became extremely hostile and, true to type, began spitting frightening volumes of venom at us. The snake man received a faceful, but thankfully only a very little got into one eye. I received some on my left cheek and arm. Luckily for me I had not shaved that morning, otherwise the venom may well have entered a shaving nick.

With his eye smarting and venom dripping off his face, the snake man had no trouble identifying my passenger as a Mozambique spitting cobra. Then he turned to me and said rather unnervingly: 'The angels were with you, my friend.'

I believe he was right. We had driven for over seven hours with this snake at my feet, and we often wonder how or why I had not been bitten. Likewise, what would have happened if it had bitten me? And what if I had been wearing jeans that day – would the snake have crawled up the leg, then panicked at the first movement I had made? I still wonder about all this and my blood runs cold.

The story of our journey back that day was very soon picked up by a local reporter who was a friend of one of the birdwatchers who'd helped us. It was published in the local Lydenburg paper and from there the story spread like wildfire. The day after getting home, reporters from the Beeld, Pretoria News, The Sun and a host of other papers too numerous to mention were on the phone. It made me feel like a celebrity for a day. I gave a journalist reporting on behalf of the British papers my story, and from there it literally went worldwide. Practically every country in the world had an article in one or more of their papers. There was controversy too, of course. After a radio interview, a female listener accused me of being selfish and inconsiderate for the danger I had put my wife in. Perhaps she was right.

More light-heartedly, some amusing comments were made in different countries. A French chap wrote that he agreed it was a dangerous situation, but that was nothing: he drove 50 kilometres every morning with his ex-wife in the car! An American woman, skillfully combining both ignorance and jingoism, wrote that the Mozambique spitting cobra wasn't that bad; after all 'it only spits,' she said, and doesn't bite 'like our rattlesnakes'.

What would you have done and how would you have managed a situation like this? I have asked many people their thoughts on being in a similar situation – all have been uncertain. One thing that was for sure though: I was not going to abandon my beloved Hyundai Terracan!

13

HIJACK ON THE BRIDGE
Andrew Clark

SOME YEARS AGO, I NOTICED a sign at either end of the bridge over the Sabie River near Skukuza that said something along the lines of: 'This is an experiment. You may get out of your car between the two yellow lines'. I chuckled to myself at the thought that this seemed to imply that if you didn't get attacked or eaten, then the experiment would be judged a success.

Nevertheless, I was driving along the bridge with the car's right rear window and the two front windows open to circulate the air, as it was getting close to 40°C. Having just changed a flat tyre earlier that morning, the entire contents of my boot were still on the back seat, as I had had to move it all to retrieve the spare wheel.

Spread out languidly on the tarmac towards the middle of the bridge was a large troop of baboons, watched over by a big male sitting on the railing. Knowing how dangerous baboons can be, I realised that partaking in any bridge 'experiment' would not be happening that day – in fact I did not even dare stop. That did not seem to bother the alpha male, though. With one bounce from the railing onto the road, he jumped in through the back window of my moving car.

As fast as the baboon got in, I got out. However, in my haste to evacuate, I failed to switch off the ignition. I also didn't have time to put my shirt on or even grab my camera – mostly because the baboon was sitting on it. So there I was: shirtless, running around the car from the passenger side to the driver's side, trying in vain to scare the baboon back out of the car. Every time I tried to put my hand into the driver's window to switch off the engine, the baboon went for me. With the engine still running, I was terrified that he would knock the lever into gear and the car would go careering through the barrier and down into the Sabie River below.

So I watched helplessly as the baboon ate my apples, then opened my box of buttermilk rusks and, bar two, ate the lot. A packet of sweets was then opened, shovelled into its mouth and the wrappers spat out. He tried to eat a camera lens but found that a bit hard.

This is not a quiet area of the Park, and by that point I had attracted a fair few onlookers, who were all taking videos and photos of the uninvited passenger – and me. They weren't entirely unhelpful, though. One couple gave me an apple to place on the railings of the bridge in the hope that it would lure the baboon out of the car. No such luck. The hairy hand of one of the hijacker's extended family appeared from nowhere, made a grab for it and in a flash disappeared off the bridge and into the bush.

More cars streamed past and had a good laugh at my expense. About a quarter of an hour later, an open safari vehicle full of tourists came into view. For whatever reason, upon seeing the driver's khaki uniform, the baboon knew that the game was up and beat a hasty exit from the car. Relieved, I climbed back in. But just as I sat down, another smaller cousin clambered inside the same way the big male had done earlier and, as if to add insult to injury, grabbed my last two remaining rusks. I screamed at it and it screamed back – and because its teeth were bigger than mine, I got out again. As the safari vehicle drove past, the guide slammed his hand against his door, and the rather nervous young baboon burst out like a shot.

I had definitely learned a lesson that day. Now, whenever I see baboons, I make sure all the windows are wound shut.

Due to the fact that the big guy had been sitting on my cameras when I abandoned ship, I was sadly unable to get any photos of my misadventure. But I do know that there are a few photo albums out there somewhere with some shots of a naked ape running around a car in a pair of shorts on the Sabie River bridge, while a hairier ape sits inside polishing off a box of rusks.

Whether all of this added to the outcome of that bridge 'experiment' or not, I don't know – but I notice that those signs are no longer there, and getting out of your car on the Sabie River bridge is now strictly verboten.

14

HOW THE ELEPHANT GOT ITS TRUNK
Johan Opperman

KRUGER'S ORPEN DAM, between Skukuza and Satara, may be several hundred kilometres from the 'great grey-green, greasy Limpopo River' – as Rudyard Kipling famously described it – but it was here that I captured a remarkable series of photos that, perhaps because they so closely resembled Kipling's timeless tale of how the elephant got its trunk, were published in newspapers across the world soon after.

During a day trip to the park early on a February afternoon in 2007, I was at the lookout point above Orpen Dam. Down below, a family herd of elephants on the far bank were browsing amongst the reeds, drinking and rolling around on the muddy edges of the water.

I was particularly amused by a young calf that had ventured off away from the herd like a curious child and was ambling along the water's edge towards the far right side of the dam. Just then, there was a sudden splash and a gigantic crocodile, twice the elephant's length, surged out of the water and grabbed the youngster by the tip its trunk.

With a high-pitched squeal, the calf dug its heels into the mud and flapped its ears in panic while the croc tugged and tugged on its trunk. The commotion soon caught the attention of the rest of the herd; they suddenly went crazy, running around and trumpeting and stamping their feet before quickly surrounding the struggling calf and somehow wrestling it away from the croc's grip.

After it was saved, all the other elephants in the herd huddled around the youngster for a while, some gently brushing it with the tips of their trunks, as if to make sure that it was all right. It was a deeply touching scene.

They say an elephant never forgets. So it was a bit of a surprise when, a short while later, the whole herd began walking through the dam, which wasn't much deeper than a metre at that point. They passed the area where the crocodile was last seen – and was probably still lurking – without much of a care. I suppose they knew the crocodile would not have been foolish enough to try its luck a second time against the collective force of an entire herd.

I did not realise exactly what I had caught on film (to use an old expression, as I was actually using a digital camera) until I got back to my lodge outside the Park that night and looked through the photos on my computer. When the crocodile had lurched out of the water, I had just started clicking away in typical amateur fashion, hoping to capture at least something of the action. So it was quite a surprise to discover that I had, in fact, caught one remarkable shot where the crocodile, its body almost fully out the water, had its jaws clamped onto the baby elephant's trunk. The elephant in turn was pulling back firmly like the anchor in a tug o' war, with its feet dug in, ears flapping, mouth agape and its trunk stretched taut like a rubber band – a shot that so closely mirrors the many different book covers of Kipling's *The Elephant's Child* that it could easily have been used as an illustration itself.

After returning home I posted the pictures on an online photography forum, where they were praised for the subject matter, if not for their technical brilliance. Eventually, they were removed to make way for other photographs and were largely forgotten about.

For three years the pictures just 'gathered dust' on my computer's hard drive, until 2010 when I decided to repost them. This time, a UK-based news agency saw the photos and sought permission to sell the publishing rights and split the profits 50/50. I enthusiastically gave the go-ahead, hoping that I might make a few hundred rand or so. Two days later they contacted me with the news that the story had become 'big'. Just how big I only found out later – when the payouts started coming in.

The pictures were published in just about every major newspaper in the UK. This was unsurprising, given that Kipling was British and his stories are well known there. But they were also published in mainland Europe, the USA, Australia and New Zealand, as well as in local newspapers where it made it to the front page of a large Afrikaans national. It even appeared on television in Australia.

In the end the payouts to me totalled the euro equivalent of almost R25 000 – not bad for an afternoon's game viewing at Orpen Dam.

There is a curious little side note to this story. While I had never set out to deliberately recapture Kipling's children's tale and would never be so bold as to compare myself with the man, it is an odd coincidence that Rudyard Kipling and I share much in common. Rudyard Kipling was a Freemason, and so am I. What's more, when Kipling wrote *The Elephant's Child* he was 36 years old – precisely my age when I took those pictures. But most intriguingly, Kipling's birthday is the 30th of December. And so is mine.

15

THE NEWLY DEPUTISED OFFICIALS
Beukes Geldenhuys

A NUMBER OF YEARS AGO, as part of a group of tourists in an open-topped safari vehicle, we came across a lone Kruger veterinarian who had just darted a tuberculosis-infected lion not too far off the road.

He called over to us and asked whether we could give him a hand getting the lion onto the back of his flatbed *bakkie*.

He had been alone when he came across the lion, he explained, and knowing that it may be a long time before he'd get the opportunity to dart the ailing lion again, grabbed the chance to do it there and then. However, despite not being fully grown, the lion in its comatose state was still too heavy for him alone to lift onto his vehicle.

Naturally, we were very keen to help and thrilled to be allowed out of the vehicle on 'official duty'. We were handed some gloves, but before we'd even had time to put them on properly, other cars had begun arriving – as is often the case in the busier sections of the Park – and their occupants, noticing a bunch of civilians standing around out of their vehicle, took it as an indication that they too could get out of their cars to have a look. Before long it was total chaos.

The vet cried out: 'Oh dear, what have I done? We need to get these people back into their vehicles now! The rest of the pride are all still lurking in the bush close by!'

So, relishing our role as newly deputised 'Park officials', we began to chase the wayward civilians back into the vehicles, with our guide – a huge *boertjie* with long hair like a heavy-metal rocker – leading the charge; the white gloves and khaki outfit making him look like a traffic officer. With great results he stormed the people one by one, stabbing the air with his finger and shouting 'You! Get back in your car! You, get back in your car! And you, dammit man, get back in your car!' when he suddenly came to a really pretty, blonde bombshell of a lady. 'And you!' he bellowed at her. 'Come see this lion!'

16

BATTLE AT KRUGER
David Budzinski & Cheryl Dowds Budzinski

IT IS A DELICIOUS IRONY that 'Battle at Kruger' – the eight-minute amateur video that astonishingly became one of the most famous pieces of footage ever shot in the Park – was almost never filmed at all because I was in two minds about taking the video camera with us on that trip.

'Of course you should take it – it is your first trip to Africa,' said my wife, Cheryl, unknowingly altering the course of our lives. 'And you need to practise with it.' She was right – about taking it, and about needing practise. I had only ever used it once or twice before, always briefly, and unquestionably did not quite have the hang of it.

Cheryl had been to Africa twice before, both times before we were married. But for Linda – Cheryl's old college roommate who was joining us – and me, it was our first trip: a 12-day whistle stop tour (as we Americans like to do) stretching from Cape Town to Victoria Falls in Zambia, taking in a couple of nights at Kruger. We all had a feeling it would be a pretty good trip. We really had no idea just how good, or quite how profoundly it would change our lives.

By the time we reached Hazyview, on the outskirts of the Park, and met our trusty guide, Frank Watts, all three of us were champing at the bit to see some wild animals. It was September of 2004, and there was still a late winter chill in the air as Frank drove us into the Park for a short game drive before checking us in at Pretoriuskop rest camp for the night. Friendly, good-humoured and with a remarkable eye for game spotting, I realised very quickly that Frank was no rank amateur – he knew the Park and he knew his animals. Clearly 'this was not his first rodeo' as we say in Texas.

Our time in the Park flew by, and with Frank's patience and keen eye, we saw plenty of game. But by the end of our final afternoon, we still had not had any close cat sightings. Knowing this, Frank stayed glued to his VHF radio, and with just an hour to go before gate closing time – and the end of our Kruger trip – word came through of a pride of lions lying in the grass near Transport Dam. Despite it being late in the day, Frank thought it might be worthwhile to check it out. So we rumbled along to the dam and found a good parking spot, parallel to the water's edge. About 50 metres away to our right, perched on the near-end of a dusty mound that formed the dam wall, lay five or six lions doing what lions do best: napping. The clock ticked by, vehicles came and went, gate closing time loomed, and the lions did not move. But Frank encouraged us to be patient. Was he somehow clairvoyant?

This was almost like watching a play. Within a few minutes, the key characters started taking their places on stage. The first, a mature lioness, walked right in front of our vehicle and crouched down in the grass. To our left, and on the opposite side of the water, a herd of 100 or more buffalo were grazing, but a handful of them began making their way downwind and onto the dam wall, traipsing directly towards the resting lions. This play was starting to look interesting. The lions saw them coming, probably smelled them too, and quickly slipped into attack mode, crouching eagerly and locking their eyes on the targets. With the encroaching buffalo oblivious to the danger in their path, I pulled out the video camera and began filming – or at least I hoped I was filming.

When the buffalo – two adults and a small calf – got halfway across the dam wall, about 25 metres from the lions, the excitement in the air was palpable. I was using the zoom feature on the camera and did not want this home movie to show my shaking hands, so I stood up in the vehicle and braced myself against the left side of the uprights. With the buffalo blindly tramping ever closer, I nervously checked the camera to make sure I had hit the 'record' button, not 'pause' or 'play'. Just then, barely a bus-length from the lions, the lead buffalo – a big male – stopped and began nodding its head up and down, like it was smelling the air. How it could not see the lions crouching prone and unobstructed straight in front of it, I do not know, but it finally seemed to have caught whiff of them.

I had zoomed in to watch this, but sensing something was about to happen, I zoomed out again. Good thing I did, because the lioness hiding in front of us suddenly took off on a dead run, straight at the three buffalo. The other lions took the cue and set off too, but were quickly passed by the female. The buffalo had, meanwhile, turned tail and were kicking up dust as they lumbered back across the dam wall. The lioness disregarded the huge bull, passed the second somewhat smaller buffalo, and leapt onto the hindquarters of the calf, sending them both tumbling into the dam with a big splash.

Seconds later, a male lion leapt feet first into the water too. Together the pair began suffocating the calf: the lioness clamped onto its muzzle, and the male clamped around its neck. Gradually, the others – about six in all – waded in and helped drag the limp young buffalo out of the water and onto the bank.

But just then, another sinister player joined the fray. Swimming in from stage left, an enormous seven-and-a-half-metre long crocodile surged from the water and grabbed onto the side of the limp calf, readjusted its grip to get a hold of one of the hind legs, then dragged it partly back into the water. There were gasps from the vehicle. 'Look at this,' spluttered Frank, incredulously, 'the crocodile is taking the baby away!'

An almighty tug o' war ensued: the crocodile thrashed in the water, pulling backwards; the lions, side-by-side, jaws locked on the calf, paws dug deeply into the embankment, pulled upwards; while the poor calf was stretched and yanked from both ends. The tussle seemed to last a deathly long time – so much so, I was tempted to stop filming. This was not the kind of movie I wanted to show my grandchildren some day, what with all the blood and gore to come. But in the end there wasn't any, and my decision to keep filming turned out very much to be the right one.

Even a crocodile of that size was no match for the combined strength of the lions. It eventually gave up, released its jaws and swam away. Up on the bank, all I could make out was a thick huddle of lions; the dark shape beneath them could surely not have survived that ordeal. Or could it? Thundering in from the left came the cavalry. The entire herd of buffalo had reformed and looked to be about to attempt a rescue.

'They're going to come and try and chase the lions – but I think they're too late,' said Frank.

'I think you're right,' replied Linda, forlornly.

But the buffalo didn't share this hopelessness; with the strength of numbers they came charging in towards the lions, forming a semicircle around them and pinning them against the water.

'You're too late, you're too late,' pined Cheryl. But with 70-odd tonnes of angry backstop, the lead buffalo found its courage: it broke ranks and stormed forward, legs kicking, and chased one of the lions away. Seconds later it turned and charged again, this time tossing a lion six feet into the air with its horns. The lion landed squarely on top of another, frightening the life out of it and sending them both fleeing in opposite directions, with a phalanx of buffalo storming behind to see them off. Holy cow – what a battle!

In the midst of all of this, I could hear a sharp cry, almost like a sheep's *baa*. It was the calf.

'The calf's still alive!' I cried, 'It's standing up!'

Indeed, despite still being held down by the remaining lions, the calf somehow managed to stand up and tried to free itself from their grasp. Seeing this, the lead buffalo charged in and pounded its head into the rear quarters of the calf, shunting it from the lions' grip. To everyone's amazement, the calf stood up and trotted into the herd, where it disappeared behind a wall of black. What? Could it be? Did we really just see this?

With the calf safely ensconced in the herd, the rest of the lions were easily chased away. Nobody could believe what we saw. 'Did you get that?' spluttered Frank. 'Yeah,' I answered, 'I got it all!' He had never in his life seen anything like that, he told us. It was truly a once-in-a-lifetime sighting.

When we bade farewell the next day, Frank asked if I might make a copy of that encounter for him, as did another passenger in our vehicle. I said that I would and followed through with my promise a couple of weeks later.

When Cheryl and I watched the video at home, we knew without a doubt that we had witnessed something amazing. Our friends who watched the video with us felt certain that we had something truly valuable on our hands and urged us to see if National Geographic,

Animal Planet, or some producer might want to use the footage. I made a number of phone calls and sent numerous emails but, disappointingly, no one was interested. I assumed NatGeo and others received solicitations like mine all the time and were not interested in home video shot by a shaky-handed amateur. So I gave up but kept the video handy to show family and friends, who all still believed it to be remarkable. Mostly, the cassette sat in a drawer and was forgotten.

Three years later, in May 2007, I got a phone call from my daughter saying that our video clip was posted on YouTube.

'You what? What did you say?' I asked confusedly.

'YouTube!'

'What the heck is YouTube?'

I was not that familiar with social media, but I was to find out rather quickly what it was – and how powerful it could be.

What happened after that was mind-boggling, and certainly life-changing for us. I was contacted by television network ABC, the American Broadcasting Company, to be interviewed for a new TV show they were airing called *i-Caught*, showcasing unusual and remarkable footage shot by amateurs. They flew me to Washington DC, and I was interviewed by famous American television journalist, Bill Weir. I sat in the 'Green Room', which is not really green, had makeup put on me, and saw what it was like to be on TV. It still seemed so surreal; I did not know what to make of it. Our segment on 'Battle at Kruger' kicked off the first show of the season.

What came next seemed like an avalanche. A production company wished to film a National Geographic special about the sighting and contacted us about flying Cheryl and me back to Kruger to shoot some footage. This was crazy: now we were part of a movie ourselves; instead of standing behind the camera, we were now in front of it. Once again, this became an 'once-in-a-lifetime experience' for us. That makes two! Our Kruger trip was beginning to churn out once-in-a-lifetime experiences with some regularity, it seemed. On location back in the Park, it was very special to see our guide, Frank Watts, again. He was building his own reputation from 'Battle at Kruger' and had begun writing a book of safari tales. We finished filming, flew back home, and waited to hear about the 'special'. And waited… and waited…

Then in late April the following year, I heard from National Geographic that the special was going to air in early May. They wanted me to appear on TV and radio to promote the show on behalf of NatGeo. What? Me? Holy cow! A third 'once-in-a-lifetime experience'! Believe it or not, this was becoming less intimidating and beginning to feel like a lot of fun. First, I did an interview for the *New York Times*. Days later, a limousine picked me up at home, took me to Houston International Airport, and I flew to New York City where another limo took me to the hotel. A NatGeo PR person met me, arranged a few days of TV and radio interviews, and shuttled me around NYC. It was a whirlwind of studios and cameras, make-up and microphones – a far cry from the back of a safari vehicle on the banks of Transport Dam in the middle of the Kruger National Park. I appeared on *America's Newsroom*, *Inside Edition*, *Good Morning LA*, *Fox & Friends*, and more than a dozen radio shows, including the popular *Dennis Miller Show*.

It wasn't just me who got air-time. In 2010 we were asked to be a part of an NBC special on eyewitness animal footage called *Caught on Camera*, and Cheryl turned out to be the star of the show. I always said she should have been in the movies.

All the while, the video was going viral, and soon 'Battle at Kruger' had become a byword for the power of teamwork and a lesson in never giving up. Managers of professional sports teams used it to gee up their players to victory. *Time* magazine wrote about it. At last count, the video was edging up towards 75 million views online and has generated more than 65 000 comments.

With all the coverage, particularly in the United States, few people here have not at least heard of 'Battle at Kruger', and there have been many times when people we hardly know have talked about it in front of us without realising our connection. Recently at supper club, a group where you meet and get to know new people, the lady sitting next to me said: 'I googled you to see who you were. I did not know you two were famous.' But she is wrong. We are not famous. The stars of the show are the lions, the crocodile, the herd of buffalo and, especially, the calf. All we did was witness the event. We were just blessed with the gift of recording it and being able to share it with the world.

Life for us has never been quite the same, although it is a little bit more relaxed now that we are retired. We have been back to Africa, and

Kruger, and in 2012 we had a great reunion and game drive with Frank Watts. He never disappoints us, and he still has the habit of saving the best for the last part of his game drives. This time we came upon a cheetah while driving back to camp. It ran alongside the vehicle for a while, crossed in front of us, and then it took off like a rocket after some impala. What a sight. 'Not quite once-in-a-lifetime, Frank, but a great try!'

17

GRANNY AND THE WHITE LIONS
Sheenaugh-Lee Thompson

A WHITE LION IS just about the least likely thing you'll ever see in Kruger. The rare genetic mutation that leads to their distinctive snowy white coats is so localised that the few white lions alive in the wild are found almost exclusively in the Timbavati area adjoining the central region of the Park. Only a tiny handful of tourists over the years have spotted white lions elsewhere in the Park – and I am one of them.

You may think I am lucky to be part of that exclusive group, but good luck seldom runs smoothly. The most exciting thing I would ever see in my life was cut heartbreakingly short by my hysterical grandmother.

It was 1990. I was just 10 years old, and with my grandmother about to turn 72, my parents decided to surprise her and take her along with us for her first ever trip to Kruger. There was a good reason she had never been before: among her many anxieties, she had a mortal fear of wild animals. Regardless, my parents felt confident she would be just fine once she was in the Park – an immersive therapy of sorts – but to get her there would involve a few white lies. And a sleeping pill.

My father told her that we were taking her to Pilgrim's Rest, the little gold-rush mining town on the escarpment above the Lowveld. The only wild animals at Pilgrim's Rest are the wild horses in the hills around Robber's Pass, so my grandmother found little reason to object. Halfway through the journey my father coaxed her into taking the sleeping tablet – she was, after all, a nervous car passenger and the pill would relax her nicely. The plan played out like clockwork – soon she was fast asleep and we motored on to Malelane, Kruger's southernmost entry point.

My grandmother woke up as we drove under the boom at Malelane Gate and entered the Park. She took a few moments to register that we were not at the promised holiday resort near Pilgrim's Rest before blowing a fuse and going ballistic, which in turn sent my brothers and me into a fit of giggles. Somehow my father was able to placate her and explain, not altogether candidly, that now that we were in the Park, we had to stay. Less than impressed, she eventually acquiesced and we headed on to Berg-en-Dal rest camp.

The following morning was my grandmother's birthday, and Kruger had the most extraordinary birthday present ready for her. My father persuaded her to join us for a game drive, and we all happily headed along the gravel road that skirts the Crocodile River and leads eventually to Crocodile Bridge rest camp. Some distance along that road, we turned up a small side road and there they were, lying in the shade of a concrete reservoir: a pride of eight lions. But there was something very odd about the sole male and two of the seven females: they weren't the yellow colour of normal lions. Their coats were an ashen white and stood out starkly against the sand and dry grass. They were three of Kruger's mystical white lions. And there they were, stretched out in the morning sun, just metres from the car – the only car there, I should add.

We all melted in ecstasy, but the significance of the occasion was entirely lost on my grandmother, who instead began having a panic attack from being so close to a pride of lions. It started with some heavy gasping, then a few tears – and then she just went bananas. First, she feigned a heart attack, but when that didn't work she turned on the waterworks, crying and screaming and hyperventilating. She simultaneously smacked my father over the head from the seat behind, screaming at him to 'Drive! Drive!' as the lions were surely going to eat her.

This was all too much for my two brothers and me; what had started as a few barely disguised chortles gave way to a riot of guffaws, as we rolled around on the seats, barely able to breathe. This didn't do much to help my poor mother, who was trying to explain, less than adequately over the din, that the lions were clearly not going to attack us while we were encased in a two-and-a-half tonne Volkswagen Caravelle.

All the while, my poor father hung over the steering wheel, creased over in fits of laughter, trying to get at least one photo of this once-in-a-lifetime sighting. But the rocking of the car from the ruckus in the back, coupled with his own paroxysms, made it impossible to hone in on the lions; each time he steadied the camera, his mother's hand connected with the back of his head and knocked the lens out of focus.

She didn't let up until my father finally capitulated and started driving, leaving the bemused white lions behind us. That didn't stop the hysterics, though, and we had to make a rushed detour all the way up to Skukuza for the doctor there to administer her with some calming meds. It felt like a very long way, hearing over and over again how we had been the cause of her almost being eaten alive by a pride of lions.

My grandmother refused to leave the camp after that. But animals have a strange sense of humour, so even that didn't quite work out for her. The following morning a troop of baboons rampaged through the campsite, raiding the tents as they went. At the sight of this, she bolted and locked herself in the caravan. I wouldn't be surprised if she piled furniture up against the little door. I can still see her horrified face peering out through the window at us kids all sitting outside, unperturbed by the marauders as they scampered past. She truly believed the animals were out to get her, and on the final day, as we left the camp and drove towards Malelane Gate, she kept herself hidden well below the window line – just in case the animals saw her and mistook her for food.

My father never got any photographs of those white lions in the end. And, of course, I have never seen another white lion since then – nor is it likely I ever will. I don't mind so much about the photos, and by the time my grandmother died a few years ago, we had all long forgiven her. But thinking back, it would have been nice to have spent more than just a few minutes with the world's rarest lions – perhaps without the histrionics, too.

18

PULLING A BABOON'S TAIL
Riël du Toit

AT A BEND IN THE ROAD a short distance east of Skukuza rest camp, my wife and I came across a large troop of baboons fanned out along the tar. It is always fun to sit and watch baboons. It can be instructive too – you can identify with their antics and even recognise in them some of the traits and mannerisms of your very own friends. Worryingly, you may even recognise some traits of your own. Certainly, what we did a few moments later falls firmly into the category of monkey business.

Ahead of us in the road, in amongst the baboons, was a stationary open-backed Isuzu *bakkie* with two ladies sitting frozen with fear in the cabin, their windows wound shut. For perched behind them, on the side of their *bakkie*, sat two big baboons with their legs inside and their backs facing the road.

I quietly rolled forward a bit and stopped alongside them. There must have been something very interesting in the back of that *bakkie* because, despite being just inches away, the two baboons remained oblivious to our car. Meanwhile, behind us, cars were beginning to roll up, full of holidaymakers and tourists captivated by the peaceful antics of the troop on the road.

When my wife quietly wound down her passenger window, the baboons didn't even glance back. The biggest of the two sat closest to the *bakkie's* cab and, with its backside just inches from our open window, the temptation became too much for me. The situation was so ideal and the challenge so provocative, I couldn't hold it in. I whispered to my wife, 'Pull his tail!'

To my surprise, she responded immediately and reached through the window and gave the baboon's tail a swift tug.

I would never have imagined a baboon could do so many things at once. It barked thunderously, let out a terrified scream, evacuated its bowels, bared its teeth and executed a perfect somersault – all in one swift motion. It would be safe to say it got a bit of a fright.

Almost simultaneously, its terrified companion performed more or less the identical routine, soiling the *bakkie* further and doubling the uproar. You would think a leopard had pounced on them, the way they carried on. The whole of Kruger echoed with their clamour – it was as if they were being murdered and the world was coming to an end. Scampering away, they were so upset they began fighting one another, each pinning the blame on the other and neither seemingly able to work out just who had pulled whose tail. The rest of the troop, meanwhile, had got the message loud and clear when the uproar began and had scattered into the bush. In a trice, the road was cleared of all baboons.

It was suddenly very quiet. All that remained was a handful of tourists in their cars, a dung-splattered Isuzu *bakkie*, and my wife and I feeling sheepish and embarrassed. Even we had got a fright. We certainly hadn't expected a reaction quite like that. Worse, our actions had left someone's *bakkie* befouled, and we had thoroughly destroyed the harmony in the troop – most probably for quite some time. To try and excuse it would be churlish. Who would have thought my wife would even do such a thing? She never listens when I ask her to do *anything*!

Our embarrassment was compounded by the fact that we do voluntary work in the Park as 'honorary rangers' and had large signs on my car doors signalling that fact. Worse still, I was even wearing a uniform. What sort of example was I setting? I was supposed to uphold the correct attitude towards conservation and ensure visitors enjoyed the Park peacefully, but here I was doing the complete opposite. I was too ashamed to even look into my rear-view mirror and see how the people behind me were reacting. They would surely have been flashing their lights and shaking their fists at me.

Feeling as guilty as the wood of the gallows, I gritted my teeth and squinted my eyes, kept my head locked dead ahead, took a deep breath and slowly drove forward as if nothing had happened. A little further on, when we were almost out of sight, my wife and I burst into a fit of hysterics. It was perhaps more from the shock than from any impertinence. After all, wc had just made huge asses of ourselves in front of a bunch of strangers.

A short while later at Nkuhlu picnic spot on the banks of the Sabie River, we were enjoying a drink when a group of tourists who had been driving behind us and seen it all happen walked up to me and stopped. I braced myself for a ticking off. *'Jislaaik Oom,'* said one of the boys, suddenly breaking into a wide grin, 'you really gave that baboon a fright!'

19

SPAT ON FROM ABOVE
Christa Niederer

WHEN A BIRD DROPPING LANDS ON YOUR HEAD, they say good luck is just around the corner. I suspect this is more to placate the poor victim who has just been splattered. But if luck is the reward, I am yet to find out what great fortune awaits me after getting showered on from above by something that was neither a dropping, nor from a bird – it was far more disturbing than that.

With our children having recently flown the nest, my husband and I treated ourselves to a few nights in one of Lower Sabie's furnished safari tents. Mounted on stilted platforms in thicker bush to the north of the camp and far from the hubbub of the chalets and bustling camping area, we knew as soon as we arrived that we had made a good choice. From our veranda we could just about see the Sabie River, and not far from the tent a large lizard basked on a stone in the afternoon sun. Even though the bush around the tents was quite dense, it was visibly becoming dry – autumn was approaching fast. Inside the tent's en-suite bathroom, a small frog had found its way up to the basin in search of water. I carefully took it into one hand and transferred it to the grass outside. We watched it hop away and then turned our attention to the river and horizon. The sun was beginning to set and was painting the sky with the deep hues of red, orange and blue which are so characteristic of Kruger. Things couldn't have been more perfect – but that was about to change.

Walking into the tent, I was puzzled to find a couple of bats flying around in circles inside. I opened the door to let them out, but they didn't seem to sense the opening and continued to flap around in a gyre. Suddenly, I got sprayed on from above. The bats? As I contemplated the possible quantities of guano that bats might excrete – for this was no light sprinkling – I received a second dose of spray on the top of my head. I stepped away from the door towards the opposite side of the tent to survey the scene, tracking the bats with my eyes. And then I saw it: a Mozambique spitting cobra with menacing black eyes, facing me angrily from the top of the wooden door frame. It lunged forward threateningly. For a split second, I thought it would make a dash for me.

'Snake!' I hissed to my husband, who spun around and followed my gaze to the top of the door. Our minds raced and my husband fought an immediate reflexive urge to flee. 'Let's get out of this tent!' he spluttered, with a barely disguised undertone of urgency. 'But then we won't know where it might go next,' I protested, not forgetting the fact that we would have to pass under the snake on our way out.

We fled the tent as soon as the snake withdrew its head – my husband to go and find help, and I to keep an eye on it from the outside. I wasn't convinced by the wisdom of this decision, though, because it had already become quite dark and I felt somewhat vulnerable, wearing only a t-shirt, Bermuda shorts and a pair of slip-slops. It had also dawned on me that this snake belonged to the spitting variety, and I longed for some kind of glasses to protect my eyes.

So I remained on the veranda, waiting. Every now and again, I stepped towards the door and peered through the mosquito-netting to see whether the snake had plans to relocate – specifically in the direction of my bed, which would have been the worst of all possible scenarios. But I noticed that it was equally apprehensive. Occasionally, it would gingerly protrude from its hiding place somewhere at the top of the doorframe to see what was going on. It didn't seem to harbour any plans for resettlement and had probably only spat at me to warn me not to let its dinner out through the door.

Even though the snake and I seemed to have reached some kind of truce, I was not unhappy when a Park's vehicle eventually pulled up and a ranger approached, armed with two long rods and a pair of protective goggles. By now, a small crowd of neighbours and inquisitive bystanders had gathered on our veranda.

We were asked to stand at a distance while the ranger carefully placed the looped end of his rod against the door frame at the spot where the snake had just disappeared after squirting some venom in his direction. We waited in suspense, but it took only a few minutes for the snake to reappear and examine the loop with its tongue. Then, to my surprise, it slid its head straight through the loop. The ranger pulled the noose tight and attempted to remove the snake from its hiding place, but it put up a valiant fight, resisting with every muscle in its long body. It was a formidable – and well-fed – specimen.

But a snake is no match for a sturdy ranger, and in the end he was able to uproot it from behind the doorframe and transfer it carefully into a plastic bucket, where it continued to bang against the closed lid. Bidding us a good evening, the ranger placed the bucket alongside him and drove off to release it some kilometres further away in the open bush.

Our adrenaline levels remained elevated for quite some time, but we felt relieved at the prospect of not having to share our tent with a Mozambique spitting cobra, one of Africa's most venomous snakes. To be on the safe side, I took a shower and rinsed my hair thoroughly; the venom of this cobra, even in tiny quantities, can cause immeasurable problems if it gets into your eyes or seeps into a small cut or nick in your skin. I felt grateful that we had emerged from the adventure unscathed – and I suspect our sentiments were shared by the two bats that had left our tent in the meantime.

20

LEOPARD IN THE TORCHLIGHT
Gavin Black

BEFORE WE HAD EVEN HAD A CHANCE to shake out our bones following a long drive up to the Park from Durban, we were presented with a dilemma at the Berg-en-Dal rest camp reception.

The Duty Manager was jittery about our plans to camp at nearby Malelane, as there had been a problem there the previous night. A leopard had jumped the fence and chewed on some tent ropes, a few car bumpers, some other things left around and, ominously, the corner of an occupied caravan tent.

But, it being the last day of a long weekend, our options for somewhere safer to sleep were limited; the Berg-en-Dal camp site was fully booked, our budget didn't extend to the family cottage they offered us, and it was too late to push on to one of the other camps in the Park. So there was little option but to risk it in our tents at Malelane.

Malelane rest camp is a small, unmanned, gem of a camp in the far south of the Park, lying just above the banks of the Crocodile River. For those who have never visited Malelane – and if you haven't you really should – the most striking thing is the incongruously low gate into the camp. While other camps have electrified cattle grids, a guard on duty and, by comparison, a virtual portcullis to protect them, the guests at Malelane are shielded from the wilds of southern Kruger by nothing more than a rickety old farm gate.

I suppose with a gate like that, anything more than the rudimentary farm fence – three strands of barbed wire and a single steel cable along the top – surrounding the camp would be superfluous. If I recall correctly, the fence is not electrified either. After all, with a gate that you could hurdle over with a decent run-up, what would be the point?

We were greeted at Malelane a short while later by a congested sea of tents and caravans in the camping area. Although we had a reservation, it initially appeared that every campsite space was occupied, but we eventually put up our tent in a small clearing near the gate. The road into the camp was to our left as you face the gate, and the camp fence was about 15 metres in front of our tent.

Having been in the car all day, we relaxed that evening. We made our customary first fire, had our *braai*, then sat quietly watching the goings-on around us, as most people in the camping area were up late packing and readying themselves to head home the next morning.

Around our fire there was no talk or overt concern about the leopard; not because we were not interested – on the contrary. We just didn't want to frighten our two daughters – or, if I am honest, ourselves – into having a sleepless night. A few well-intentioned campers did come and chat to us, though, and showed us the evidence of the leopard's deeds and damage from the night before, as well as some preserved pugmarks in the sand. Nevertheless, we had a good, uneventful night and were relieved the next day that there were no signs of the leopard having returned to the camp while we slept.

That first morning, we went on an early drive and had breakfast at Afsaal picnic spot. On returning to camp at about 10 AM, we were met with an incredible site: the camp was empty. With the exception of our solitary tent, there was not a single car, caravan or tent anywhere. It was unbelievable – from the heaving bustle of the camp the night before, we now had the entire place to ourselves. By lunch time, an elderly couple had arrived with their caravan and pitched camp down in the far corner near the river – but that was it.

Later that evening, at about eight o'clock, all was quiet in the camp. The children were fast asleep in the tent, and I was just sitting and relaxing, enjoying the bush smells and listening to the occasional grunting of impala rams, as it was right in the middle of the rutting season. From my camp chair, I switched on my handheld spotlight and shone it up beyond the gate. The beam revealed a large herd of impala grouping together on the gravel road, settling in for the night.

Suddenly, there was a commotion and the impalas began snorting in alarm. Illuminated by the spotlight, I could see them all looking up the road. Then, without warning, they burst into action and fled in all directions, snorting and bounding away. What on earth had scared them?

My relaxed state had rapidly drained and the hairs on my arms were sticking up. Standing up and shining my spotlight further up the road, I saw a set of green eyes looking directly at me. When the eyes blinked, they reflected back at me with an eerie red colour. At the same time I could see only one eye, then two, then one, as if the animal was winking or moving its head from side to side. I kept the torchlight locked on those eyes and stood firmly, but my legs felt hollow. Whatever it was, it was about 100 metres away and walking straight towards the gate. I still couldn't see what it was, but I didn't need to – from the way the large eyes shone in the light, and perhaps from pure gut instinct, I knew it was a leopard.

I told my wife to get up slowly and come and have a look. We moved a few steps forwards and, with the spotlight now illuminating a larger area, sure enough, walking casually down the road towards us was indeed a leopard. Standing about 10 paces from the fence, with our tent about five paces behind us, I whispered to my wife that whatever we do, we must not take our light, or our eyes, off the leopard.

When it got to about 20 metres from the gate, the leopard cut away into the bush in front of the fence line and crouched down behind a small shrub. Every time my wife or I moved, we could see its head rise up to stare back at us. This behaviour was not right, I thought, and it was unquestionably not what I wanted to be seeing with only a four-foot fence between us. I should really have listened to the bloke at Berg-en-Dal and taken that family cottage instead.

It was too late for regrets, though – it was time for action. I did not want to lose sight of the leopard, so I told my wife to quietly and calmly get to the tent and take our two small children and lock them into one of the empty huts adjacent to us. The leopard's behaviour seemed unusual and I was worried that any sudden noise or movement might provoke it into unwanted action. So I decided, rightly or wrongly, that it wouldn't be wise to shout at it or clap my hands to try and frighten it away.

Carefully, my wife managed to pick up both my daughters and carry them, still sleeping, to one of the huts, open it and put them safely on the beds. Quite how she managed this I have no idea, but she did it with no fuss from the girls, who didn't so much as stir.

For the duration of the translocation operation behind me, the leopard had not moved and was still watching me intently. With my wife and children safe, it was my turn to back away and get myself into that hut too.

Before I could make my exit, out of the corner of my right eye I saw another spotted animal at the fence, walking in my direction along the tract dividing the fence from the bush. I froze and my heart somersaulted in my chest. Another leopard! But as it moved into the clear light of my spotlight, I saw that it was just a large civet cat, nose to the ground, sniffing along and oblivious to the predator a few metres away. In the blink of an eye (literally – I now really know what that expression means) the leopard began slinking up towards the civet – which, disturbingly, also happened to be right in front of me. With a sudden explosion of speed, the leopard completed its ambush and leapt onto its prey. A high shriek from the civet, a low rumble from the leopard, and it was all over. Clasping the kill in its mouth, the leopard bounded off into the bush. Gone.

With my legs close to buckling and my hands shaking with adrenaline, I wasn't prepared for the shock of what happened next. Something moved behind me and before I could turn, it had me by the shoulders. For a terrifying second I thought the leopard was on me. But, spinning around, I came face to face with my wife; she had quietly moved in from behind while the kill had been unfolding in front me. I had no idea that she had returned in time to see it all too.

I was not amused, to say the least, but after a few minutes I began to see the funny side of it, especially every time she collapsed with laughter imitating my terrified reaction. It was good to unwind and laugh as we talked excitedly about what had just happened.

If you're wondering where we slept the remainder of the night, I confess that it was most definitely in the hut. Kruger Bookings Department, you may send me the bill.

I fondly recall many details of that night, but my daughters' puzzled expressions when they woke up the next morning to discover that they were inexplicably in a hut, and not a tent, were priceless. And as for my wife, I don't think she will ever know quite how close she came that night to having my torch used as a weapon against her.

We reported the incident that same evening to the ranger staying in the residence next to the camp. He and a student went out in their vehicle with a spotlight, and in the area we had pointed out, not far from the camp, they found an adult female leopard with an approximate year-old cub.

I mention this because there is a sobering and tragic footnote to this tale. A few months later, barely three kilometres from Malelane rest camp, a newly-qualified Kruger guide stopped one evening to allow the tourists on his night drive to stretch their legs. While he sat drawing on a cigarette on the railings of the bridge that crosses Matjulu River, rifle on his lap, a female leopard crept out from the darkness and attacked him from behind, killing him instantly.

21

AN ACCIDENTAL TRANSLOCATION
Elfie Barker

OVER THE YEARS, many animals in Kruger – particularly elephants – have, for one reason or another, been translocated out of the Park to new stomping grounds in reserves around southern Africa. Well don't mention it to anyone, but my family and I once undertook a translocation of our own Kruger animal – entirely unwittingly, of course, and admittedly nowhere near as big as an elephant.

It was some years ago now, and after a few days camping at Lower Sabie rest camp, the time came to pack up and head home to Johannesburg.

Normally, we are meticulous about making sure that there are no creepy crawlies trapped inside our tent before folding it up and packing it into the lower bunk of the caravan. But a thunderstorm had been looming the previous evening, and the tent had been hastily folded into its bag and stashed away. The next day we got up early and made our way through the Park and down to Malelane Gate, from where we headed back home to Johannesburg.

About six weeks later our trip to the Park was all but a distant memory, and it being a beautiful Highveld summer's day, we decided it was a good opportunity to pitch the tent against the caravan in our yard and give them both a good hose-down to get rid of the dirt and bird mess.

Out came the tent and, to our astonishment, hidden between one of the mesh windows and the cover was a pale but very much alive gecko. Miraculously, it had not been crushed and appeared very pleased to see the light again, despite being almost 500 kilometres from home.

Our children promptly christened him Jacob, and he was gently caught and placed on the wall in our back yard near a light – the rationale being that if he lived, he could at least try and catch some food. 'Will he survive?' enquired my two boys of eight and six. That was the big question.

Well, Jacob did survive and indeed seemed to thrive in his new home. As it was summer, there were a lot of bugs for him to eat and the weather was not too harsh. I suppose, incredibly, he had gone into semi-hibernation for his six weeks in the dark, otherwise I cannot explain how he lived for so long bundled away inside the caravan.

Jacob quickly became part of the family, and many nights were spent watching him stalk and capture his prey. I am pretty sure not one of us ever walked in or out through the back door without looking for Jacob. Even friends and family soon got to know about the now not-so-little gecko and would ask to see him every time they came around. And so, life continued, with the summer eventually turning to autumn.

Unfortunately, with a Highveld winter on its way, concern was raised as to whether Jacob could handle the cold weather we get in Jo'burg. He was, after all, from the sub-tropical climes of the Lowveld, where anything below 20°C triggers a mad scramble for scarves and jerseys.

Some friends of ours had mentioned that they would be spending a few nights at Orpen rest camp in the late autumn, and it was decided – with broken hearts – to return Jacob to Kruger. After much chasing and squeaking, he was eventually caught and put into a shoebox for safe translocation back to the Park.

We were pleased to hear from our friends upon their return that Jacob had travelled well and was safely released back into the wild at Orpen.

Thus a valuable lesson was learned: no matter how hurried we are, the windows in the tent are always thoroughly checked before packing up. As much as we loved having our little Kruger refugee that summer, we wouldn't wish to put even the smallest of creatures through that again.

As for Jacob, he would have had some very interesting tales to tell the other geckos about life in The Big Smoke. And while he may not quite have been back at Lower Sabie, he was at least close enough to say that he was home.

There is an intriguing addendum to this tale – one which suggests we may be making a habit of accidental translocations. A few days after our most recent trip to Kruger, I was surprised to see a slender mongoose popping its head up in our Johannesburg garden – something I had never seen in all my years living there. Had it come back with us from the Park? There was much speculation as to how that could have happened; the most feasible explanation being that it crawled onto the water tank under our caravan and huddled there like a stowaway until the caravan eventually came to a standstill in our driveway. For a week it hung around in the garden, revealing itself now and again and terrorising the local insect population. Then one day it simply disappeared, and I've never seen it again since.

22

LION ROAR UPROAR
Derek Conradie

AS A NATURAL BORN PRANKSTER, I am the type who never passes up the opportunity to pull someone's leg. But many years ago, in Skukuza rest camp, I got a taste of my own medicine when a little lion-inspired prank backfired spectacularly.

We had travelled up to Kruger from Velddrif on the West Coast with a bootful of *snoek* and crayfish, lightening the load as we progressed, but saving some to enjoy in the Park. When we finally arrived in Skukuza, where we were booked into a rondavel on the perimeter fence, we immediately set about enjoying our first *Weskus*-style fish *braai* – much to the envy of our neighbours.

Not long after dinner, with the sun set and a not inconsiderable volume of tipple under my belt, I spotted an opportunity for a brilliant prank. Our foreign neighbours sitting in front of their rondavel alongside us had become noticeably nervous and jittery now that night had drawn in, and were jumping and starting at each mysterious night sound. This was too good to pass up. I whispered to the others that I was going to give the poor tourists a little scare.

Our rondavels were right on the perimeter of the camp, with a short, steep slope in front of them running down to the fence. That would provide the perfect cover. So I quietly slid down the slope and stalked along the fence line until I was just in front of the neighbours, who sat huddled around a little fire, still wide-eyed at the sounds of Kruger after dark.

Very quietly, I leopard-crawled up to the edge of the slope to within just a few metres of the couple, took a deep breath and bellowed out the loudest, most terrifying lion roar I could muster.

The poor tourists just about jumped out of their skins – chairs went tumbling as they fell over themselves and jostled to be the first back inside the rondavel. But rather than making me feel bad, their panicked exodus just fired me up, and I let out two further loud roars to see them home.

It was precisely then that my plan backfired, and it was suddenly my turn to run like crazy. From right behind me came the bone-bending roar of an extremely unhappy lion, drawn to investigate this strange-sounding intruder on its patch. I scrambled out of that ditch like two rockets had been fired from my heels and hurtled back to the rondavel, pale-faced and breathless, where my friends were all rolling around in hysterics at my delicious (and well-deserved!) comeuppance.

23

A CLOSE SCRAPE WITH POACHERS
Keegan Lloyd Steward

WHEN THE RESCUE WAS ALL OVER and we were safely deposited by helicopter at Skukuza, it turned out that nobody even knew we were gone. We'd been discovered entirely by accident. Tragically, this was only because three rhinos had been shot and mutilated by poachers just 300 metres from where we had become stranded in a riverbed the previous day.

I had just turned 21 years old, and as a present, my parents had treated my girlfriend, Meghan, and me to a seven-day trip to Kruger. If 21st birthday gifts are supposed to be memorable, this one turned out to be firmly unforgettable. In truth, we were lucky to have come out of it alive.

It was on the fourth day of the trip and raining heavily when we left Pretoriuskop rest camp early for the long journey up to the big baobab tree, just south of Satara, which Meghan had been eager to see. We eventually reached the tree at around two o'clock in the afternoon, before deciding to head back via the gravel road down towards Skukuza, where we would be spending the night. Soon, though, it was bucketing down, and our decision to take the scenic route back was beginning to look unwise. We made a pit-stop at Hamilton's Tented Camp and asked whether there was a quicker way back to Skukuza, but the rangers advised us that with some of the roads closed due to rain, our best option was to just keep driving south. So we pressed on.

Eventually we reached a point where the road dipped and cut across a sandy riverbed. In dry weather, the crossing wouldn't have troubled even a small car, but with all the rain it looked worryingly muddy. Meghan and I both let out a soft 'uh-oh' as I slowly drove forward and down into the riverbed. Our instinct was correct: almost immediately the car became bogged down in the soft sand. I accelerated a little, but while the wheels tore up the sand and mud behind us, the car didn't budge. I revved a little more, but nothing – we were stuck.

It was fast approaching sunset and I had no intention of us spending the night in the car, so I got out and attempted to dig it free from the sand. With me pushing and Meghan in the driver's seat, we tried every manoeuvre possible, but the car remained stubbornly bogged down. Time ticked on. I jammed branches and wood under the wheels, but that too proved fruitless. In the end, exhausted, soaked through and covered in sand and mud, with the light fading, I accepted the inevitable – we would not be sleeping in our beds in Skukuza that night.

We hadn't seen another car for hours. But in the vague hope that our non-arrival at Skukuza had triggered a search party, we sounded the horn over and over and kept the hazard lights on for as long as possible. Eventually, the car battery ran down and the lights slowly dimmed and died. We were stuck in the middle of the Kruger National Park with a dead car, no cell phone reception and no sign of any search party coming our way.

That night, while trying to sleep across the two front seats, I heard a trickling of water under the car and realised, to my horror, that with all the rain the dry river had begun to flow. I covered my ears and tried to ignore it and not tell Meghan – things were bad enough as they were without having to contemplate abandoning the car in the middle of the night and pitting ourselves against the Park's predators. Moments later there was a loud thump on the car. I froze, shut my eyes tight and dared not move a muscle.

Waking up the next morning, we saw that the river had indeed started to flow and was streaming around the car – though mercifully not strong enough to cause any concern. Also, there was a pile of fresh elephant dung not more than three metres from the car. That would have explained the thump in the night.

With the sun up, and our estimation that we were not much more than 25 kilometres from Skukuza – the busiest camp in the Park – we figured that the first of the morning's tourists would very soon be heading up the gravel road towards us. But nobody arrived. The sun rose higher and still nobody came. This didn't make sense. I started to second-guess myself: were we on the road I thought we were on? Had we unwittingly taken a detour in the rain the previous day and landed up on a disused road? Panic set in. We began shouting for help, but soon realised this was futile. In the thick bush, our voices would have barely carried a few hundred metres at best.

The morning passed slowly. Eventually, at around noon, we heard a chopping in the distance and realised a helicopter was coming our way. Meghan jumped out of the car, shouting, and attempted to flag the helicopter down, while I clambered onto the roof and waved my arms like a madman – but it just flew right past. They had missed us. But rather than being crestfallen, it gave us hope: either the receptionists at Skukuza, or perhaps our parents, had alerted the authorities that we had gone missing, and the helicopter was on a rescue mission to find us. We couldn't have been more wrong.

As the hours slowly passed, our hope faded, and the thought of spending another night in the wet, cold and dead car started to haunt us. Would it be better to abandon the car and trek towards the main road somewhere to the south-east?

I was mulling the pros and cons of such a perilous plan when, suddenly, there was that chopping sound again in the distance – the helicopter was back. This time we shouted even louder and made as much noise and movement as possible. It worked; the helicopter turned in a wide arc and landed in the riverbed. We were saved.

Two rangers emerged from the chopper and rushed over to us. They checked that we weren't in shock and assured us that everything was going to be all right. There would be no additional charge for the airlift, they joked. Within minutes we had unpacked the car and were in the helicopter waiting to head back to some form of civilisation.

As we flew out over the bush back to Skukuza, I finally saw why nobody had come along the road that morning. The turnoff onto the gravel from the tarred road, just a few kilometres south of where we had been stranded, had been closed off because of the rain.

It was only when we were back at Skukuza that we smelled the rot on the rangers' clothes and discovered that not only had we been found by accident, but that our position was chillingly more perilous than we imagined. When they had flown over us the first time, the rangers hadn't been out looking for us at all; they had been on their way to the spot, a few hundred metres from our car, where three rhinos had been slaughtered in the night.

'You're very, very lucky you didn't run into the poachers,' said one of the rangers, gravely, 'especially with all your shouting and hooting'.

It didn't bear thinking about. As if the flowing river under our car and the mysterious thump in the night wasn't enough, we'd been within earshot of some of the most ruthless and barbarous people on the planet – people who surely wouldn't have thought twice about offloading a further two cartridges.

But there is a warming ending to our story. Not only did the experience of being stranded for 24 hours in a riverbed in the depths of Kruger make us both stronger as individuals, it brought us closer together too – four months later, we announced our engagement and are now happily married.

24

GOOD TURN TURNS BAD
Bertus Meiring

RUSTY OLD CYNICS will say that no good deed goes unpunished. Over a long weekend with family at Lower Sabie rest camp a few years ago I came frighteningly close to proving this dictum correct, when a good turn almost got me eaten by lions.

Over that long weekend there were a few prides of lions around the camp all competing for territory. Each night we fell asleep listening to them trying to outroar each other, and in the daytime we were spoiled rotten for sightings, frequently chancing upon them on the roads around the camp.

During one of our morning drives, we ended up slowly following three teenage males plodding along the road. As traffic started to build up from both sides, an elderly gentleman coming from the opposite direction decided he had had enough of the lions and needed to get to camp, so he pulled forward slowly to try and pass them. Teenage lions are often boisterous and full of mischief – not unlike teenage boys – and, as the man passed the lions, one of them began sniffing at the slow-turning wheels of the car, before casually sinking its teeth into the tyre.

When the man reached my car, I rolled down my window and told him that his tyre was unfortunately completely flat. He groaned at his bad luck. Because he was alone in his car, I offered to help him change it as soon as the lions and their entourage of vehicles had moved on a bit. My parents, who were in another car, decided to carry on following the lions, so I told them I would catch up with them as soon as I had helped the man.

When the procession was almost out of sight around a bend further down the road, the man and I both got out of our cars and set about changing the tyre as quickly as we could. There were lions in the vicinity after all, and I did not want to spend a minute longer outside my car than was necessary. We had got the tools out and were just about to jack up the car when I heard hooting and a choir of people screaming and shouting. Above all the voices I could hear my mother's voice the clearest: 'Get into your car now, they're coming for you!' The panic in her voice could have melted glass. And looking up, I understood why: all three lions had turned around, burst through the traffic, and were running straight for us.

Tools went flying as we abandoned the wheel, jumped up and bolted back into our respective cars, slamming the doors behind us. I sat there breathing hard and was overcome with an intensely uncomfortable feeling as I reflected on what could have just happened. This, I suppose, is why they tell you to always stay in your car in Kruger.

I turned my vehicle around and drove back to camp, where I soon found a ranger who could help the man change his tyre. That, after all, seemed like a much wiser way to help – and one far less likely to end with me becoming lion feed.

25

A BITE AT BERG-EN-DAL
Diederik Harmse

SOMEWHERE BETWEEN PRETORIUSKOP AND BERG-EN-DAL rest camps, our morning game drive – which had already been quite productive – suddenly became a lot more interesting as we rolled up to a large puff adder sunning itself in the middle of the gravel road. We coasted up alongside it, turned off the engine and watched it quietly for a while, little knowing that this was not going to be our last close encounter with a snake that day.

My eight-year-old niece, Mecyla, was with us in the car that morning. Like me, she is a real bush fanatic, always exploring the camps and passionately interested in every aspect of life in the animal world. She is always first in line when a weekend to the bush is planned. On this particular trip she was at her game-spotting best again, helpfully pointing out well-camouflaged animals that we'd have otherwise gone whizzing past.

When we pulled in through the gates of Berg-en-Dal a short while later, Mecyla's excitement at seeing a new camp for the first time was fizzing over. So, when we got out of the car, I suggested that before we sit down with some drinks, we should stretch our legs and all take a stroll down the walkway that follows the camp fence in front of the restaurant.

Mecyla was in her element. After seeing some hippos and a few crocs really close to the fence, she turned around and skipped back towards the restaurant where the promise of an ice cream beckoned. Just as she reached the front of the restaurant, close to where the animal skulls are on display, she let out a piercing scream. My mother, who was right behind her, shouted, 'Snake!'

Mecyla had been bitten.

I had been standing further down the pathway snapping away at the hippos, but with my adrenaline surging I bounded up to where Mecyla was lying on the ground, screaming and holding her left foot. My heart sank when I saw the puncture wound on her little toe.

The first thing on my mind was to get help but also, very important-ly, to find the snake, as I knew any treatment would rely on a positive identification of the culprit. I looked around frantically for my fiancée to tell her to take a picture of the snake, but I needn't have panicked; she was already on its trail. As Mecyla wailed, you could really hear the pain in her voice. Even the birds scattered and called out from the trees – the same way baboons do when a leopard gets too close. Visitors at the restaurant had heard the commotion, but rather than help us they just sat there staring, watching the drama like it was just another Kruger sighting.

I picked up Mecyla and ran straight to the camp's reception area for help. As we ran I tried to squeeze out the venom, but this only made her scream louder. My fiancée was still in hot pursuit of the snake and, much to our relief, eventually found it not too far from where it had struck. Carefully aiming her camera at it, she snapped a number of clear photos.

In times of tragedy, things are supposed to happen in slow motion, but here it felt like it was all happening in a flash. With Mecyla still in my arms, the receptionist directed us to the small town of Malelane. While running to the car, we tried to identify the snake in the picture – but I didn't recognise it at all. My brain was still trying to catch up with the rapid escalation of events, and I went cold as the gravity of the situation set in: the nearest doctor was a good 20 minutes away, in Malelane – outside the Park. Would we get there in time? How much time did we even have?

As we drove we all prayed that the venom would not have any further effects on Mecyla's foot and body. She was clearly in a lot of pain, and while we tried to remain calm, my mind was racing: Neurotoxic? Cytotoxic? Do I suck out the blood? Should I make a tourniquet like in the cowboy movies? Was it a puff adder? No, I am pretty sure a puff adder is larger in diameter and has a bigger head. Maybe it was a juvenile *puffy*, then? I was sure it was not a black mamba.

My fiancée, meanwhile, was on her phone searching online for pictures of snakes to compare against the photos she had taken. My mother was doing her very best to help Mecyla remain as calm as possible, despite the pain.

Now, normally I find people who speed in Kruger to be a disgraceful bunch. But on this occasion I felt that if ever there was an excuse to exceed the 50 kilometres per hour limit, this was it. However, the bush alongside the road was thick, so there was no way of knowing what was going to jump out in front of the car at any point. How disastrous would it have been if we had collided with something?

In the back of the car, blood had started flowing from Mecyla's toe. Despite it being barely five minutes since the snake had struck, the swelling had become pronounced too, and the colour in her toe had turned a nasty deep red.

Our prayers on that drive were no doubt being heard, as we only passed one car all the way to the gate and were very glad not to find any traffic jams at a big sighting on the way. The staff at Berg-en-Dal had forewarned the guards at Malelane Gate that we were on our way, and they were ready for us, clearing the road as we approached and waving us through like a presidential motorcade. I did not even have to slow down as we passed under the boom and zoomed out over the bridge across the Crocodile River and out of the Park.

In no time we arrived in Malelane – truly a one-horse town, just beyond the gates of Kruger. The staff at Berg-en-Dal had given us rough directions to the nearest doctors' surgery and said they would call ahead to let them know we were on our way, but in the heat of those panicked moments I hadn't quite taken it all in. So I parked the car and got Mecyla out to carry her to the front door of the first practitioner we could find, only to discover the place deserted; I had forgotten it was the Easter weekend. Where to now? My fiancée saw another medical sign just two houses down the road. I did not even bother to drive there; I just ran towards it, with Mecyla in my arms.

I can hardly remember now, but I think we found a further two practitioners closed, so I just kept running with her until we eventually ended up at the only doctor on duty in Malelane that day. There was a very long queue, but they were expecting us. I burst straight into the doctor's room, Mecyla in my arms, to find her busy with a patient, who very kindly didn't hesitate to put his shirt back on and leave the room so that Mecyla could be seen immediately.

I was absolutely exhausted but also relieved that we got her to the doctor, who was very quick to get Mecyla on a drip and give her something for the pain. After a while she calmed down, but she was certainly not out of danger yet – not by a long chalk. We still had to identify the snake.

The doctor peered at the picture on the camera display. Her immediate reaction was that it was a puff adder, but worryingly she was not sure. Straight away, she got on the phone to get hold of any snake specialists in the region. However, after a few minutes of calling around, she told us apologetically that they had all gone away for the long weekend. The initial relief at having got Mecyla to a doctor suddenly drained away.

My fiancée, meanwhile, had been consulting a few patients in line waiting to see the doctor. They too all thought it was a puff adder. I am no snake expert, but I refused to believe this, especially as the image of a puff adder was still fresh in my mind from our sighting on the gravel road a couple of hours earlier.

With the doctor's hands tied, so to speak, there was little she could do but call for paramedics from Nelspruit to come with an ambulance and move Mecyla to hospital and get her into intensive care as soon as possible. They arrived about 40 minutes after the phone call, stabilised Mecyla and loaded her into the back of the ambulance. One of the paramedics took a look at the photo of the snake and tentatively identified it as a night adder because of the dark arrow behind its head. But, like the doctor, he was not entirely sure.

I travelled with Mecyla in the back of the ambulance all the way to the hospital. It felt like the longest drive of our lives, made worse by the fact that her toe was turning blue and the swelling was visibly increasing by the minute.

Safely in ICU, the doctors treated Mecyla's symptoms and, mercifully, she had no difficulty in breathing – although she was both dizzy and nauseous. The doctors said it was a good thing that we did not restrict the blood flow to her toe by using a tourniquet, as her symptoms were identified as those of an adder or viper bite, meaning that it was a cytotoxic venom, which leads to rapid swelling of the bite area. Just to be sure, though, they called a nearby snake specialist to come and identify the snake accurately. In the meantime, the doctors showed us that there was only one puncture wound on her toe, meaning she only received half the dosage of what both fangs would have delivered.

When the snake specialist arrived, he identified it immediately as a night adder. The paramedic had been right. Night adders are considered less venomous than their cousins the puff adders but should not be underestimated. He told us that a full dose from two fangs into an adult can cause such excessive swelling that the skin can burst open. For an eight-year-old, where the body's immune system and resistance are not as strong, the consequences could have been fatal. But the sunny prognosis didn't end there; the swelling would continue up to about knee height, he said, and in the worst case scenario the tissue damage to her toe could lead to her losing it.

Mecyla's mother and father arrived from Gauteng and stayed with her for the duration of her spell in hospital – which would amount to another three days in the end. We, on the other hand, had to head back to Pretoriuskop, where we were camped. It was very quiet that evening as we reflected on the day. Our Kruger holiday was on its back, and the conspicuous absence in Mecyla's spot around the fire only served to reinforce our decision to pack up and head back home the next morning.

I'm pleased to say that Mecyla eventually made a full recovery and, despite some difficulties walking for a while, she suffered no long-term ill effects. She was, however, armed with the most thrilling story to share with her school friends. Despite the ordeal, she is still as eager as ever to visit Kruger and, remarkably, does not fear snakes at all.

26

BULL ELEPHANT AND THE MINI
Tyla Jade Veenendaal

I HAVE VISITED KRUGER every year of my life, but this story didn't happen in my lifetime – it took place many years ago, back when the Park's roads were all gravel and nobody drove around in big cars the way they mostly do today.

My great grandparents, who started the tradition of visiting the Park every winter, were staying in the southern region along with my grandparents.

Now, my great grandmother had a well-known fear of elephants, which makes this story all the more amusing. They had been viewing game the whole day and were on their way back to camp along the Lower Sabie–Skukuza road, which my great grandmother always said was the only road one needs to drive to see the Big Five.

As is common on this road, they came across a few elephants crossing and stopped the car to let them pass. As they watched the procession from a relatively safe distance, my great grandmother's worst nightmare materialised in the form of a curious bull elephant which had emerged silently out of the bush alongside them. It slid down an embankment right next to their car and, with a thud, flopped its trunk across the roof. To the utter horror of my great grandparents inside, the elephant began rocking the car from side to side, gently at first then progressively harder and harder until the whole car rattled and creaked.

My great grandmother began screaming and, in her blind panic, came close to jumping out of the car and running away. Fortunately, the bull elephant was just being curious and, thankfully, before my great grandmother had had time to eject herself from the passenger seat, the rocking stopped and the perpetrator melted away back into the bush.

The fact that they were in a tiny old Mini – a car not much taller than four-and-a-half feet and almost ten times lighter than a bull elephant – did not make the experience any more enjoyable for my poor great grandmother.

The sight of this gigantic elephant rocking such a tiny car must have been shocking for any onlookers. In this instance, those onlookers were my grandparents, who were driving in the car directly behind. They always insisted that it was even more frightening for them, as they did not know exactly what the elephant was going to do. They genuinely thought that the tiny car and its occupants would be crushed in front of their eyes like an old tin can.

Luckily, cars back then – even tiny Minis – were a lot tougher than the ones we drive around in today, and incredibly, at the end of it all, there was barely a scratch or dent on it – just a smear of dust along the roof from the elephant's trunk, and a bit of wear-and-tear on the old shock absorbers.

The encounter did not stop them from subsequently returning every year to the Park, but it did make the already significant fear of elephants far worse for my great grandmother – which she then duly passed down to my grandmother. Today, this makes driving with my grandmother and viewing game almost impossible. If there is even a whiff of elephants in the air we have to drive on quickly, even if it means abandoning a pride of lions on a carcass, or a leopard posing in a tree.

The elephant phobia has thankfully become diluted as it has trickled down the generations, and I suffer no 'hereditary' unease, so to speak. What has been passed down, though, is a boundless love for the Kruger National Park – the smells, the sounds, the animals, even the people – and this is one family trait that I will happily pass on to my children and my grandchildren. I would, however, always advise them to avoid driving through the Park in a little old Mini!

27

DOG DAY MORNING
André Liénard

RAINY MORNINGS IN KRUGER often produce wonderful cat sightings. Leopards will use the haze and the pitter-patter of raindrops as cover to hunt their prey, and lions may well move onto the roads to keep out of the wet grass. But it wasn't a cat we saw one rainy September morning on the circle route around the *koppies* near Pretoriuskop. It was a dog. An ordinary, domestic dog with a collar and a tatty leash around its neck.

Quite how somebody's pet had found its way into the Park was unclear. But here it was, running around aimlessly in and out of the long grass alongside the muddy road. It was clearly a mongrel, however, no larger than a border collie, with a dark coat, light brown legs and the distinctive snarl of a cur. Were it not for its rudimentary collar and leash, you'd be forgiven for thinking this was an alleyway stray raised on a diet of snatched morsels and rubbish-tip meals.

What happened next was so extraordinary you couldn't make it up.

On the crest of the *koppie* to our right, a pair of large dog ears appeared. It was an African wild dog – one of the Pretoriuskop pack which roam the vast area between Afsaal to the east and Phabeni Gate to the west – and it had spotted the domestic dog. Silhouetted against the grey sky, it stood at the top of the rocky dome and stared down with its ears pricked and head cocked, in the same curious manner that all dogs share. Who knows what signal it yelped, but soon it was joined by one of its pack mates, and they both trotted down across the rocks towards the trespasser on their patch.

Every now and again they would stop in their tracks and glance down in the direction of the dog. They seemed as incredulous about it being there as we were. We could sense that a dogfight of violent proportions was about to play out, and it wasn't going to be pleasant; what chance would a small domestic dog have against a pack of much larger African wild dogs, schooled in the art of hunting, and no strangers to ripping apart their prey while it's still alive?

By the time they reached the bottom of the *koppie* and made their way onto the road, the domestic dog had disappeared into the long grass. The *suurveld* grass around Pretoriuskop grows taller than a man in places – but when you have the nose and ears of a wild dog, that is no barrier. We followed them as they sniffed their way along the road, ears erect and scanning like radars for any tell-tale sounds of their target crashing through the grass nearby.

Eventually, they found it. The domestic dog came bursting out of the grass on the right with such ferocity it took the wild dogs by surprise. Outnumbered and outsized, the mongrel drew deep from its street-fighter lineage and firmly stood its ground, curling its lips and baring every single one of its fangs. It growled and barked and snarled, crouching down and lunging forward at the wild dogs, which growled and whooped back at it. Never have we seen a dog behave quite so ferociously and show such little fear, even when a third wild dog – drawn to the ruckus – joined the other two. The domestic dog stood rooted on the edge of the road while the three wild dogs churned up the mud around it.

But wild dogs are no chumps. Gradually, they edged the dog backwards, away from the open space of the road and into the longer grass, where the advantage would clearly move into their favour.

Out of sight, the brawl continued and we could hear the barks and snarls reaching a vicious crescendo from somewhere in the depths of the grass. We knew the domestic dog stood little chance; there was no way it could hold off three larger, stronger wild dogs in their own domain. It would be like trying to fight off a group of dockyard muggers in a thick fog. With the wild dogs' legendary stamina, which they regularly use to outrun and exhaust their prey, turning and running would have been fruitless too. But just as we were imagining the little animal being torn to shreds some way off in the bush, something completely unexpected happened: the three wild dogs came crashing out of the grass, onto the road, with their tails between their legs. They scampered off, glancing back now and again as if to make sure they weren't being followed.

Quite what had happened in the long grass we'll never know, but a few moments after its surprising victory, the mongrel hobbled out onto the road, limping slightly on its rear leg, before disappearing off into the bush further up ahead of us.

My wife and I had been visiting Kruger from Belgium every year since our first trip in 1997, and we had never before seen anything like this. When we reported it to the ranger at Pretoriuskop later that morning, he told us he would need to track the dog down and destroy it; the dog could be carrying rabies which would have a devastating effect on the Park's natural citizens. Where it had come from was anyone's guess. Pretoriuskop lies not more than 10 kilometres from the densely populated settlements on the south-western boundary of the Park, and it is possible that the dog had found its way in through a hole in the fence and got lost. It is far more likely, however, that this was a poacher's dog. Sadly, the presence of a white rhino just 50 metres from where the fight had taken place was perhaps an ominous indication of that.

28

SLAPPING A HYAENA IN THE FACE
Raymond Hewson

IT MAY BE HARD TO IMAGINE NOW, given how some of the rest camps in Kruger resemble small towns, but in the 1930s they were very different places indeed.

My wife's late uncle, Dillon, loved Kruger. As he lived on the Reef, he visited the Park frequently and would often regale us with tales from those early days. What is clear from those stories is that there were none of the luxuries we enjoy in the Park nowadays. There were no electric lights – only candles or paraffin lamps – and certainly no fans or air conditioners in the huts. There were no locks on any of the doors – including the shower cubicles in the ablutions, where, when taking a shower, you would drape your towel over the door to show that it was occupied. Significantly, there were not only no electric fences around the camps as there are today, there were not even any fences at all!

Uncle Dillon told the story of when at Skukuza with a friend in the early 1930s, they had a leg of lamb hanging in the open window. With no fridges in the huts, of course, and it being a particularly hot night, he felt that hanging the leg of lamb in the window would keep it fresher. As his bed was in front of the window, Uncle Dillon felt the prized leg would be quite safe.

In the deep of the night he was awoken by a snuffling sound at the window. To his horror, the moonlight revealed a hyaena, mouth open, at the point of helping itself to an easy meal. With no time to think of a plan, and fuelled by a determination to not lose tomorrow's roast, Uncle Dillon sat up, leaned forward and with all his might slapped the hyaena in the face. With a yelp, the hyaena – alarmed that the leg of lamb apparently had some fight in it – darted off into the darkness, and a startled Uncle Dillon was left with a stinging hand, an intact leg of lamb and a fireside tale to be retold countless times over the years to disbelieving friends and relatives.

29

LEOPARD VERSUS CROCODILE
Hal Brindley

I WAS A COMPLETE AFRICA-NEWBIE when I took those now quite famous shots. Come to think of it, I was a bit of a photography-newbie as well; when my then-wife and I arrived in Kruger from America, my 600mm lens barely had a scratch on it. By the time we left a few days later, however, I was heading towards the kind of recognition and reward even a top wildlife photographer would envy, and my life's trajectory had been unknowingly redirected.

It was our fourth day in the Park and the sun was refusing to shine. When it is cool and dreary like that, everything appears in shades of grey, and I knew the photos I had taken were going to look miserable. Worse still, it seemed that most of the animals had decided to take the day off, too.

When we pulled up alongside Silolweni Dam – just south of Tshokwane picnic spot – the clouds had formed a dense blanket, and I wasn't holding out much hope for the pictures I was about to take of a group of hippos resting on the far bank. I had just loaded a new 36-exposure roll of slide film and was clicking the shutter lazily when my wife gasped loudly, 'Omigosh, what's that?'

Glancing up from my viewfinder, I saw a blurry shape darting breathtakingly fast across the sand next to the dam, trailing a cloud of red dust behind it. The blur hit the edge of the water with an audible splash, sending a shower of spray in all directions. Without thinking, I swung my lens around and began firing. The shape reappeared on the shore as a flailing ball of limbs and dust. I was four photos into the sequence before I realised what I was seeing through my telescopic lens.

It was a leopard. And it had caught a crocodile.

Was this even possible? Adrenalin was surging through me and my finger remained firmly pressed down on the shutter release. I didn't know it, but the next 60 seconds were about to change my life.

Despite the crocodile's berserk thrashing, the leopard dragged it away from the water, and they began tumbling and twisting around in the dirt with such fury it was difficult to make out exactly what was going on. One moment the crocodile's tail was pointing straight into the air, waving like a flag, the next it was rearing its body upwards, with it jaws snapping at thin air and the leopard riding it like a Buckin' Bronco.

You wouldn't think it, but a leopard and a crocodile are apparently pretty evenly matched. While a crocodile possesses a mouth full of sharp teeth, a muscular tail, armour-plating, one very crafty wrestling move, and explosive, cold-blooded fury, the leopard makes up for any disadvantage with agility, pure strength, and single-minded determination. Having said that, there is no way a leopard – even a big one like this – could have taken on a full-grown adult crocodile. But its opponent here was perhaps in its seventh year and only half its potential size. As such, these two heavyweights were in roughly the same weight class and there was no way of knowing how it was going to turn out.

That is, until the crocodile attempted its secret move: the death roll. With the leopard straddling it from above and biting firmly into its neck, the croc slapped its tail to the ground and twisted its body violently, rolling the cat clean off its feet. While a move like this may have brought results in the depths of the dam, on dry land the leopard was too fast and spun nimbly again back onto its feet, consolidating its position and bettering its grip on the softer nape of the croc's neck. The death roll turned out to be a bitter miscalculation for the croc; the leopard was back on top, its feet were now more firmly dug in and it pinned the crocodile to the ground.

The pendulum had swung in favour of the leopard. Sensing this, it began dragging the crocodile further from the water, where any more sneaky death rolls would see them both back in there with advantage firmly favouring the croc. So, step by step, the leopard heaved the crocodile towards the bush, awkwardly straddling it between its legs and lifting the croc's front legs clear off the ground to avoid giving it enough purchase to perform another roll. Slowly, it heaved that almost three-metre long crocodile up into the grass and out of sight. Was it over? Did the leopard win? Where were they? What was happening?

With the spectacle apparently over, I lowered my camera and scanned the area. The hippos I had originally been photographing were all on their feet and looking decidedly edgy. I hadn't even noticed that a herd of elephants had appeared on the opposite bank for a drink, oblivious to the battle that had just been fought across the water.

Only three cars witnessed the fight along with us, but now more cars were arriving. As word of what had just taken place spread, there was a frenzy of excitement and activity, and one guy jumped onto the roof of his big van for a better view. Seeing this, my wife judged it to be a good idea and jumped onto the roof of our small rental car, caving in the roof.

'Look!' she yelled down to me.

The leopard had appeared again and was still dragging the crocodile through the grass. But the battle had been won out of sight; with blood running from the wound in its neck, the crocodile hung limply from the leopard's mouth. Setting down its prize and panting deeply through its bloody mouth, the leopard simply stood there for a moment, victorious and exhausted.

We too were breathing hard, and with shaking hands and craned necks we all strained to see what would happen next. Would it drag the croc up a tree? Would it try and eat it? We never found out, as the leopard simply picked up its kill and dragged it off into the bush and was not seen again.

And with that, it was all over. My wife climbed down from her rooftop position and we banged out most of the dents from the inside, hoping the rental company wouldn't notice. Elated at how a slow, overcast day in Kruger had delivered the sighting of our lives, we drove away.

That was certainly the most amazing thing I'd ever seen in my life and, quite possibly, ever will. Just my fourth day in Africa and I was forever spoiled.

Six months later, after completing our round-the-world trip, I finally processed my film. There it was – proof that it really had happened. After some research I soon learned that I was the only person ever to document such a thing; apparently these remain the only photos in existence of a leopard attacking and killing a crocodile. Since then, there have been occasional reports of similar sightings in Kruger, but to date, no photos or video have been forthcoming. If the sightings are true, perhaps it is the very same leopard doing the killing each time and it has become Kruger's own specialised croc-killer.

As I said, those 60 seconds at the edge of the dam changed my life in ways I could never have imagined at the time.

The images won a competition on a popular conservation-related television show, and I managed to trade my prize for enough cash to buy a plane ticket back to South Africa. Meanwhile, a short video I compiled from the photo sequence and put online was watched over three-and-a-half million times and continues to tick over.

A few years later, though, things really took off when the images somehow found their way into a major London broadsheet newspaper. From there they exploded worldwide in what I could only describe as a bit of a media frenzy. Papers in over 20 different countries ran the story, earning me more money in two weeks than in my previous three years of photography combined. But the biggest surprise was yet to come. One of these stories appeared in a newspaper in Dublin, where a Spanish zoologist working there at the time discovered it and got in touch with me. We corresponded for a while, and a year later we travelled to Africa together for seven months and wrote a book about it. Oh, we also fell in love and are now very happily married.

So, in addition to everything else, those extraordinary 60 seconds brought me the love of my life – which makes me wonder what on earth that leopard and crocodile at Silolweni Dam have in store for me next?

30

ROCKING THE CAR TO ESCAPE THE RHINO
Pieter Colyn

THERE ARE FEW THINGS MORE ANNOYING than being joined at a sighting in Kruger by a car of tourists who refuse to cut their engine, letting it idle away in neutral, belching out exhaust fumes and disturbing both the animals and the people around them. But sometimes there is a valid excuse for it.

It was in the late 1980s, somewhere near Berg-en-Dal rest camp, and just two cars were parked up at a very rare sighting. Barely 50 metres from the road, and unobscured by bush or scrub, stood a herd of three or four black rhinos – of which there were just several hundred in the Park at the time, having only been re-introduced a decade earlier. Furthermore, black rhinos are typically solitary animals, so it was quite something to see them grouped together like this.

The next vehicle to join the two cars was an old Toyota Corolla driven by a couple of twenty-something-year-old men. They slowed down and came to a halt, but annoyingly they did not switch off their engine. Soon, even the rhinos became irritated by the whirring noise and began staring agitatedly in the direction of the cars, twitching their ears. Black rhinos are not a species you want to annoy. They have a most fearsome reputation and, with their terrible eyesight, are inclined to charge indiscriminately at the slightest whiff of provocation.

With the agitated rhinos drifting nearer and nearer to the cars, and amidst questioning stares from the other motorists, the guys in the Corolla eventually got the hint and, with great reluctance, switched off their engine. For a brief moment there was silence again.

Just then, one of the rhinos, which was now standing little more than a few bus-lengths away, became aware of the three cars and burst forward a few steps with a mock charge. The first two cars rapidly started their engines and prepared to leave in a hurry. But not the guys in the Corolla. To everybody's surprise – not least the rhino's – they swung open their doors, jumped out, and began rocking the car forward and backward four or fives times before hastily jumping back in, starting their engine and whizzing off.

That Corolla was mine.

The reason I had been reluctant to turn off the engine when we pulled up at the sighting was because sometimes it would not start. Whenever this happened, I had to put it in fourth or fifth gear, then get out and rock it forwards and backwards a few times. The rocking apparently turned the ring gear just enough to allow the bendix gear of the starter motor to kick in and turn the engine over to start the car. I am technically challenged and just accepted this explanation as the truth for as long as the proposed solution worked. I never anticipated that I would have to employ it to escape an angry black rhino, though.

When I think back to that trip, I chuckle to myself. Not only at what the occupants of the other vehicles must have thought of these two idiots jumping out of their car at the most inappropriate time, but at some other shenanigans we got up to as well.

We were young back then – and very naughty. We had rigged up a PA system in the Corolla and had a cassette tape of animal sounds in the glove box. I cannot remember exactly where, but at some remote picnic spot, demarcated by just a few stumps in the ground and where hot water was supplied from a 'donkey', a young boy was playing in the sand with his little toy car some distance from his parents and near to where the cars were parked. As we left, we flicked on the PA, inserted the cassette and, at full volume, broadcast the sound of a roaring lion.

I can still see the dust kicking up behind the boy's shoes as he fled in terror across the picnic site.

31

TOO BUSY FIDDLING TO NOTICE
Alma Sparrius

WAY BACK IN 1960 I treated myself to what was then a state-of-the-art cine camera. I couldn't wait to use it, so when a friend from England urged me to take her to Kruger, I figured that would be a perfect opportunity to test it out.

I thought I was the bee's knees with this magnificent, modern film camera. Modern it may have been at the time, but both antiquated and extraordinarily complicated it seems now. For starters, it did not record audio, but the real bane was the fiddly way it had to be operated. The light meter had a black vertical line that had to remain steady in the middle of the lens. Simultaneously you had to keep the object you were filming centred at all times too, and just to complicate things further, in order to zoom you had to focus on the subject and then move backwards or forwards to follow the moving object.

So, every day we drove around in the boiling hot sun – there was no air-conditioner in my Renault – looking for anything worthy to capture on my camera. I was driving along a winding dirt road not too far from Skukuza when we came upon a family pride of 12 lions lying on a raised bank alongside the road.

The budding producer in me was all excited to film them, and I focussed in on the subjects. The large male lion stood up and moved towards the car. *Jeez*, this was hard work. I had to focus and set the light metre and move backwards or forwards. With all this fiddly business going on I did not notice the lion, drawn to the whirring of the camera, sidling up right next to my half-open window. I heard a gargled whimper from the passenger seat next to me, but it was only when my view through the lens became blurry that I moved the camera away from my eyes to see why: the lion's yellow eyes were staring at me – 12 inches from my face!

Thank heavens I had left the engine running with the car in gear and my foot on the clutch. I dropped the clutch, and the car jolted forward and pulled away so fast that the lion jumped backwards with fright.

Glancing in the mirror, I was horrified to see that it had given chase and was bolting along right behind us. I willed the car to go faster as the lion tore along through the clouds of dust at a significantly faster rate of acceleration than my Renault could muster. But, after about 100 yards, and with the car finally at full tilt, the lion gave up and we disappeared off down the road.

With that, my friend dropped any semblance of her English reserve and rebuked me so harshly she must have used every insulting word in the dictionary. Admittedly, I deserved the tirade. I had acted foolishly and without thinking; recording through an open window and becoming so engaged in the camera's mechanics and so enraptured by the lions that I had forgotten to keep an eye on their movements.

And the camera? I never used that stupid thing again. But should I ever buy a top-of-the-range video camera again, I'll make sure it is one that requires perhaps a little less fiddling about.

32

BUMBLING LIONS IN THE JACKALBERRY TREE
Steve Farrell

WHILE THE LIONS of the Vurhami pride near Crocodile Bridge may have mastered the art of climbing trees and are often seen slumped high in the boughs of a marula, this rare skill set has seemingly not been passed completely intact to two zealous teenaged lions a little further north, closer to Lower Sabie.

In the late winter of 2010, my then-girlfriend and I drove up from Cape Town to spend a week in the Park. The trip was special for two reasons: it was to be my girlfriend's first time in Kruger, and there was also the other minor detail that I planned to propose to her.

If a few days of brilliant game viewing was to soften her up to say yes, I figured the game-rich area of Lower Sabie would be the place to do it – and I wasn't wrong. It's hard to tell if those two lions played a role in enchanting her, but at the very least they served up one of the most remarkable – and entertaining – sightings of our lives.

Driving back along the tarred Crocodile Bridge to Lower Sabie road after our first afternoon's game viewing, we drew up to what must have been 50 cars all jostling for position. High up in an ancient jackalberry tree alongside the road, a leopard was standing guard over a fresh impala kill. It had pulled the carcass a good seven metres up into the tree and slung it between a fork near the upper end of a long, thick bough. Having already seen rhino, elephant, a few lionesses, and a huge herd of buffalo that afternoon, we couldn't have asked for a better way to end our first day in the Park.

As soon as the gates opened the next morning, we made a beeline for the kill, roughly five kilometres south of the camp, to see what the leopard was up to. All we found was a tree and the hanging remains of the well-eaten impala. The leopard was nowhere to be seen.

Later that morning we decided to swing past the tree for one more look. Barely a kilometre before the kill, we pulled up behind two healthy young male lions walking purposefully along the road. We drove slowly alongside them, following them on their march, and noting how every few metres they would stop and mark their territory, the scent of the leopard evidently fresh in their nostrils. Then we realised: these lions were walking directly to the impala kill. Knowing that lions aren't renowned for their tree-climbing prowess, we wondered how they would react when they came across a dead impala hoisted seven metres up a tree.

We soon found out. The lions arrived at the tree, peered up into the branches and immediately set about devising a strategy to get to the carcass. With the prize slung up so high, on the far end of a steep branch not much more than 30 centimetres in diameter, I was convinced that these two burly males didn't stand a chance of getting anywhere near it.

Well, try they did. For over an hour, the clumsy brothers had their ever-growing gallery of onlookers in stitches as they scrabbled and contorted themselves into a right old pickle. As one lion nervously made its way up the tree, the other followed, only to block the first's descent, leaving them both clawing at the tree for dear life.

Eventually, after many failed and comedic attempts, the larger of the two lions got within a paw's length of the mostly-consumed impala. It was an extraordinary sight to see a big lion so high in a tree. But then it just stopped and stared at the measly remains, as if finally realising that all this effort was not going to fill their tummies. In fact, they had probably burned more calories getting to the carcass than any meat on those bones could ever have provided. The round-bellied leopard was probably sitting in a nearby tree 'roaring' with laughter at these so-called kings of beasts.

It took the lions a while to work out how to get down again. Finally back on *terra firma*, they sniffed around awkwardly for a bit; cats are so bad at hiding their embarrassment. Eventually, they ambled off into the bush – pride dented and still hungry.

I would like to think that my proposal a few days later, in one of the luxury safari tents at Tamboti tented camp, was performed with a touch more elegance and grace than displayed by those tree-climbing lions. She did, after all, say yes.

33

REVERSING A CARAVAN
Julius Kunzmann

GROWING UP, caravanning was in my family's blood, and over the years our Sprite Musketeer caravan, trailing behind my father's Chrysler Valiant Safari estate, saw most of southern Africa and, not least, many trips to Kruger.

When my mother was in the driving seat, the only thing she had a problem with was reversing the caravan, as the Valiant was a long car and she never quite got her corners right. Being the oldest of three brothers, I was ever keen to help out in manly activities, so whenever she needed to reverse, I would run to the back of the caravan, seize one of the grab handles and help swing it in the right direction.

It was the final day of one of our Kruger holidays, and after two sighting-rich weeks, we packed up, hitched the caravan and left Skukuza for Graskop via Hazyview. Just outside Skukuza the road signs used to be a bit confusing – which is how we mistakenly landed up on the road to Pretoriuskop instead of the one to Paul Kruger Gate.

Time to turn around.

My mother was driving, and so, as usual, I jumped out to help turn the caravan. This was a narrow road and, as I say, reversing the caravan was never her specialist subject. From my guiding position behind the rear left-hand corner of the caravan, I was completely obscured, so my father – in the passenger seat – had his window open to hear my shouted commands, which he would then relay across to my mother.

We had to push the caravan halfway into the *veld* to be able to turn around. I was anxiously watching the thorn tree that my mother was pushing me towards when, in my peripheral vision, I saw movement. I turned my head for a closer look, and there, lying in the shade of a bush barely 10 paces away, was a pride of five lions, keenly eyeing me up.

Being distracted by the lions I forgot about the task at hand, and mother proceeded to push me – and the caravan – into the trees. As luck would have it, the corner of the caravan struck the tree first, but it still managed to trap me firmly against the boughs of the tree's v-shaped trunk.

The collision knocked the breath out of me and I found myself unable to shout for help – not that I wanted to anyway, as the male lion stood up and looked at me very intently. The two females and the two cubs were still lying down, but they too had their eyes locked on me.

My father, in the meantime, got out of the car and walked up to see what was happening, muttering threats under his breath about damaged vehicles and children being grounded for life. He stopped next to me and had just started asking what the hell I was up to when he saw the expression on my face – and my breathless pointing at the lions behind me. His face changed rapidly from anger to astonishment and then to panic before he plucked me from between the caravan and the tree, leaving behind half of my shirt – and a significant chunk of skin off my back! Half carrying, half dragging me behind him, he threw me through the open back window on top of my brothers, jumped into his seat and shouted at my mother to 'Go! Go! Go!'

Mother, in a flat panic, drove off at speed and, of course, in the wrong direction. Only after my brothers stopped crying and I got my voice back could we explain what had happened. My back was smarting terribly and oozing blood, but she refused to stop until we reached Pretoriuskop, where I finally received medical attention.

Back at the tree, I suppose that unless those lions had a use for some t-shirt fabric and a generous slice of teenage skin, both items would have remained pinned to the bark for quite some time, flapping in the wind as a little landmark to my scrape with a caravan, a thorn tree and a whole pride of lions.

34

BOUNCING OFF THE FENCE
Ursela Klitzke

IT'S NOT ALWAYS EASY to understand the cruelty of nature – which is why my brother spent that entire first evening in Kruger sulking in the car rather than sitting by the fire with my father and me. He couldn't accept that we had let it all happen in front of us and not done anything to intervene. I can't blame him though; the incident just on the other side of the fence at Pretoriuskop was as gut-wrenching as it was grisly. But, for all its brutality, it was a sighting to beat all others, and the fact that it all took place within touching distance made it all the more remarkable.

It was summertime and we had only just pitched our tent alongside the fence at Pretoriuskop's camp site after a long drive from Johannesburg. The bush beyond the fence was dense, and the grass grows famously high around Pretoriuskop, so we knew there was little chance of seeing much game from our prime spot. However, there was always the promise of a hyaena or two showing themselves once the *braai* fires were lit and the smells of meat wafting out into the bush had drawn them in.

But it wasn't that late yet and the sun was still up. So it was a huge surprise when a bushbuck ram crackled out of the bush and ran full throttle into the wire fence right in front of our tent. There was a tremendous crash as it hit the wire and fell backwards. But just as fast as it had collapsed it was up again and bolting leftwards along the fence line away from us. It wasn't long before we realised what was causing its panic: five or six wild dogs came yelping through the bush right behind it. This bushbuck knew it was in trouble and, like a trapped bird trying to bash its way through a glass window, threw itself repeatedly at the fence. The camp must have somehow looked like a safe haven – or perhaps in its blind panic it was fixed on one sole direction of escape and, disastrously, Pretoriuskop was stonewalling its route.

As the bushbuck cut back and disappeared into the bush again with the wild dogs bouncing behind it, a lone hyaena ambled onto the scene, no doubt following the action in the hope of picking up a piece or two of the kill. It was in no mood to join the chase, though, and settled instead for sniffing around where the bushbuck had first struck the fence.

We could hear the excited chirping and squeaking of the wild dogs some way off as they chased down their quarry, but with the thick bush and high grass, there was no way we were going to see the kill. Just as well too, we thought, as wild dogs are said to be the cruellest of hunters and will chase down their prey to exhaustion, often disembowelling the poor creature while it's still on its feet.

But, as it turns out, it wasn't going to be the wild dogs dining on bushbuck that evening. Having run full circle, the bushbuck bolted back out of the bushes to our right and slammed straight into the fence again. It veered leftwards and repeatedly bashed itself against the fence as it scrambled in our direction. Just as it reached the point where we were standing, it glimpsed the hyaena immediately to its right and threw itself so ferociously at the wire that it bounced off again and landed straight into the open mouth of the startled hyaena.

My brother and I, along with my father and a handful of other campers, gasped as the hyaena wrestled the bushbuck to the ground and started eating it alive. It tore open the stomach, and as the insides spilled out onto the grass, we could see the bushbuck had no fight left in it. Its eyes rolled around in its head for several minutes before its rasped breathing eventually stopped.

We never saw the wild dogs again. They must have cut their losses and gone away hungry. The hyaena had scored without having to do a thing, and I suspect it could barely believe its luck. Meanwhile, the wild dogs must have been rueing their misfortune; all that hard work, only to deliver the prey straight onto the plate of a lazy scavenger which hadn't even bothered to keep up with the chase.

By that point the sun had set, and in the fading light we watched the shadowy figure of the hyaena – just a metre in front of us – tearing into its free meal with gusto. As the darkness thickened there were only sounds – and the most ghastly smell of stomach contents and raw flesh.

We went to sleep that night listening to the crunching of bones, and at one point in the early hours, my sleep was disturbed by some cackling and commotion at the kill site.

As soon as morning dawned I was back at the fence. To my amazement, there was nothing there: not a single bone, not a scrap of hair, not even a single drop of blood. But for some flattened grass, nobody standing at the fence that day would ever have guessed that a large bushbuck ram had been killed and consumed on that very spot just hours earlier. But for me, and for my poor traumatised brother, the sounds and the smells were still very much with us, and even now, many years later, they remain strikingly vivid.

35

THE SHOCKING DEATH OF A LEOPARD
Nigel Aitken

THE ELECTRIC FENCES around Kruger's rest camps have been controversial ever since they were introduced back in the late nineties. Proponents of the live wires insist that they are necessary to keep dangerous animals out, while the critics say they are unnecessary, as wily animals like leopards, baboons and monkeys regularly find their way into the camps anyway. Right or wrong, what is certain is that the electric fence around Lower Sabie – when coupled with that fatal ingredient: thoughtless human behaviour – was responsible for the appalling death of a healthy male leopard right in front of my eyes.

It was around lunchtime on a Sunday when my son and I returned to Lower Sabie following a morning's game drive. A handful of cars had stopped at the turn-off towards the camp's old entrance, which lies about 60 metres or so south of the current camp gate. But, with it being April, the bush was still dense, so it wasn't immediately obvious what they had all seen. When I asked one of the people parked up, they pointed through the bush towards a very handsome male leopard wandering along the outside of the fence, barely 20 metres in from the road, heading directly towards the new gate.

Knowing that this gate is normally manned by an unarmed guard – who is often found sitting in a chair in front of his sentry station just outside the cattle grid – my blood ran cold. We abandoned the sighting and accelerated towards the gate to warn him of the approaching leopard.

Before we had even reached the gate, I realised I needn't have worried; the guard was not there and the sentry station looked shut. Just then, a car leaving the camp passed over the grid with a loud rumble and startled the leopard, which turned around sharply and headed back towards the old gate.

Sunday is always a busy day in the southern parts of the Park, and lunchtime particularly so, as visitors head to camp to eat and perhaps snooze a bit before heading out again in the afternoon. So unsurprisingly, the small number of cars that had originally been watching the leopard had multiplied considerably; some were parked down the old entrance road and many more still along the main road, all eager to catch a glimpse of a leopard so close to camp.

Windows were wound down, voices were being raised in excitement, cameras were clicking and the inevitable rule breakers started leaning out of their open windows. And that was when the problems started.

With the ruckus of the assembled crowd, the leopard clearly felt trapped. In a panic, it turned away from the onlookers towards the relative quiet of the camp and tried to jump the electric fence. In doing so, it somehow got itself entangled in one of the ground-level electric wires. With the pulsing current shocking it repeatedly, the leopard bolted towards the short section of curved wall – the bit that bears the large 'Lower Sabie' lettering – just outside the main gate. It must have seemed like the only place offering some cover.

Sadly, this was a tragic miscalculation for the leopard, as it only got itself into a far greater, and ultimately inescapable, tangle with the live wires between the wall and fence. What had been a glorious sighting of a leopard slipping through the grass minutes earlier had now become a nightmare, with the leopard in a blind panic, being shocked over and over again by the array of high-voltage wires.

I couldn't just watch the leopard die so cruelly. Someone had to do something. As nobody else appeared to be stepping up, I drove into the camp, parked up just inside the gates and ran around looking for anyone official-looking. I soon found a man who, fortuitously, turned out to be an electrician employed by the Park. He knew the electrical architecture of the camp well and revealed that the mains switch for the electric fence was in the guard's hut – the hut which was locked shut.

After at least five minutes of jimmying, the electrician broke open the door of the hut, ran inside and flicked off the mains switch, which shut down all power to the fence. It was too late though; the repeated pulses delivered through the wires wrapped around the leopard had been too much even for this stout male. Although its flinching from the shocks had stopped, the leopard was only barely breathing in low, pained rasps. It died shortly afterwards.

It was sad to realise that we Park visitors had unwittingly been the cause of this animal's ghastly death. Of course, nobody has exclusive rights to any sighting in Kruger, and the build-up of cars at a sighting like this so close to a busy camp is inevitable. But I can't help thinking that had everyone behaved a little less selfishly and a little more discreetly – keeping their distance and allowing the leopard a path to escape – the outcome would have been entirely different.

But selfishness and stupidity are unfortunately not painful, so there was no shortage of either that day. It still upsets me to recall what must have been the very last thing the leopard saw as it gasped its final few breaths. A handful of tourists had got out of their cars – completely ignoring the demands of the Park officials to return, and oblivious to the danger to themselves or the stress they would cause the leopard – and just stood there right in front of it and watched it die.

36

DRAGGING A CARCASS
Gabi Hotz

IF THERE'S ANY DOUBT as to which is the toughest creature in Kruger, a sighting I had one morning near Skukuza should settle any scores on the matter.

That morning, we had taken the gravel road towards N'waswitshaka waterhole to see if anything exciting was happening there. Barely 500 metres down that road, the excitement found us instead. A cluster of cars had all stopped, and it wasn't long before we discovered what they were looking at: on the side of the road, seemingly untouched, lay the carcass of a large impala.

A man in one of the cars wound down his window and explained to us that the impala had been killed by a leopard; but as more and more cars had arrived on the scene, the noise and the chatter and the idling diesel engines had forced the leopard to abandon its meal and disappear off into the bush.

Some cars decided that there were better things to see elsewhere and soon pulled away. But we were in no hurry. Knowing that the leopard would unlikely want to just abandon its hard-fought meal, we decided to sit and wait for its return.

A good twenty minutes passed and, unless you counted the flies, nothing had come for the impala. The bush was quiet, the temperature was getting up and just as we were wondering whether we really had the patience to sit and wait hours for a leopard that was probably sleeping off the morning's exertion deep under cover half a kilometre away, there was a distinct rustling in the bush. Whatever it was, it was coming straight for the carcass with some determination.

Everyone jumped to attention. Our patience had paid off – the leopard was surely coming back for its meal. But then, from the depths of the dry grass, the source of the rustling revealed itself with little fanfare but a lot of attitude. It was not the leopard at all. Instead, out marched a honey badger with a determined swagger.

Not much phases a honey badger, and no amount of excited chatter nor the *click-click-click* of the cameras from the assembled audience was going to bother it. This tough guy was there for a reason – breakfast.

When the honey badger approached the carcass, the head of the dead impala was facing the road. This clearly did not suit its plans. It sank its teeth into the impala's stomach, and then, like one of those tiny tug boats that somehow turns around a giant cruise liner, it swiftly spun the impala around 180 degrees with astonishing ease. I had always known that honey badgers were vicious little things, but I had no idea they were anywhere near as powerful as this. However, that was just the warm up.

With the carcass now facing the opposite direction, the honey badger grabbed it by the neck and, like a dog with a blanket in its mouth, dragged the carcass – which probably weighed a good 50 or 60 kilograms further into the bush with such ease we could barely believe what we were seeing. Satisfied it had found a nice spot comfortably away from the crowds and with a little bit of shade, the honey badger released its jaws from the dead impala's neck, scuttled around to the belly area and wasted no time in tearing right into it.

We stayed and watched, fascinated, for another hour. In that time the honey badger left the carcass and disappeared a number of times, but it always returned to feed a little more. Once, it even scurried across the road – going to where, I have no idea – before doubling back a few minutes later, straight to the carcass.

All the while, a large bateleur eagle was watching impatiently from a nearby low branch, desperate to get stuck in too. But despite there being enough meat to feed 100 birds of prey, this eagle had decided it was going nowhere near that honey badger. Given what I had already seen of this particular specimen, it was, I thought, probably a very wise decision.

37

TIDAL WAVE OF ELEPHANTS
Lourens Durand

ON AN EVENING in the dry September of 2009, I sat alone outside my tent at Lower Sabie rest camp contemplating a red glow on the northern horizon – the glow of a vast bushfire; one that would eventually burn for three days. With a shudder, I relived the narrow escape I had made earlier in the day.

It had been late in the afternoon and I was returning to camp along the gravel road from the Ntandanyathi hide – one of my favourite spots in the Park – when the sky suddenly turned unnaturally dark. My nasal passages tingled and my eyes watered as a faintly acrid smell filled the air. It was the smoke from a faraway bushfire that, I learned later, had started well north of Lower Sabie. From the fire billowed thick clouds, ushered along by a stiff breeze, carrying fragments of sooty grass and blotting out the setting sun.

Ahead of me, the driver of a fast-approaching car flashed his lights and made exaggerated and urgent pointing gestures into the *veld* to his left and behind him. I assumed he was pointing out a sighting ahead. 'Nice guy', I thought as he sped past me, 'but a little excitable.' I scanned the area he had been gesticulating towards, but seeing nothing of real interest, I shrugged it off.

A little further on, the driver of a stationary vehicle some distance ahead also flashed his headlights at me, so I idly looked to my right again. Then I saw it – and heard it. It was an unbelievable sight, the likes of which I had never before seen in all my years visiting Kruger, nor ever seen again since: an immense, rumbling, black, undulating, tidal wave of hundreds upon hundreds of stampeding elephants running shoulder to shoulder across the valley, crashing through the bushes to escape the threatening fire.

And there I was, sitting just 100 metres away, smack-bang in the middle of their intended path across the road.

In the panicked moments that followed, questions raced through my mind: If I stayed where I was, would they run around me? Was there any truth to the story that elephants run around an obstacle? That didn't seem likely, given the way they were flattening the bushes. Was there time to turn the car around and retreat? Would it be better to carry on and try and get past them?

With few options and all out of time, I went with my gut and hastily accelerated forward.

Moments later the enormous herd thundered across the road behind me. Mercifully, there was room to spare, but as I watched uneasily in the rear-view mirror, I couldn't but help ponder what might have happened had panic set in and the car stalled...

38

WRONG PLACE, WRONG TIME, ON A RHINO'S TURF
Angie Shackleford

THIS IS A TRAGIC AND UNCOMFORTABLE TALE; one that I take no pleasure in recounting. Out of respect to an animal that was greater than all of us in that group put together, and to the men who saved our lives, I have carefully taken only the facts from the group's recollections and present them here as an account of that ill-fated afternoon.

In the dusty spring of 2001, I was part of a group of seven reluctant managing directors – all 'business thinkers' at the height of our careers, deeply engrossed in our corporate worlds – invited to attend a walking trail in Kruger's south-western corner. Now, well over a decade later, as I have sought their recollections in putting this account together, many in the group still recall the horror that unfolded on that walk as if it happened yesterday.

All of us were, at that stage, responsible for managing a number of diverse companies within the same group. The chairman of the group – a dynamic, forward-thinking woman – had decided that putting glamour and mobile phones aside for a weekend and sending us off into the bush would result in some innovative thinking to move the group into the new financial year. But in the end there were to be no innovative ideas and no balance sheet-altering moments from that weekend – just shock, cuts and bruises, and a deep, disquieting sorrow.

When we first entered the Park, it was after midday and sticky with heat. I recall walking through the sand at the entrance gate and watching my casual shoes making circular patterns in the sand; I could not really remember the last time I had worn casual shoes. We all climbed into an open safari vehicle and were driven into the bush to the Wolhuter Wilderness Trails camp. There were seven wilderness trails in the Kruger at the time, but the Wolhuter Trail had been the first – established in

1978 in the vast tourist-free wilderness area between Pretoriuskop and Malelane rest camps, and named after one of the Park's first rangers.

The bush camp was very primitive and a far cry from the luxury we were accustomed to as seasoned business travellers. Small two-man tents, with scarcely enough place to store a suitcase, blistered in the heat, while two narrow paths behind them led to tiny corrugated iron-clad toilets and bush showers. There was no electricity, no power points and no laundry facilities. But by early evening, seated around a fire with drinks on ice, we had all started to relax. The peace and gentle surroundings were overwhelmingly beautiful.

The following morning we were lined up early, told not to talk and to follow all directions – not an easy task for a group of people accustomed to always taking the lead. Nevertheless, with an armed ranger leading and an armed guide following, we walked silently into the bush. The morning was long and hot; game was scarce in the heat, and at one point I found myself behind the ranger marvelling at how he was able to walk through the scrub in flip-flop sandals. Eventually, we returned to camp. It felt like it was going to be a very long weekend. Unaccustomed to the slow pace of the bush, by mid-afternoon we were all getting bored and decided that we would like to walk through a dry riverbed. Humour had started to become infantile by that stage, and at one point one of the senior managers ran out in front of the group, posed and exclaimed, 'If you like it charge it!' – a well-known advertising line from a retail store at the time. None of us realised how ominous those words were to become in the next hour.

As we walked further, the sun dipped a little lower. Suddenly, ahead of us appeared the large dark shapes of two white rhinos just breaking the skyline above the reeds. The group crackled with excitement. Whispering and shuffling, we moved a little closer. The two rhinos continued grazing without paying the slightest bit of attention to us. When the ranger ascertained we had got close enough, he led the group up a sandy path towards the top of the riverbed to give the rhinos a wide berth. The single file followed him. I was third from the back, with the guide taking up the rear again. At the top of the path, the riverbed immediately disappeared from view as the sandy trail meandered towards the brush along the banks.

All of a sudden the ground began to shudder as though a tube train was about to pull into a station. In confusion, we all stopped – just as the rhino's horn appeared above the horizon. The creature charged at the line with full force. There was really nowhere for us to go.

My recollections of what happened next are like flashbacks from a dream. I remember people screaming, dust everywhere and the sound of shots so close it was like being on the front lines of a war zone. At one stage, four of us, including two large men, took cover behind a metre-tall sapling. Again and again I could hear people screaming that it was coming back. One of the group fell, and in slow motion, the big man – who had been my companion behind the tiny sapling – turned around and picked her up from the ground, moments before the rhino thundered past. Through the clouds of dust, I recall watching the ranger aim and fire and, in the confusion, fall to the ground as his heavy weapon threw him backwards. The rhino, just a blur of blue and grey, rumbled past him, tearing his shirt with the edge of its horn. The noise, the shooting and the thundering footsteps seemed to last an age.

Then, all of a sudden, it was deathly quiet. In the bush there is always noise of birds and insects and life, but the stillness was complete. I had somehow found my way up a small acacia thorn tree, but had no recollection of climbing it. I slowly descended and walked through the thorns to the edge of the riverbed. The rhino lay on its side, facing the sinking sun. As I watched, it took a deep breath and died. There were so many oozing bullet wounds that it was impossible to count how many shots it had taken in the mêlée. In protecting the group, the ranger and guide had had precious little time to react – they had boldly held their ground under terrifying circumstances, first firing warning shots before tragically being forced to do the unthinkable. I later discovered that this was the first time an animal had ever had to be shot on a walking trail in the Park.

Watching the life fade from such a magnificent animal will be a moment I will remember for all my days. The rest of the group moved like shadows until we all stood in this animal's terrain and watched its life end. I remember glancing up and seeing a camera bag still slowly swinging from a branch above us where it had hooked as it had been thrown into the air.

There were a few cuts and bruises and very little chatter as we limped in the swiftly descending darkness some distance to reach the safari vehicle. After hurried discussions through the radio, we were driven to the section ranger's post where we had to individually recount the events that had just happened. It was never clear to me why the rhino had charged. In all probability it was just defending its territory, despite us keeping a respectful distance. After all, this was the rhino's turf, not ours. Its crime was to follow its instincts – ours was to be in the wrong place at the wrong time.

We all left early the next morning and did not discuss the incident beyond a few occasional words. As I said, there were no innovative ideas and no balance sheet-altering moments that weekend. Over time, the group have moved on and are occupying positions in various businesses around the world. But for everyone, the memories still cut deep. I doubt that any of us will ever be able to shift the vivid image of that magnificent, two-tonne beast lying motionless in the dust as the sun set over the bush.

39

A CRY IN THE NIGHT
Lesley Henderson

THESE DAYS, the neighbourhood trouble-makers in Kruger's rest camps are mostly baboons, vervet monkeys and the occasional marauding honey badger. Back in the early years, however, scavenging hyaenas were a real problem.

I particularly remember, as a small child in the late 1950s and early 1960s, that hyaenas, with their inordinately powerful jaws, were known to break open the food cupboards on the verandas of the huts at Orpen rest camp, where we often stayed. At night-time, we always had to look out for hyaenas when visiting the ablutions, but for the most part we were quite safe in our huts. However, this can't be said of people sleeping in tents.

My mother would often recount the terrifying tale of our neighbours from Benoni when they visited Kruger in about 1951. At that time, accommodation in the Park consisted of simple rondavel huts and canvas bell tents. With no electricity, there were no fridges or fans. Paraffin lamps were used for lighting, meat was hung up inside to keep it safely off the ground, and water was cooled in canvas bags strapped to the bumper of the car – in fact, my grandfather was once fined by an honorary ranger for getting out the car at Leeupan to get some water to drink!

Our Benoni neighbours were staying in one of the canvas tents at Skukuza when they came within a whisker of what would surely have been the most horrifying thing ever to befall visitors in the Park.

During the night, a lone hyaena, probably lured by the smell of the hanging meat, entered their tent. In the darkness, it skulked past the sleeping adults, completely ignored the meat – which was hanging near the back of the tent – and picked up their baby boy instead.

The hyaena was on its way out the tent with its 'meal' between its jaws when the baby's distraught cries alerted the sleeping parents. In a flash, the father shot up and snatched his son from the hyaena, which scuttled off into the night. Amazingly, the baby suffered no serious injury.

What unspeakable tragedy had been averted doesn't bear thinking about.

That baby boy grew up to be a healthy young man. I lost contact with the family soon after he finished high school, but I remember, with a smile, that he and his older brother were well known as the neighbourhood trouble-makers – ironically, not all that dissimilar from those troublesome hyaenas back in the Park's rest camps.

40

GOOD MORNING, *GROOT KROKODIL*
Bertus Meiring

GROWING UP ON A FARM in the Free State, our annual Kruger trip during the winter school holidays was by far the highlight of the year. Even as a young boy I realised that when you spend that much time with your family and friends, driving around all day long, there are bound to be some funny moments you will never forget.

During one of these trips in the mid-eighties, my grandfather Hennie unknowingly found his rhythm as the group clown and gave us many good chuckles – often without intending to. He was a very unassuming, down-to-earth man with a wealth of knowledge on most topics. He had also lost an eye earlier on in his life in an accident at work and wore a bad glass eye for as long as I could remember. A few months prior to our trip, he had walked up to a lady in Durban asking for directions and was promptly told that she 'does not support beggars and bums', which was one of the funniest moments of my young life.

Although he could speak English very well, he instructed a fellow tourist that if he used his 'far looking glasses' – a literal translation of the Afrikaans word for binoculars – he would be able to see the lion lying about 100 metres into the bush. I don't know whether we or the people in the other car laughed most, but it infuriated him – which only made us laugh even more.

One of our most memorable moments, however, was at another lion sighting on the road between Lower Sabie and Skukuza rest camps. The bush alongside the road was very dense, which made it quite difficult to see the lion. To make matters worse, the whole family was jam-packed into an old Toyota HiAce minibus which sported homemade curtains to cover the windows for when the vehicle doubled up as sleeping quarters. Needless to say, I hated driving around in it, and we were often mistaken for a taxi taking a shortcut through the park to Mozambique.

While sitting at this lion sighting, which had not become any clearer, another minibus stopped next to us to see what we were looking at. At first we did not take much notice of the elderly man and woman in the vehicle, until my grandfather suddenly called out loudly in his friendliest tone: *'Goeie môre, Meneer President!'* (Good morning, Mister President).

We all swung our heads across to the minibus next to us and could hardly believe our eyes: sitting in the seat behind a lone driver was the serving State President P.W. Botha – *die Groot Krokodil* himself – and his wife, Elize. Of course, President Botha returned the greeting politely and, after learning that we were looking at a lion that we could not even see, said his goodbyes and instructed his driver to move on.

We all remarked afterwards on the surprisingly ordinary way in which they were travelling, which, looking back now, is all the more remarkable as this happened in the winter of 1986 at the very zenith of Botha's tenure as president, and just weeks after his controversial declaration of a state of emergency in South Africa.

Nevertheless, my grandfather was the butt of every joke for the rest of the holiday, but made a valid point in saying that the right thing to do was to greet the man.

41

IMPALA IN THE MUD
Wendy Abadi

THE KRUGER NATIONAL PARK is not a zoo. So when misfortune strikes an animal, and so long as it is not man-made, it is the Park's policy to let nature take its inevitable course – no matter how heart-wrenching or cruel it may seem. This is as it should be, I suppose. But we are human too, and human empathy is a powerful thing – which is precisely why I still feel so torn about the incident of the impala stuck in the mud.

Like everywhere in Kruger, you never know what you are going to see when you get there. So, when I walked into the Ntandanyathi hide, to the south of Lower Sabie rest camp, I was shocked. Having last visited the hide in the rainy months, the difference now at the end of a dry winter was stark: where there was once a healthy pool of water in front of the hide, full of hippos and darting kingfishers, now there was just a dried up waterhole with a small puddle in the middle, surrounded by a wide ring of well-trodden mud. Barbel flapped away in the slush, while a delighted saddle-billed stork strutted around amongst them, picking off the small fry.

From out of the bush on the far side of the waterhole, a series of animals began filing down towards the puddle, only to find their path to the water thwarted by the band of thick mud surrounding it. This was no big deal for the warthogs; they threw themselves into the mud and wallowed around. But for a handful of wildebeest it was a different story. With their awkwardly long legs and high centre of gravity, they sank knee-deep into the mud as soon as they stepped off the dry edge. With each additional step, their legs sank deeper. It wasn't long before they accepted there'd be no drinking for them today – not at this waterhole at least – and they turned around and scrambled out of the mud, up the bank and back into the bush.

Being daintier and lighter than their clownish companions, the impalas that had arrived at the waterhole with the wildebeest were able to venture further towards the puddle in the middle. But the mud there was softer – and deeper – and very quickly a couple of the ewes found themselves sucked into the mud right up to their necks. Only their heads and the uppermost part of their torsos remained above the surface.

At first they seemed a little perplexed, but they were in no way panicked. They looked around confusedly as, I suppose, they tried to make sense of just quite how they'd found themselves in this pickle. A good number of people had trickled into the hide, and collectively our eyes were all fixed on these stricken impala. Hides are normally quiet places – or they should be, anyway – but there was much excited chatter about the drama unfolding in front of us. How were these impala going to get out of the mud?

The ewes' composure didn't last long when they realised they were well and truly stuck. While their initial predicament had at first been greeted with some mirth by the onlookers in the hide, the mood changed quickly as time wore on. With the sun beating down hard, and their frantic attempts to free themselves only serving to suck them deeper into the mud, it dawned on us that these impala were in some considerable trouble.

It was difficult to watch. Their eyes were huge with fear, and it was heartbreaking to see the methodical way in which they struggled to break out. For long periods they would do nothing at all. Then, as if a command had been bleated from the sidelines, they'd suddenly jiggle and heave. You could almost see them taking deep breaths then going for it, trying their hardest to somehow push themselves up and out of the mud. But their struggling only made things worse.

Other impala continued to sidle down to the waterhole, strangely unperturbed, and all I could do was shout at them in my head: 'No, stay away – can't you see what's happened to your friends?'

Where they got their willpower from, I don't know, but the two stricken impala just wouldn't give up. In the two hours I had been watching, they must have made at least a dozen exhaustive attempts to free themselves. That persistence eventually paid off for one of them. With an almighty heave, it broke the seal and dragged itself up and staggered out of the mud, looking almost embarrassed. There were stifled cheers from everyone in the hide. I was so happy I wanted to shout and clap, but the other ewe was still firmly stuck, watching silently as the luckier one teetered off into the bush.

In the distance a troop of baboons started barking – the way they do when a predator approaches – and there was much panicked movement in the trees and clumsy crashing of branches. The animals that were at the waterhole turned on their heels and scattered – and my heart sank. Was I about to witness the most horrific thing?

But the remaining stricken impala decided it wasn't going to stick around to see what had startled the others. With that added injection of adrenaline, it too forced itself free from its stranglehold and clambered clumsily up out of the mud to the safety of the hard bank. But, as it hobbled off to join the rest of the herd, it turned around and looked back. I followed its gaze and my heart sank once more.

A young impala ram – its horns nothing more than two little spikes – was also stuck in the mud several metres from where the other two had been struggling. We had all been so busy watching the ewes in front of us, we hadn't noticed that there was another victim, sunken much deeper than they had been and only barely visible above the surface.

There was no way this little guy was going to get out – even if it had been able to free itself from the mud, how would it have been able to get enough of a firm footing to jump up the low bank immediately in front of it?

I waited for a while longer, praying for some small miracle. Some elephants arrived and even they battled with the mud. But time was ticking on, and in the end I left the hide with a heavy heart and returned to camp. All evening and into the night I thought about the poor impala. I decided that I wouldn't go back to the hide the following day; it would just be too traumatic seeing the remains and thinking about its last few moments on earth.

By about four o'clock the following afternoon, though, I figured it would be safe enough to return to the hide. The hyaenas, vultures, black-backed jackals, and other scavengers would have cleared away any evidence of the attack that had surely gone down in the night.

As I say, you never know what you are going to find in Kruger, and when I walked back into the hide again and scanned the mud, to my huge surprise the impala was still there. But there was no movement and, sadly, its eyes were closed. It had been stuck in the mud for over 26 hours – how could it have survived, really? Predators hadn't found it as I had assumed they would, but instead fatigue and shock must have taken its toll on the youngster.

I squinted at the lifeless body. Suddenly, it opened its eyes, blinked listlessly a few times and took a weary look around. My heart jumped. I couldn't believe it – the impala was alive!

Two couples arrived at the hide, took a quick look around – missing the stricken impala completely – and muttered, 'Nothing here today.' As they were about to walk out, I called them over and pointed out the little head barely sticking out above the level of the mud and related the goings-on of the previous day, before turning my attention back to the impala. I wasn't paying much attention to the whispered conversation the others were having behind me – until, that is, two of the men came over and asked me whether I would object if they attempted a rescue of the impala.

As much as I wanted to see the impala rescued, this did not sound like a good idea at all. After all, I had in the past arrived at Ntandanyathi hide a number of times to find people sitting in their cars because there were lions in the grass alongside the entrance. But the two men, in their shorts and casual shirts – one even in sandals – assured me that had there been any predators about, the impala would not still be alive in the mud 26 hours later, and off they went.

As they approached the impala, it began to panic and jerk around, but so firmly was it stuck that not even the sight of these two casually-dressed giants looming towards it could propel it from the mud.

Standing on either side of the buck's head, each man grabbed a horn and, making sure they had a solid footing, they began to heave. They pulled and pulled and pulled until eventually, after a good minute of tugging, the mud let go and, with a plop, the young impala was pulled free. It shook itself a bit before wandering off into the bush, looking as though it had been dipped in chocolate.

It is difficult to say how I felt about what had just happened. I left the hide that afternoon knowing that those men were probably wrong for interfering. Nature is indeed cruel, and the circle of life is, I suppose, as inevitable as the sun rising behind the Lebombos, or the sausage tree dropping its fruit. And yes, Kruger is not a zoo; tragic things will happen to helpless creatures and sometimes they will die in ways that seem neither fair nor humane. But, I must admit, I slept better that night knowing that that little *bokkie* was no longer stuck in the mud, waiting for thirst to consume it or, worse, for something to come along and rip it apart alive.

42

MONKEY MAN AND THE SKUKUZA OFFENSIVE
Romey Doubell

THIS IS THE TRUE TALE of how I got lumbered with the most unfortunate nickname of 'Monkey Man' – and how I have had to add yet another species of animal to my growing list of antagonists.

I had spent the latter half of one January in the Park on my own, starting at Mopani in the north and ending with three days at Skukuza. On my very last afternoon, after a light meal at the restaurant, I was joined by an old friend and his wife who I had coincidentally bumped into at the camp's reception area a few days earlier.

It was one of those perfect summer evenings in the Park, and we sat on a bench near the restaurant overlooking the Sabie River, chatting about this and that and enjoying the tranquility of the setting.

My friend's wife remarked that a troop of monkeys had entered the area around the open-air restaurant, but I didn't pay much attention to them. I should have, really, as the monkeys were apparently paying a lot of attention to me.

The next thing I knew, I was under attack and quickly outnumbered.

The tranquility on the bench had turned to bedlam in a matter of seconds. Beneath me, two monkeys were biting at each of my ankles, another two were clamped to my back, while the leader sat perched on the fence in front of me, baring its teeth in a frighteningly unfriendly manner. The attackers were clearly not interested in my friends, who rapidly backed away as the monkeys continued their offensive on me.

My only option was to fight. Soon, the scene was a real-life version of Whac-A-Mole, with me swatting at one monkey, while three or four others flung themselves at me from different angles. No sooner had I swatted one than a bunch of others would pop up. The bench area had become a whirlwind of snarling and slapping and screeching and shouting. I stomped around, flailing my arms and kicking out at each wave of attack. But unperturbed, they just kept coming at me in numbers.

People sitting on the deck of the restaurant were snapping away with their cameras, and above the pandemonium I could hear shrieks of laughter. It may have looked comical, but being on the receiving end of a co-ordinated monkey attack was no laughing matter for me.

You would think an attack like this would last no more than 30 seconds or so – but it didn't. The ordeal had been going on for a good few minutes when, eventually, my friend, resolving that while we may be outnumbered we weren't going to be outgunned, removed the leather belt from his trousers and unleashed a frenzy of cracking locker-room lashes at the monkeys. The sound and the fury of his improvised whip did the trick. The monkeys high-tailed off into the branches above us as quickly as they had appeared at the start of the battle.

I cast a disapproving frown at my audience of tourists, thanked my friend (what would I have done without him – and what if he had instead worn braces that day?) and inspected my wounds. Despite the duration and intensity of the attack, I got off quite lightly: a bite on each ankle, a bite on my back and an assortment of scratches all over.

With the tranquility ruined and wounds to tend to, we said our goodbyes and went off to our respective bungalows. I treated myself by applying lashings of antiseptic to the bites and scratches and hoped for the best.

As I made my way home to Johannesburg the next morning, I was swamped with phone calls from friends and family. It seems my rescuer had spread the news of the attack and it wasn't long before the name 'Monkey Man' had stuck.

What is strange about the whole incident is that the three of us had no food, drink or anything the monkeys could possibly have wanted. More importantly, why were the monkeys only interested in me? This was not the first time I've been attacked – in fact, I go to great lengths to steer clear of animals wherever I can, and where I can't, I make sure I don't provoke them in any way. I have been bitten by all sizes and breeds of dogs, numerous cats, a baboon once and have even been chased several times by elephants in Kruger, despite sitting quietly a safe distance away in my car with the windows closed.

Family and friends say it is my 'aura'. I don't know anything about that, but I do know that I will continue to be on guard and extremely cautious around anything with fangs, claws, horns, beaks, tusks, teeth or venom. And monkeys!

43

LION CHARGE MIRACLE
Leon Maré

ON THE PAGES of a Pretoria newspaper in 1999, our Kruger miracle was extracted from my film footage and laid out, frame by frame, for everyone to see. With no obvious rational explanation that I can think of, was it divine intervention that had saved us from that lion?

But I am getting ahead of myself. I haven't told you what happened yet, never mind how the incident inexplicably wormed its way to the BBC in London, before eventually being recreated for a television documentary and aired in 85 countries.

It was early morning in February, and my fiancée and I were in the car, idling at the gates of Skukuza rest camp. My brother and his family were in the car behind us. As is always the case just before the camp gates open each morning, there was an air of restlessness amongst the early birds gradually queuing up. With the sun just rising way off in the east, and the heavy clouds from the previous day having cleared, we could feel it was going to be a good day in Kruger.

The gate opened on the hour, and we headed in the direction of Lower Sabie before cutting south onto one of the gravel roads running parallel with the tarred road that follows the Sabie River.

We had barely covered four kilometres from the camp when my brother spotted a very large lion and a lioness mating in the grass, just off the junction with a narrower detour road. We turned into the narrower road, which we felt would give us the best view of the pair, and decided that would be a good place to enjoy our morning coffee.

The lioness, tiring of the night's lovemaking, lifted its body from the grass bed and sauntered over to the shade of a thorn tree, where it flopped down, closed its eyes, and lightly whipped its tail affectionately for its lion king.

The male lion was looking most pleased with itself and stretched its broad legs and gigantic paws out in front of it. Holding up its head, crowned with a dark brown mane, it looked with distaste at the rapidly gathering crowd of cars and tourists alongside the two dirt roads to the left and right of it. A lion sighting near Skukuza – the largest and busiest of the Park's rest camps – is always going to attract the crowds.

On the other side of the gravel road, my brother and his family were watching the lion through their binoculars. From the other cars, a cluster of cameras were clicking and flashing away, and people chattered excitedly – as they do at sightings like this.

Clearly annoyed at the intrusion into its intimate affairs, the lion lifted its head and let out a roar so powerful its mane seemed to vibrate. Guinea fowl scattered in panic, and whatever that was in the grass behind us crashed away off into the thick bush. Then, singling out some noisy tourists in a large 4x4, the lion jumped up and, with a loud groan as warning, charged at the vehicle with such strength and aggression I thought it would send the car somersaulting sideways across the road. But it was just a warning, and the lion skidded to a halt – letting the occupants know, in no uncertain terms, on just whose doorstep they were squatting.

With order restored, and knowing full well that all eyes were on it, the lion strolled slowly to the bushes where its princess was resting. It singled out three or four strategic points in the bush, turned its back, lifted its tail and unambiguously marked its territory with several strong blasts of urine. Happy with the established discipline and silence of the onlookers, the lion gently nuzzled the lioness and, with an elegance that belied its size, padded around in a circle a few times before lying down alongside the female and closing its eyes.

And there they lay, in peace, barely 15 metres from our car. I slid the windows down, turned the engine off to keep the noise down and, from my position in the driver's seat, began to film the pair with my video camera through the passenger window. Through the lens, and zoomed in, I could clearly see that the lion was not snoozing. Rather, it was staring directly at me. Watching back at the video, you can hear me say presciently: 'It seems he doesn't like us. Look at those piercing eyes.' Then, with its strict stare fixed on us, the lion made a couple of low grumbling sounds in our direction. Nothing stirs up suspense quite like the menacing rumblings of a lion – particularly when they're directed squarely at you.

A large male lion like this one could easily weigh as much as 250 kilograms – as heavy as three men – and its paws are the size of paddles. While its walking speed is on par with that of a human, it charges at an astonishing 80 kilometres per hour. I say all this because of what happened next.

It was like a switch had been flicked, and bushveld idyll turned to bedlam. Letting out a terrifying growl, the lion jumped up with savage intent and, in a whirlwind of dust, charged towards us. Through the camera lens I could see it, its mane seemingly dancing in slow motion, as it hurtled towards us, getting bigger and bigger by the second. My fiancée clambered over onto my lap, away from the open window, and began frantically pushing the master button for the electric windows, yelling, 'It won't close! It won't close!'

I had always wondered how people ended up filming disasters rather than dropping the camera and attending to the ensuing fiasco, but here I was, frozen by shock and fright, studiously capturing those terrifying seconds of the lion's onslaught; the violent thud as it reached the car in full stride, its gigantic head with open jaws filling the entire window, its enormous right paw on the window frame. We did not even hear the screams and yells of the other tourists.

It was over as fast as it had begun – somehow we'd survived the charge. The lion dropped back down onto all fours alongside the car and walked away groaning under its breath, before coming to a standstill. It was not yet done. It turned its head and looked directly at my brother's car on the other side of the road. There was clearly something about the Maré family that this lion did not care for.

For a few seconds there was a chilling silence and nothing moved, then the lion exploded off its blocks and charged a second time – straight at my brother's car. With the engine of his car still running, and the selector lever ready for maximum acceleration, he took off like a cork from a bottle, and rocketed past us. In the meantime, I had started my engine and quickly reversed as fast as I could some distance away. My hands were shaking and we were both white with shock.

Now, with both targets having shown due obeisance, the lion seemed to calm down and slumped back down next to the lioness with a humph.

The driver of a minibus filled with tourists pulled up alongside me and asked if there is anything he could do for me.

'A new pair of trousers will help,' I quipped. I was only half joking.

Some weeks later, I received a mysterious call from the BBC in London. Word had inexplicably reached them of the dramatic footage I had captured of the lion charging our open window. They were commissioning a production company to film a documentary series, and they were interested in re-enacting our incident and using the footage I had filmed.

My fiancée was not willing to perform in front of the cameras, so the production team brought in a British actress to fill her role. I, on the other hand, proudly played myself, and our lion encounter became part of the first episode in a television documentary series about man-eaters, which was shown all around the world, including several times in South Africa.

But, on watching it, the programme raised some questions in my mind about what had really happened that day. There is a point in the programme where the narrator says: 'Luckily the lion's head was too big to fit into the window. It was a close call.'

Was it luck? Certainly, the lion's head was big – but was it really too big to fit in a window almost half a metre wide? I doubt it.

Then, a few seconds later, a prominent British authority on animal behaviour comments on the incident, saying: 'Leon got too close, it was making too much noise. The lion got fed up and gave one warning charge, and Leon did not move away. So the second time the lion charged, it was actually trying to get into the car. It was fed up and would have got them – if it physically could.'

But why didn't it get us? The window space in my vehicle is large, and the window was fully wound down; the lion could have easily pulled enough of itself into the car to grab my fiancée.

The question was perhaps answered in the pictures printed in the Pretoria News, a daily newspaper, of each of the frames extracted from my film footage. In the first few frames, the car's window can clearly be seen to be open. But just at the moment before the lion's head comes through the window frame, a mysterious 'screen' – like a sheet of glass – appears, covering the lower half of the window. At the moment of impact, the lion's cheek appears to be pushing flat against this 'screen' – despite the fact that its giant paw is on, and partially inside, the window frame. In the later frames where the lion pulls back, the 'screen' is missing.

I should be clear, my wife and I are in no doubt about the intervention of God, saving not only both of us, but indirectly saving the lion too, as it would most surely have been hunted down and shot had the incident become a tragedy. To everyone else we ask, what else could explain this but a miracle in the divinest sense of the word?

44

NOT AN EAGLE OR A BIRDIE – BUT A WILD DOG
Andy Crighton

NOT MANY PEOPLE KNOW that there is nine-hole golf course in the middle of the Kruger National Park. Built in 1972 for the Park's staff, the course lies just west of Skukuza rest camp, midway between the camp and Lake Panic. These days the course is open to Park visitors too, and with it being completely unfenced, you must contend with sharing the course with crocodiles in the water hazards, grazing impala on the fairways and – if the 'Be Careful - Dangerous Animals' sign is anything to go by – a lot more besides.

When my parents moved to Nelspruit in the early nineties, my father joined a group of golfers there called the 40+ Strikers. Every month they played golf at different courses around the Lowveld, and one of the highlights of the year was to play at Skukuza.

I happened to be down in the Lowveld at the time of their Skukuza golf day and was invited to join them for the day. This was my first time playing at Skukuza, and I was a touch nervous about wandering around in one of the Park's most predator-rich areas armed only with a nine-iron and a little pencil. My father didn't help by recounting the story of a friend of his who arrived at the second hole to find a pride of lions occupying the green. Needless to say they moved straight to the 19th hole.

But it was a busy morning and man-eaters on the second hole seemed unlikely. However, as we stood around near the first tee in front of the clubhouse, waiting for our turn to tee off, things quickly turned interesting.

From barely 100 metres away, an impala ram burst out of the bushes to the west of the clubhouse and barrelled straight towards us in marble-eyed panic. To our amazement, snapping at its hooves barely a metre behind it was a lone African wild dog.

With the large lake in front of the clubhouse blocking its path, the impala veered left suddenly and made a beeline for the golf club car park. A low wooden pole fence, barely waist height to a man, separates the clubhouse and car park from the golf course, and, as the impala and the wild dog got to within a stone's throw from where we were standing, the impala tried to leap it.

It got halfway over, two legs over and two behind, when the wild dog caught the impala's hind leg in its mouth and stopped it in its tracks, right on top of the fence. And so began a frantic tug o' war – the dog wrenching the impala back off the fence, and the impala heaving equally hard in the other direction, trying to get over and away.

We all stood rooted to the spot, too shocked to utter a sound. But when some of the golfers' wives standing nearby began shouting 'Wild dog! Wild dog!' and calling others to see, the dog suddenly realised how close it was to us and let go of the impala, before turning and scampering briskly back into the bush.

The lucky impala – terrified, and oblivious to the fact that its pursuer had given up – bolted into the car park, ran diagonally across the tar and slammed straight into a wire fence. It bounced off and landed flat on the ground, almost knocking itself unconscious. A little stunned, it lay there for a few moments before clambering back onto its feet. Realising it was no longer being chased, the impala located the gate and, showing few signs of its double calamity, teetered off out of the car park and away into the bush.

I don't remember much about the game of golf that followed. We never encountered lions on the second hole, of that much I'm sure. Just as well too, as an attempted wild dog kill *and* a lion encounter in the space of nine holes would have definitely given me the yips.

45

SAFARI TENT SPITTING GAMES
Philippa Spruyt

I'VE BEEN TOLD ONCE OR TWICE that when staying in any of Kruger's rest camps, you can never rule out the presence of a snake anywhere. With a ready supply of small rodents, plenty of nooks and crannies to hide in and comparatively fewer predators than outside in the bush, it is easy to see why. Thankfully, they go about their business silently and without fanfare and so are seldom seen by visitors, particularly in the colder winter months. You'd have to be very unlucky indeed to come eyeball to eyeball with one – so I suppose I can consider myself a little bit unlucky then.

It was July – that time of the year when my friend and I would leave the men at home and head off for our annual girls-only weekend in the bush. We arrived on a Saturday afternoon at Lower Sabie and checked into one of the safari tents tucked away in the northern part of the camp, overlooking the Sabie River. After giving my friend – who had never before stayed in one of Lower Sabie's safari tents – the grand tour of the tent, which includes a large en-suite bathroom, I excused myself and headed into the bathroom to heed nature's call.

Sliding the door closed behind me, I switched on the light. Then, just as I was about to sit down on the toilet, I looked up and found myself staring straight into the eyes of the biggest snake I had ever seen – a snake, I might add, that happened to be draped leisurely over the casing of the lightswitch I had flicked just a few seconds earlier.

I screamed like a little girl and, with my shorts around my ankles, retreated rapidly into the shower enclosure, where I watched the snake perform a cartoon-like double-take and disappear up between the wall and the tent tarpaulin. Now I am no herpetologist, but this looked to me awfully like Africa's most feared and deadly snake, the black mamba.

Meanwhile, my friend, who had heard my panicked cries of 'Snake! Snake! Snaaaaaaake!' and had rushed to the other side of the closed door, was being really inquisitive and urging me to let her in so that she too could see it. The more I said she shouldn't come in as the snake was at the door, the more she wanted to come in. But somehow the urgency in my voice kept her on the other side.

Eventually, I figured that the snake had probably retreated out of biting distance, so it may just be safe enough to make a run for it. Calling to my friend to slide the door open from the bedroom side so that I could run straight out, I pulled up my pants – which were still at my ankles – and prepared to make the dash. But just as she slid the door open, a huge black thing as big as my hand scuttled across the floor, and I nearly wet myself again. So there I was, hopping around like I'd just taken to the stage on opening night of *Riverdance*, screaming 'Spider! Spider! Spideeeeer!' and wondering what on earth else this bathroom could throw at me.

With that, I heard the wooden door of the safari tent slam shut, followed by quick footsteps across the deck and down the wooden stairs. It turns out my friend was significantly more petrified of spiders than snakes.

Plucking courage from nowhere, I made a dash for the door, my eyes not moving from the black thing now resting against the plinth beneath the basin. In the peripheral blur of my record-breaking run from the shower to the bathroom door, I detected that the black thing crumpled up to my right was not a spider at all, but something even worse: a bat!

Standing outside, a safe distance from the tent of horrors, with me shaking like a leaf and my friend still looking disappointed that she had not seen the snake, I somehow found the phone number for reception and made a frantic call to them to break the news that there was a black mamba in our tent.

When one of Lower Sabie's intrepid female rangers and her colleague arrived to help us out with our visitor, I spluttered out a rough account of the previous ten minutes' game viewing. She smiled and said that it was unlikely to be a black mamba and more likely a spitting cobra, as though that was somehow a much better thing. I told her that whatever kind of deadly snake it was, it was a very large one, and she smiled again, no doubt thinking I was exaggerating.

Exaggerating I was not. A few minutes later when she found our visitor, we heard her shout out – with some choice expletives – that our slithery friend was indeed very, very large.

My friend and I had retreated to a safe distance of, oh, 300 metres or so when our neighbours pulled up. Curious as most people are, they asked what was going on. So we recounted, in great detail, the story of our unexpected roommate. The result was that the wife would not get out of the car and insisted that her husband have their accommodation changed immediately. We didn't see them again.

After much effort trying to capture the snake, the rangers decided they'd give it a break for a while and turned their attention to capturing our undercover spider – the bat – instead. Apparently, it was the reason for our intruder. With the tent finally bat-free, the rangers said that they would return later. And with that, they left us with our giant spitting cobra secreted somewhere in the folds of our tent's canvas.

Worryingly for me, I still needed the loo. So, each armed with a pair of sunglasses, we tip-toed into the bathroom. Seeing our eyewear, the snake must have known that we meant business because it didn't reappear, and I was finally able to relieve myself while my friend looked the other way and kept a beady eye on the surroundings.

If ever there was a good time for a beer to calm the nerves, this was it. So we gingerly sat down on the chairs on the tent's decked veranda and cracked open some cold ones. As we chatted, my friend announced in a very calm and even tone that the snake was behind me. Thinking she was joking I turned around laughing and found myself, for the second time that day, eye-to-eye with Mr Mozambique Spitting Cobra. That was it – in a single gymnastic leap, I somehow managed to clear the table and evacuate the veranda without even touching the floor.

When we called the rangers back, they arrived in numbers. This time there were three of them. While two were busy in the bathroom, the other one kept us calm outside. Inside the tent, however, things were far from calm. There was much clattering, yelping and shouting as the snake darted up, down, left and right all around the bathroom before eventually making its dissatisfaction known by spitting a shower of venom straight into the female ranger's face.

This rather escalated the conflict, and the other ranger was relieved of his minding duties with us and took up arms alongside his colleagues inside. For a further 30 minutes, they wrestled with the cobra before eventually walking out triumphantly with it wriggling and dangling one-and-a-half metres – longer than the female ranger was tall – from the noose-end of a capture rod.

I am glad to say the snake was released back into the bush that evening a safe distance from the camp, and I believe the ranger who had received the faceful of venom made a full recovery, despite some of the venom having penetrated a crack on her lip. Needless to say, our sleep that night was fitful at best, and for the rest of our stay, every shadow, every creak and every unexpected movement made us jump right out of our skins.

46

CROUCHING LEOPARD, SILLY FOOL
Lorraine Mollentze

SADLY, IF YOU SPEND LONG ENOUGH IN KRUGER, you will get to see all kinds of rule breaking by tourists: kids hanging out of car windows, cars driving way too fast, litter being thrown or people tossing bones over the camp fence to hyaenas at night. But it was a special kind of rule breaking – and a special kind of stupidity – that really shocked us at a leopard sighting near Pretoriuskop one year.

It was mid-December, and with the late gate closing times at that time of year, we were enjoying an early evening drive. On the way back to camp we spotted a teenage leopard on the road in front of us, rolling around on the warm tar. As we drew nearer, it darted into the long grass on the side of the road and crouched down to watch us. With the grass lush and high, it was quite difficult to get a good view of it, even though it was sitting just a few metres away from us.

As we snapped away with our cameras, the leopard became agitated and started hissing at us. So, on urgent instructions from the two teenagers in the back, I pressed the button to close the windows. But the noise of the glass sliding shut scared the leopard a few metres further back into the bush, where it stopped at the foot of a tree and peered back at us over a mound.

Just then, an elderly man in a white car drew up alongside us and asked what we were looking at. We showed him the leopard, and to our astonishment, he opened his door, got out of his car and pointed his camera in the leopard's direction. We all hissed at him to get back into his car, but he ignored us and went on trying to get a photo.

From his vantage point it was unlikely that he could see the leopard at all, given the height of the grass. We, on the other hand, were sitting high in our vw Kombi and could see quite clearly that the leopard was less than pleased at the man's presence. Its angry hissing stopped. Then, to our horror, it crouched down into a stalk – much like a cat does seconds before it pounces on a sparrow – and locked its eyes on the man and his camera. As he fiddled with his zoom, it was clear he had no idea that the cross-hairs of an agitated leopard were in fact locked on him.

The next few seconds seemed to slow down to a crawl, as my grandson shouted to us to drive the Kombi between him and the leopard. There was a grinding of gears and we lurched forward, forming a shield between the man and the predator. The noise and the motion spooked the leopard, and it spun around and disappeared off into the bush. As we pulled off – shocked at what we'd seen and what could have happened – the old guy got back into his car, shaking his head and muttering under his breath, totally oblivious to the fact that he had been just seconds away from becoming a statistic.

We may have ruined his shot, but as my grandson earnestly commented as we pulled away: 'We didn't come to Kruger to see an old man getting chowed!'

47

AN UNUSUAL SIGHTING DOWNSTREAM
Arshad Bhamjee

MOST KRUGER VISITORS make a habit of stopping on bridges and causeways to look up and down stream for anything interesting. Often they'll be rewarded with something exciting like a leopard padding down along the dry riverbed, or a saddle-billed stork strutting around in the shallows. But I'd hazard a guess that not many people ever see what we came across at the N'waswitshaka River crossing one Easter weekend.

My family and I left Skukuza rest camp that morning and cut down the gravel N'waswitshaka Road, renowned as one of the Park's best roads for sightings. If you've ever driven it, you'll know that about roughly halfway along, the road fords the N'waswitshaka River – a tributary of the Sabie – via a low, concrete causeway.

There had been heavy rains the previous few days, and as we approached the dip, we knew immediately that there was no way we were going to get over it. The river had swollen in the night and was raging over the drift with such velocity that I doubt even a large safari vehicle would have safely made it across. Just as we were about to turn around and head back the way we came, my cousin in the back noticed something unusual in the water further downstream.

'There's a car in the water!' he yelled.

We could not believe our eyes. There was indeed a car in the water. Some 60 metres downstream a small, white hatchback lay submerged almost to its windscreen, with the water roaring around it. From our position it was difficult to make out whether there was anybody in the car or not, but suddenly the car's window opened and a man began clambering through it. Rather implausibly, he was pulling his suitcase out with him.

They say that in moments of panic we do the strangest things, which would perhaps go some way towards explaining what the stricken man did next. Now out of the car and standing on the edge of the open window, with the water rushing by just a few inches below him, and the vehicle starting to bob precariously, he spread his suitcase out on the roof of the car, calmly unzipped it and began gingerly rifling through the contents as though he was in a hotel room searching for his glasses.

There are crocodiles and hippos in that river, but even more frighteningly, the strength of the water that day was such that the car looked as if it was on the verge of being washed further downstream at any moment. Worse, the man could so easily have been swept off his perch to an almost certain death.

My father, who was in the front passenger seat, got out of our car and yelled as loud as he could over the din of the water to the trapped man and told him to stay calm and that we would phone for help. Having told him this and all having grabbed our phones, we discovered a small problem: there was no cell phone coverage. Just then, another car – a large 4x4 – pulled up behind us. We discussed the situation with them and decided that the best thing to do would be for them to stay behind and keep an eye on things while we would drive the 13-odd kilometres to Paul Kruger Gate to raise the alarm.

As we hurried back up along the gravel road closer to the gate and civilisation, we noticed there was signal on our phones again. We didn't waste a moment in calling both Skukuza and the office at Paul Kruger Gate. Having given them as much detail as we could, we turned the car again and made our way back to the causeway with a dreadful sense of trepidation as to what may have happened in the half hour that we had been gone.

To our amazement, the other people had somehow managed to rescue the man, who was sitting wrapped in a blanket in the backseat of their 4x4, dripping wet and visibly shocked. To this day I have no idea how they actually rescued him, but thanks to their efforts he lived to tell his rather extraordinary tale. About 10 minutes later, two rescue vehicles arrived and took the man back to Skukuza for some medical assistance, dry clothes and, I imagine, a sweet cup of coffee.

We later found out through the 'bush telegraph' that the man was a Canadian national who had been visiting the Park on his own and, having misjudged the strength of the water over the causeway, attempted to cross it in his small rental vehicle. Given that he was an overseas tourist, I suppose it was his passport that he had been rummaging for on the roof of the stricken car, but that's just my guess. What I can predict with complete confidence, however, is that he most definitely lost his rental deposit!

48

BARELY IN THE PARK
Penny Legg

FOR MOST KRUGER VISITORS, the very first animal they see upon entering the Park is an impala. One October some years ago, that is exactly what we saw too. Except in our case we were barely even in the Park – and the impala we saw was about to be ripped apart in front of our eyes.

It was well after 6 PM when we left the sugarcane fields of Komatipoort behind us and drove onto the low concrete causeway over the Crocodile River, which forms Kruger's southern border. We were barely halfway across when a large impala ram burst over the bank to our left and tore down towards the river, with three wild dogs in pursuit just metres behind it. All the cars on the causeway ground to a halt, and through sheer luck we found ourselves immediately adjacent to the sandbank where the dogs brought the ram to a standstill.

The dogs kept looking back up towards the bush. It soon became apparent that they did not have the numbers to deal with such a large prey and were waiting for reinforcements.

It did not take long for the rest of the pack – all in all, the final count of dogs was 10 – to arrive. Even though the ram got away a couple of times and tried sweeping its horns at the dogs, they eventually managed to overpower it and, before our eyes, began their feeding frenzy.

Meanwhile, our best friends were sitting waiting just a few hundred metres north in Crocodile Bridge rest camp, where they had arrived ahead of us an hour or so earlier. Their brother, who was in the car with us, was excitedly dialling his sibling's cell phone to tell him that we were watching this kill within shouting distance of the camp. Unfortunately, his brother's phone was switched off and went straight to voicemail. The call was hilarious, nevertheless: 'Hey *boet*, you're not going to believe it:

we're sitting next to a whole pack of wild dogs that have brought down an impala. Sorry, we're going to be late meeting up with you!'

And late we were. We stayed until the dogs had reduced the carcass to a mere backbone and a set of ribs, before we left the causeway and drove the short distance into camp. There we found our best friends tapping their fingers and looking at their watches.

When we explained the reason for our delay, their scepticism was glaring. So out came the digital camera and, frame by frame, we showed them the whole sequence of photos. This did nothing to allay their doubts. 'Rubbish!' they said. 'That's the footage you took of the wild dog kill you saw last year in January.' But when we revealed the date and time in the camera settings, their shoulders sank and their disbelief turned to deep disappointment. If their cell phone had been switched on, they would have been able to drive down to the bridge in minutes and they too could have seen the kill. Aside from the fact that being the early bird had failed them completely, our late start setting out from home that morning had ensured that we had landed up in prime position for the sighting.

It's still a sore point to this day, and whenever we go to the Park together – which we still do regularly – they never let us out of their sight in case we see something and they do not.

Incidentally, a lot of South Africans eventually did get to see this kill too, as we submitted our footage to a popular environmental TV show and it was aired one Sunday evening. While we won no prize for the footage, it remains one of our most memorable sightings ever. More so, we've learned that the very best Kruger sightings can happen at any time – even before you've properly entered the Park itself.

49

A HISSING IN THE ENGINE
Marlene Swart & Leon Swanepoel

ON ANY GIVEN DAY IN KRUGER, you are, at best, one of almost 4 000 tourists taking to the roads around the Park in search of something special. So when my husband, Leon, and I entered via Phabeni Gate one Sunday morning in May 2012, we would never have imagined that our little Renault hatchback – just one of many cars in the Park that day – would somehow become the star attraction. I will never forget the sight in our rear-view mirror of the phalanx of cars, *bakkies* and safari vehicles throwing up clouds of dust as they followed us, bumper-to-bumper, up the winding hill to Mathekenyane lookout point. Everyone wanted to see our stowaway.

My late father loved Kruger dearly, so it is befitting that all of this happened on his birthday, of all days. It began innocently enough, with news of a lion sighting on a stretch of tarred road about 15 kilometres south of Skukuza. We were not far from the area, so decided to go and check it out.

On our way there, we drew up to a handful of stationary cars and safari vehicles and assumed it must be the lions – but it was something far more exciting. One of the drivers motioned to the grass on the side of the road about three metres in front of us. 'It's a python,' he said.

We craned our necks and scanned the grass but couldn't see anything. Suddenly, the python sailed out of the grass and, reaching the tar, cut sharply right and slithered along the verge straight towards our car. To say that this python was big would be doing it a disservice. It was enormous. We lost sight of its head long before the rest of its body had even emerged fully from the grass.

'Move back!' shouted the driver of one of the safari vehicles, with more than a hint of urgency in his voice, as the snake sniffed around our front bumper. We couldn't do a thing, however, as we were boxed in. I frantically waved to the driver in the car behind us and screamed at him to reverse – in Afrikaans at first, then English, and when that didn't work, French. But he couldn't understand what everyone was looking at and didn't move. With that, the python disappeared underneath our car.

A minute or two later, with all eyes on our car, the tourists in the vehicles around us started laughing nervously as they realised that the snake was not emerging on the other side. Leon opened his door, leaned out and peered cautiously under the car. What he saw shocked him – there was nothing there!

'I saw the snake going up,' said one of the safari operators, as my blood ran cold.

'We are driving to Skukuza *right now* to get this thing out of my car!' I shouted to Leon, who wasted no time in starting the engine and driving off. A few seconds later a flashing of lights in our rear-view mirror caught my eye and I looked back: a convoy of vehicles made up of every single car at that sighting, plus a few newcomers, was trailing behind us. We stopped, and the driver of the safari vehicle at the front told us that there was a lookout point a few kilometres up the road where we could get out of the car, and where he would help us look for the snake.

Like the Pied Piper of Hamelin, we headed towards Mathekenyane lookout point – the famous granite *koppie* south of Skukuza – with an ever-growing string of vehicles on our tail.

As we drove, Leon and I began arguing about the possible location of the snake. He was worried that it could be coiled somewhere underneath or on top of the petrol tank, where it would be impossible to get it out, whereas I told him I had previously seen a snake on top of a car engine. Either way, what baffled us both was quite how such an enormous snake could just disappear into such a small car.

When we parked on the hill, I pulled the lever, and Leon bravely opened the bonnet. There was a brief silence, then he shouted to me to bring the camera.

I had been correct after all. The python lay bundled up on top of the engine, just as I had imagined, eyeballing all the commotion around it. Our entourage had parked up haphazardly around us, and all but the bravest of the bystanders stood at a very safe distance, snapping photos and cracking nervous jokes. I failed entirely to see the funny side of it.

The safari guide who had promised to help us get the snake out had inexplicably gone very quiet; he hovered around at a comfortable distance from the car. Leon showed far more mettle. He leaned in gingerly and patted the snake, making sure he touched it as far from its massive triangular head as possible. It didn't move. So he leaned in again, lifted the body of the snake a bit and gave its tail a firm tug. That did the trick – the snake bolted head-first down through the engine the same way it had come up. As it shot out from under the side of the car, the assembled crowd scattered, screaming as they dispersed. The unhelpful safari guide led the retreat, bolting straight to his vehicle and desperately trying to start it, while one of his American guests leapt up onto the bullbar at the front.

As the snake sailed across the top of the *koppie* to freedom, we finally got an idea of just how big it was; four metres long and as thick as a telegraph pole would not be an overestimate. Thankfully it survived its ordeal unscathed, as we received word later that day that someone had spotted a very relaxed python on Mathekenyane.

We survived the ordeal too; the incident made front page news, and the photos are still popping up in inboxes around the world. But the lions we had originally sought that morning were all but forgotten, as Leon had to drive me straight to Skukuza so that I could get some sugar water – and visit a loo!

50

AN EXTRA NIGHT IN THE PARK
Sauda Omarjee Amojee

THE ONLY PROBLEM WITH MAKING WISHES is that sometimes they come true. And in the Kruger National Park, the consequences of that can end up being rather precarious – as we discovered one July just as my parents and I, along with my brother and nephew, were reaching the end of our annual jaunt to the Park.

The trip had delivered the most wonderful sightings, as you'd expect in the middle of winter in the Park when water is scarce, the temperatures are cooler and the bush is less dense. We saw a lioness with cubs, huge herds of elephants, and were thrilled – if not a little chilled – when a ranger showed us fresh leopard prints right in the middle of the Afsaal picnic spot. On one day we'd stopped at Nkuhlu picnic spot between Lower Sabie and Skukuza, and while walking down to the tables, a ranger ran forward and shoved my dad out of the way; a boomslang as thick as my wrist was slithering down from a branch just above our heads.

Despite our earlier brushes with nature, we were not prepared for an altogether closer one on the final day of our trip. My mother was saying she wished we didn't have to leave that day, wishing she could stay another night, while I wished we didn't have to leave the Park, as I would have loved to have gone on a night drive. As I say, we should be careful what we wish for.

It was around four o'clock in the afternoon – two hours before the exit gate at Crocodile Bridge would close and the Park outside the rest camps would return to a tourist-free wilderness. Wanting to maximise our remaining hours in the Park, my father decided to take the gravel Bume Road back towards the gate, calculating that we'd make our exit just before gate closing time.

As we were driving we saw ahead of us what seemed to be a shallow puddle covering the entire width of the road. Seeing tyre tracks on the other side of it, we casually assumed it was not very deep, so we trundled slowly into it. Halfway through, however, we made the unfortunate discovery that there was a deep dip in the road and that shallow puddle was, in fact, anything but shallow. Our wheels sank deep into the mud. My father is a city driver and the car was no off-roader, so after some frantic revving and a few desperate reverse manoeuvres, it dawned on us all that we were well and truly bogged down. In the middle of Kruger. At the very end of the day. Now what?

A short crisis meeting later and the bravest of us had stepped out of the car and attempted to shove some rapidly gathered branches and rocks from the side of the road underneath the wheels to give the car some traction. But sadly the old Honda Ballade would not budge.

With less than an hour before the gates closed and just a single bar of signal on the cell phone, we managed to get through to the Skukuza police station. But because of bad reception and a bit of a language problem we struggled to make any kind of headway with them. We all watched in a kind of silent panic as the battery on the phone went from low, to red, to dead.

Meanwhile, the air had become cool and the sun was now very low in the sky. We knew there was now nothing we could do but wait. Someone else may have had the same idea of driving that road before gate closing time and would stumble across us sooner or later, we hoped. But as the last glow of daylight petered out and night approached, we knew we were there for the long haul. Everyone would be back at the rest camps by now, and the last day visitors would already be out of the Park. We wound up the windows, as much to keep the mosquitoes out as to keep our body heat in. We had food with us, but we were all far too worried to eat.

Night sets in quickly in Kruger and never more so than in winter. With darkness, the bush around us came alive with different sounds, and we could hear the low rumblings of lions grunting somewhere off in the distance. Around us there were a hundred different types of chirping and, in the near distance, an occasional snort. It would have been beautiful and exciting if we hadn't been too scared and too cold to appreciate it.

Hyaenas visited us that night, sniffing around the car and padding through the mud. But they did not stay long – perhaps sensing that we weren't going to leave the car and offer ourselves up as an easy meal for them.

Somehow the night passed, with us dozing on and off as the hours crawled by. At one point we saw headlights far off in the distance – probably a night drive returning to the camp – and signaled frantically to them with our torch, like Robinson Crusoe signalling a passing ship. But they did not see it and the lights disappeared, returning us to darkness.

Many hours later we could finally see a purple glow in the east gradually turning to orange, and then, as if by magic, day arrived. With daylight, the bush seemed far less threatening, and we figured it was safe enough to get out of the car briefly to relieve ourselves and stretch our limbs. A very young giraffe walked past but just gave us a curious glance and continued walking.

At around 8.30 AM an old brown car came rumbling along the road, and we all let out a collective cheer. The occupants of the car – an elderly couple from Johannesburg – were extremely helpful when we flagged them down and told them our story. A few minutes later, with my mother in the back of their car, they set off to Crocodile Bridge rest camp to fetch help, while the rest of us remained behind.

In the time that they were gone, our little bush hangout had turned into a bit of a party. A good number of other cars had come along and the drivers insisted that they wait with us until the rangers arrived. A few of them offered us food and drink, while others began snapping pictures of us, the accidental safari car-campers.

When the rangers arrived it was like the cavalry had rolled in, and they immediately set about pulling our previous night's accommodation out of the mud with their four-wheel drive vehicle. As the old Honda extricated itself from the mud and lurched onto the drier ground, the assembled onlookers all broke into applause. There were no smiles broader than the ones in our car, though.

As we drove out through the main gates and crossed the causeway over the Crocodile River – more than a few hours later than we had originally planned – my father chuckled and said: 'Well, Mum, you got to stay your extra night in the Park.'

'And Sauda,' he said, turning to me with a wry smile. 'You got your night drive as well!'

Somewhat true. But I did have to argue with him on that point, though, as how could it be counted as a drive? The car hadn't moved an inch all night!

51

DON'T PANIC, I'M A KINGFISHER
Andy Maclaurin

DESPITE BEING LESS THAN A KILOMETRE as the crow flies from the golf course at Skukuza, there is always something good to see from the bird hide at Lake Panic. African jacanas strut around on the lily pads right in front of the hide, and hippos slosh around in the depths. Even leopards are sometimes seen slinking down to the water's edge to drink. But early one autumn morning I saw a most unusual kill there, involving not just two, but four different links in the food chain – and an ending I never saw coming.

From my seat on the bench in the hide, I watched as a pied kingfisher flew from an overhanging branch and snapped up a fish that was clearly larger than it had anticipated. The kingfisher was nevertheless determined to hang on to its catch and flapped madly on the surface for a few minutes, which in turn attracted the attention of a great white egret. The egret calmly waded out and plucked the kingfisher from the water, the fish still firmly in its beak.

As the larger bird made its way to the shore, the kingfisher's furious fluttering eventually made the egret drop its double catch. The fish fled to deeper water – but the kingfisher clung on tenaciously and flapped wildly just above the surface, refusing to let go.

However, neither the kingfisher nor the fish had reckoned on the opportunism of a small crocodile that had been watching the proceedings patiently from the bank. Once the kingfisher and the fish had both exhausted themselves and reached a stalemate, the croc slid silently into the water and snapped them both up between its jaws.

But that wasn't the end of it. As the croc threw its head upwards to rearrange its meal towards the back of its throat, out flapped the tenacious kingfisher – looking a little worse for wear – and flew back up to its perch. The fish, however, which had survived the jaws of the kingfisher, and then the egret, and then the kingfisher again, finally ran out of luck, and the crocodile gulped it down before disappearing beneath the surface.

52

PADDLING CUBS AND THE CROC
Stella Stewart

HOW WILL WE REMEMBER our 22-day trip to Kruger in the late spring of 2013? Not for the giraffe near Punda Maria, cut down in a fight and close to death, that mysteriously rose like Lazarus. Nor for the chillingly plentiful lion spoor in the sand around the point on the eastern boundary fence where Mozambican refugees frequently enter the Park on foot. Rather, that trip was defined by an incident that happened not only on our very last day, not only within sight of the farmlands that creep right up to Kruger's southern border – but not even strictly inside the Park at all.

We had just passed under the boom at Crocodile Bridge Gate. As we rounded the bend that leads down to the low concrete bridge over the river and back out into the real world, we saw a collared lioness sitting upright in the grass to our right.

Just a few metres from the side of the road, she sat intently staring diagonally across the bridge to the far bank. We followed her gaze and saw, to our surprise, two lion cubs standing hesitantly on the opposite side of the river, right on the water's edge. They were clearly working up the courage to take the plunge and swim across to their mother. How they had become separated, I don't know, but I suspect that the lioness had earlier crossed the bridge and, like naughty children, the cubs were too busy playing to follow. Then with the arrival of some cars on the bridge, they had probably been too frightened to walk across it on their own.

From our vantage point, parked up on the left-hand side of the bridge directly opposite the cubs, we watched them debate for a while whether to swim or not.

Eventually the cubs ventured into the water. It was a calm day and the water was like glass. They were hesitant at first, even turning back briefly before they had gone out too far, but with longing glances across to their mother, they steeled themselves, wrinkled their noses and committed to the 100 metre crossing.

With their mother watching intently from the near bank on the righthand side of the bridge, the cubs paddled furiously across the water, heads just above the surface, clearly hating every second of their swim. They had barely got a third of the way across when the lioness suddenly jumped up and walked purposefully onto the bridge, growling and snarling at something upstream.

We craned our necks and scanned the water. To our horror, gliding swiftly downstream from the west was an enormous crocodile. The lioness paced up and down along the edge of the bridge, snarling menacingly at the croc, which slowed down and stopped just three metres from the bridge.

For a minute or two there was a stalemate. The crocodile didn't dare move forward for fear of the wrath of the lioness. Meanwhile, the cubs on the other side of the bridge had reached the halfway mark. But, hearing the growling of their mother and sensing danger, one of the cubs lost its nerve, turned around and began swimming back to the far bank. Fortune usually favours the brave, but not in this case. Turning around and heading back would ultimately save that cub's skin. Pressing ahead, as the braver of the two did, would prove to be a fatal decision – one aided by a miscalculation on the part of its mother.

Rather than stay on the bridge and hold off the crocodile – which was clearly working – the lioness dashed around and down to the righthand side of the bridge to face the crocodile from the shoreline instead. With the route ahead of it suddenly clear, the crocodile swam under the bridge and closed in on the cubs.

In a panic, the lioness rushed across to the left-hand side of the bridge, right in front of our car. The cub that had retreated was comfortably far away, heading towards the reeds on the other side, but the cub that had pushed on was just a few metres from the near bank. The crocodile cut a line straight for it.

The outcome was inevitable. As the croc closed in, we watched helplessly, knowing there was not a thing we could do to stop it. The lioness, on the other hand, was far more resolute. With a flying leap, she dived straight off the bridge into the water with a splash and tore through the crocodile's wake. The cub spun around in the water and snarled at the encroaching croc. But it was too late. In an instant the water frothed and the crocodile snatched the cub between its huge jaws. The lioness was just a metre from the croc's long tail.

Heroic to the end, the lioness launched herself onto the crocodile – but rescue was futile. Kruger's apex land predator was no match for Kruger's apex water predator, and the croc simply disappeared under the surface with the cub in its mouth.

As the ripples flattened, the lioness realised that the water was not all that deep and stood up. Gazing left and right, she scanned the water for the croc and cub, but there was not even a bubble or swirl to indicate where they had gone.

Looking shocked and dazed, the lioness slowly plodded through the water towards the reeds on the far bank, into which the surviving cub – which had safely made it across – had disappeared. It was heart-breaking to watch. What thoughts were going through her mind as she paddled forlornly across the channel in the middle of the river, then waded the rest of the way through the shallow water, before also disappearing into the reeds?

We sat silently for a while, unable to find the right words. Usually when you pass through the boom, wave goodbye to the gate guards and exit the Park, it is a sad occasion. And so it was here – except our sadness came not just from leaving but from the most gut-wrenching thing we'd ever seen. For our entire journey back to Durban, our conversation returned time and again to the extraordinary sequence of events at the bridge over the Crocodile River.

Some days later I read that a pride of 12 lionesses, one lion and a single cub were seen less than a kilometre from Crocodile Bridge. The heroic lioness – identifiable by her tracking collar – is the alpha female of the Vurhami pride, which is well known in the area. Tragically she originally had four cubs – two were killed in unknown circumstances, one fell prey to the crocodile in front of our eyes, and the little one, which turned back as she held off the crocodile, remains her only surviving offspring.

But just how fortunate the lioness was to have kept that last surviving cub only became apparent to me a few weeks after my return. I was poring over my photographs of the incident when, in the picture I had snapped of the two paddling cubs soon after they had set off from the far bank, I was shaken to discover something I had neither seen at the bridge nor spotted in the photographs earlier. Trailing some metres behind the cubs, churning up only the slightest of wakes, is the distinct and ominous shape of a fast-approaching crocodile. I have no idea where this crocodile came from, nor where it disappeared to after that, but quite how the surviving cub made it back to the reeds alive is nothing short of a miracle.

1. *The Leopard that Killed the Cheetah that Killed the Impala (p. 3):* A dead cheetah hangs limply from the fork of a fever tree, while a leopard sits with an impala carcass further up the branch. Earlier, the cheetah had killed the impala but was ambushed and killed moments later by the opportunistic leopard, which then hauled both carcasses into the tree.

3. *Angry Elephant's Road Rage Rampage (p. 8):* A shocked tourist tries to make sense of how his car came to be flipped by an elephant. Minutes earlier, the elephant had been challenged by the driver of a different white car, causing it to stab the car from behind and give it a shake (small pics, right). Still enraged, the elephant continued along the road and attacked the very next car it encountered.

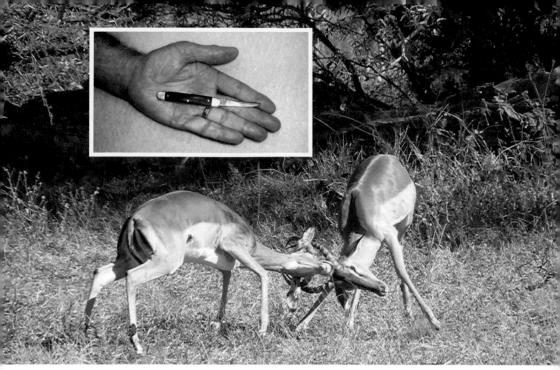

4. *A Small Knife and a Big Dilemma (p. 12):* The actual Joseph Rodgers pen knife, with its tiny 3.5 centimetre blade, used to slit the throat of a rutting impala ram that had broken its back after sliding under the wheels of a moving car.

5. *Leopard Raids the Braai (p. 14):* The silhouette of a leopard can be seen approaching the *skottel braai* just metres from a picnic bench at Afsaal picnic spot in this hastily snapped cell phone photograph (inset). The larger photo shows the location more clearly.

6. *The Hippo, the Impala and the Natural Order of Things (p. 17):* An impala is chased by a hyaena into Sunset Dam, where it swims towards a pod of hippos before being taken by a crocodile (top-right). A hippo intervenes and nudges the impala all the way to shore, where it is greeted by the same hyaena, and a stand-off ensues. Sadly, the impala is eventually snatched from behind by a different croc, which parades its kill around the dam for almost an hour (bottom-right).

7. *A Short Stroll Through Lion Country (p. 20):* The waist-high signpost, in the middle of lion country, upon which a 20-year-old girl sat waiting for rescue after abandoning her car at Leeupan and walking to the Tshokwane-Skukuza road.

9. *One Wild Morning in Lower Sabie (p. 28):* A large male lion paces around after finding itself trapped inside Lower Sabie rest camp at the busiest time of day. It was eventually rounded up and safely guided out of camp.

12. *The Biyamiti Stowaway (p. 37):* A snake expert (inset) holds a metre-long Mozambique spitting cobra soon after capturing it from under the back-seat cover of a Kruger visitor's (main pic) beloved Hyundai Terracan.

14. *How the Elephant Got Its Trunk (p. 45):* In an image that mimics Rudyard Kipling's famous story of how the elephant got its trunk, this young calf at Orpen Dam flaps its ears and pulls back desperately against a crocodile's grip.

16. *Battle at Kruger (p. 50):* The extraordinary sequence of events that became one of Kruger's most famous sightings. With a splash, a pride of lions take down a buffalo calf, before a tug o' war with a crocodile ensues. Eventually, the buffalo herd rallies and repulses the lions, tossing one high into the air. The calf survived.

25. *A Bite at Berg-En-Dal (p. 82):* The writer and his eight-year-old niece (top-left) at Berg-en-Dal rest camp moments before a night adder (bottom-left) struck. The victim is transferred to hospital where, helped by the fact that the snake only managed to pierce her small toe with a single fang and therefore half the potential dose of venom, she eventually made a full recovery.

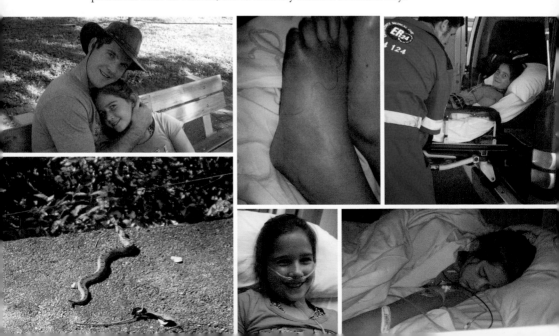

27. *Dog Day Morning (p. 89):* Possibly the only photos ever taken of a confrontation between a domestic dog and African wild dogs, snapped on a rainy morning near Pretoriuskop. Incredibly, the domestic dog, thought to belong to a poacher, fends off the wild dogs, which eventually give up and retreat down the road.

29. *Leopard Versus Crocodile (p. 94):* A brutal battle between a leopard and a crocodile at Silolweni Dam is evenly matched until the nimble leopard gets a firm grip on the crocodile's soft nape and kills it before dragging it into the bush. These are believed to be the only pictures ever taken of such an incident.

32. *Bumbling Lions in the Jackalberry Tree (p. 102):* Two teenaged lions bumble around clumsily on the branch of a tree as they try to reach the remains of an impala carcass left there by a leopard (top-left) the previous day.

35. *The Shocking Death of a Leopard (p. 109):* A male leopard, already tangled in live electric wire after being spooked by noisy onlookers, traps itself behind the wings of the Lower Sabie entrance gate, where it died soon after.

■ Leigh is a two-faced tart who only wants to jump Bradford's bones. Little does she realise that he has just come out of the closet, if one looks at the way he is sucking up to the Farmboy.

LINDSAY AND GERALDINE
■ Janine is a filthy-mouthed, sex-crazed bigot. The fact that she hasn't been nominated for eviction says a lot for the morals of the other inmates.   PETE

bade his housemates farewell, and clutched "Nando's", the toy chicken which is dear to his heart.
His heart almost skipped a beat during his interview with *Big Brother* presenter Gerry Rantseli,

surprise to most of his fans, but for Brad this is what he wanted.
"I've always been in control. Big Brother was in control when he was in the diary room, but overall I was in charge. I am sitting here today

"I have someone special in my life. She has been a part of my life for more than 11 years. I'm not prepared to put her out in the public eye."
When asked why he had stockpiled food and sweets, Brad said:

women leaving the h Zani, then Lara Plur
So the big questi will follow in Brad's it just be his fellow and Irvan?

Charging bull rhino shot to save Kruger tourists

By WINNIE GRAHAM

Seven business personalities narrowly escaped serious injury last week when, on a foot safari in the Kruger National Park, they were repeatedly charged by a bull rhino.

The animal was finally shot dead by the ranger who was with them.

The group included Angela Shackleford, MD of Europcar; Carol Scott, chairperson of Imperial Car Rentals and Leasing; Dawn Jones, MD of Imperial; Guy Stringer, MD of Maui Britz; Rosemary Moss, MD of Holiday Autos; Brendan King, MD of Swans Car Hire; and Derek van der Linde, MD of Imperial Chauffeurs.

They were following the Harry Wolhuter trail near the Berg en Dal camp in the park's southern section.

Shackleford said that when the seven went for a walk early last Sunday, they noticed there

was a large concentration of rhinos in the area. They saw four separate mother-and-calf pairs, but experienced no problems.

"On Sunday we left camp at about 4pm and were walking in a dry riverbed when we spotted a bull rhino about 300 or 400m away," she said. "Derek jokingly suggested he try to attract the rhino's attention so that we could get photos of the charge."

The ranger told them they would not be able to outrun the rhino because he could easily cover "six metres a second", despite his enormous bulk.

"We were just going up the ridge of the riverbed when we heard what sounded like an express train," Shackleford said. "Derek screamed a warning. The rhino was thundering towards us. Kallie Ubisi, our ranger, immediately pushed us behind a small tree.

"He leapt forward and shouted 'voertsek' at the rhino – apparently something that

always works – but the rhino kept charging."

The second ranger, known only as Chris, fired two warning shots. Still the rhino kept coming, this time straight for Chris. The ranger fired but the rhino turned towards him again.

"Finally we saw him drop in the riverbed," Shackleford said.

A rhino in the wild ... an animal such as this can charge at 6 metres a second, easily outrunning a human being.

"I felt sick at heart. When we saw he was dying, we walked towards him. I touched him and saw his eyes flicker and close."

She said the group were shattered. Although no one had done anything wrong, they realised the rhino had merely been protecting his turf and that they were the intruders.

Before the charge ... part of the group of seven busi personalities, with their two rangers on the left.

"We believe there are so many rhinos in the area because the recent fire destroyed their grazing further north," Shackleford said.

When the seven returned to the scene the next day to collect cameras and items of clothing scattered in the veld, they were amazed to see they had fled

through thorn bushes "an felt a thing". Their only inj were scratches and bruise

The matter was report the camp authorities, who statements. "We were told was the first time an an had to be shot on a wal trail in the Kruger P Shackleford said.

38. *Wrong Place, Wrong Time, on a Rhino's Turf (p. 116):* The tragic incident – reportedly the first time an animal had had to be shot on a walking trail in Kruger – made headlines, such as this article in The Star newspaper.

41. *Impala in the Mud (p. 124):* Two Kruger tourists (bottom-right) break the rules – and risk their lives – to pull a young impala ram from the pool of mud it had become firmly trapped in the previous day (bottom-left). Earlier, two impala ewes had found themselves in a similar predicament, but had managed to extricate themselves (top).

43. *Lion Charge Miracle (p. 132):* A sequence of three stills (middle) from the video of an angry lion charging the open passenger window of a Kruger visitor and his fiancée, now wife (top-left). The incident was later re-enacted, in a private game reserve, for a documentary about man-eaters.

47. *An Unusual Sighting Downstream (p. 145):* A stricken tourist, washed off a causeway by a flooding river, rifles through his suitcase while his car, barely arrested by some submerged rocks, bobs precariously in the fast-flowing waters.

49. *A Hissing in the Engine (p. 150):* An enormous python disappears up beneath a couple's car (top-left). They're followed to Mathekenyane lookout point by a convoy of curious onlookers, where the car's bonnet is opened and the snake is finally coaxed from the engine, sending the crowds fleeing in all directions.

52. *Paddling Cubs and the Croc (p. 159):* Two lion cubs, separated from their mother, attempt to paddle across the Crocodile River. Despite the mother's valiant attempts to hold off a croc, including jumping in and chasing after it through the water, one of the cubs is snatched and devoured (bottom-right).

54. *Battle Before the Gates of Skukuza (p. 175):* Three lions take down a buffalo just a few hundred metres from the entrance gates to Skukuza rest camp.

59. *Mauling on the Hillside (p. 181):* A lioness, barely visible over the left shoulder of a trail guide, lies in the dry grass 70 metres away just minutes before storming the group and severely mauling the guide. After a gruelling trek out of the valley, the guide is airlifted by chopper to hospital (bottom-left), where the extensive wounds to his arms, amongst other areas, are treated.

61. *At The Mercy of the Rising Timbavati (p. 196):* The Shingwedzi River (main pic, taken a few days earlier) shows the ferocity of the rivers in the Park at the time. A Kruger visitor and her two grown-up children were stranded for 30 hours beside the rising Timbavati River after driving through a flooded causeway (inset, left).

63. *A Kill from Our Veranda (p. 207):* A lioness chases an impala into the shallows of the river, where it is soon caught and devoured by a large crocodile, which is no mood to share with the lions. The sighting was captured from the veranda of rondavel 16 (bottom-right) at Olifants rest camp.

64. *And the Leopard Will Lie Down With the Kid (p. 210):* An impala ewe gives birth on some open ground but is soon disturbed by a leopard and abandons the new-born calf. For a few short moments, the leopard lies alongside the calf (bottom-left) before biting into its head and carrying it off.

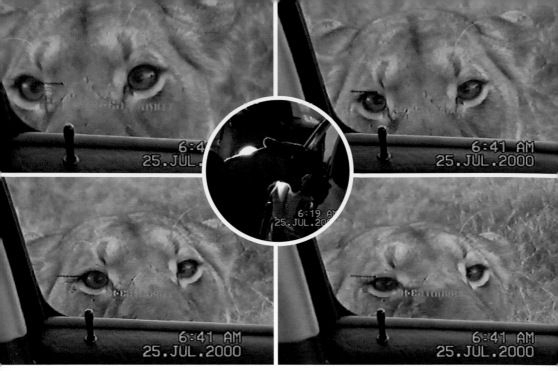

65. *The Lioness That Opened the Door (p. 212):* The horrific moment a lioness opens an unlocked car door with its mouth. Twenty minutes earlier, the lioness was snapped biting at the door handle of another car (inset).

69. *The Elephant and the Drowning Calf (p. 224):* An elephant cow saves her young calf from drowning in a rock pool, only to find herself trapped. Eventually, she heaves herself out and is reunited with her calf and the rest of the herd.

73. *The Crocodile that Stood Up (p. 235):* A crocodile and terrapins are drawn from a roadside pool to a stationary car. Moments later, the crocodile reared up onto its hind legs, lurched forward, fell sideways and scratched deep into the rear door-handle of the car with its claws.

76. *The Hyaena, the Fence and My Little Boy's Hand (p. 242):* The horrific damage to the hand of a toddler bitten by a hyaena through the fence (top-left) at Balule rest camp. The yawning hyaena (top-middle) is not the hyaena responsible, but gives a chilling indication of the animal's teeth and powerful jaws.

80. *Yes, All Cars Have Coils (p. 253):* An enormous python slithers under a car but doesn't come out the other side (top-left), so the intrepid driver uses his camera tripod to prise open the bonnet and eventually coax the python out of the engine and off into the bush.

81. *The Calculating Leopard (p. 256):* A snarling leopard paces around a car, looking to find a way inside. The photographer was too shocked to capture the moment the leopard launched itself and violently swatted the rear window.

87. *The King Cheetah (p. 271):* Sequence of stills, pulled from video, showing an exceedingly rare 'king cheetah', with its unmistakable thick spots and tyre-track markings down its back, walking through the bush then running across a road near Talamati Bush Camp in 1992. There are currently no king cheetahs alive in Kruger, though the potential for the rare genetic mutation remains.

92. *Black Mamba Hitches A Ride (p. 285):* A black mamba, one of the world's most venomous snakes, on the bridge over the Olifants River moments before it retreated up into the engine of a British couple's car. An enormous specimen, it was eventually removed by the brave staff at Letaba rest camp (inset).

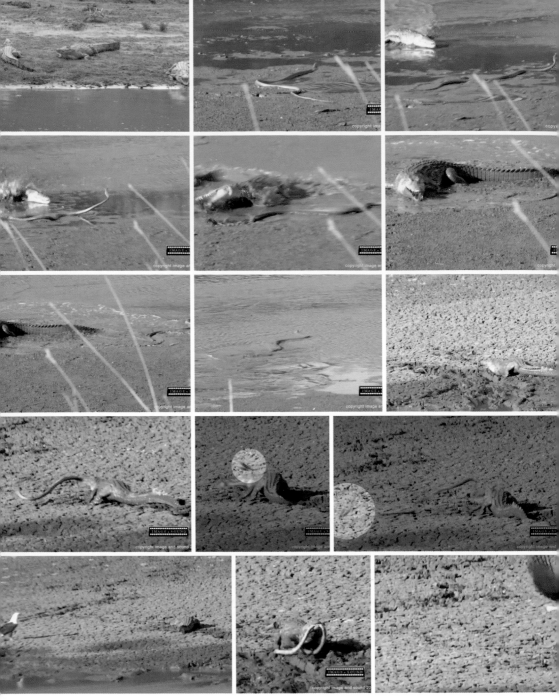

99. *Black Mamba And The Crocodiles (p. 312):* The astonishing sequence of events where a black mamba escapes the jaws of a crocodile on the near bank of the Shingwedzi River, only to get snatched on the far bank by a different croc. The darkened photos show the moment the crocodile shakes the snake's head clean from its body. The head was later snaffled by a wily fish eagle (bottom-right).

53

THE GREAT ONES DO HAVE FEELINGS
Richard Browne

THE ONLY WAY, in my opinion, to see the really special sightings in Kruger is to spend time driving. Yes, taking your time to appreciate everything may well require longish trips, and sometimes you won't see anything at all for hours. You become frustrated. The heat is often oppressive and you'll find yourself questioning whether this was the right drive. But, in the end, Kruger always rewards the patient, the persistent and the observant.

I forget the year we experienced this particularly rewarding sighting, but remember that it was in the early 2000s. I forget precisely where we saw it too, but recall that it was on one of the narrow dirt roads to the west of Crocodile Bridge and Lower Sabie rest camps. What I will never forget, though, is the poignancy of the sighting itself and how it touched everyone in the car that day.

Those dirt roads cut through so many different types of vegetation; one minute you have open plains and the next you are travelling through thick riverine bush, hoping to see that elusive leopard in a tree, or the magnificent narina trogon. But it was in a wonderfully wooded section of the road where we met a large herd of elephants with a number of small calves, spanned out along the side of the road.

We sat quietly and watched them as they slowly moved across from the left-hand side of the road to the right. Soon, most of the elephants were on the right-hand side, and we noticed that they were all standing in a group, in a clearing, sniffing the ground, then lifting their trunks and sniffing the air.

I took my binoculars and looked more intently at what they were doing. Through the glasses, I could see that there were a number of old bones lying on the ground, and the elephants were all taking turns at smelling them. Onc of the elephants picked up a large bone and carried it off a short distance, placed it down gently and continued to smell it while turning it over and over again with its massive foot.

I looked around for a skull, or something that would reveal what type of animal had died, but there was nothing.

We continued to watch the elephants and marvelled at the tenderness and apparent compassion they displayed to the grave of this dead animal. Their whole demeanour had changed from when we had first found them happily browsing on the side of the road. Some stood very still, not moving a muscle or a trunk – just like we would at the funeral of a departed friend. I still remember how one elephant lifted its trunk and caressed another elephants face. I swear it was removing a tear, but of course that's just a way they communicate.

Not a single elephant moved from that seemingly sacred spot for a long time. Finally, and only on instruction from a rumbling matriarch, they slowly began filing off into the bush.

As we restarted the engine and left the scene, you could honestly sense the grief and feel the sadness in the air. Once again, Kruger had delivered in its unexpected and rich way. It had been an incredibly humbling experience, and it only reinforced our long-held belief that the great ones really do have feelings.

54

THERE'S A LION OUTSIDE OUR TENT
Colin Lagerwall

NOT MANY PEOPLE KNOW that the high electric fences around most of Kruger's rest camps these days are a relatively new addition. When we arrived at Lower Sabie rest camp's camping area in the early spring of 1998, the perimeter fence was just one-and-a-half metres high – barely more than chest height to an average man. What's more, it seemed to be doing precious little to keep the animals out, as we were immediately greeted by the sight of a cleaner chasing a troop of baboons back over the wire.

Rather more ominous, though, was the prominent stile in the middle of the fence. This appeared to offer easy access both out of and – more worryingly – into the camp by the way of some rudimentary wooden steps on either side. What the stile was there for, I have no idea – but I couldn't help feeling that it pretty much negated the need for a fence altogether.

Fresh in our minds was the tragic incident a few weeks earlier where a junior guide had been killed by a leopard on a bridge near Malelane rest camp. In fact, that morning we had driven over that bridge and passed the very spot where it had happened. So I asked the man who had just been chasing the baboons whether the camp was safe; because, I said, pointing to the stile, it looks to me like almost anything could enter the campsite. He chuckled and assured me that animals prefer to stay away from human habitat and would not want to join us in camp.

Throwing caution to the wind and taking the cleaner at his word, we pitched our tent as close to the fence as possible, so that we could experience whatever wildlife came wandering past on the other side.

That night we settled down to our evening *braai*, with the camp bathed in the glow of a bright full moon. The night sounds were just what we anticipated. With the rumbles of some very active lions from the far side of the Sabie River, we crawled into our tent at around ten o'clock, just as the *braai* fires were dying down and lights were being switched out all around the camp.

I am not sure quite how long I had been asleep when I was abruptly woken by a disconcerting crunching sound close to the tent. My ears pricked up and I listened closely. Was it a hyaena? Earlier that evening I had seen some campers throw a few leftover bones from their *braai* over the fence to attract a young hyaena that was patrolling up and down. Was it just that hyaena crunching those bones?

It wasn't just me who had been awoken by the sounds. I could sense that my wife, Fay, alongside me was also awake and listening hard. I drifted in and out of sleep, occasionally hearing the noises that progressed from bone crunching to what sounded like brushing against a dry bush, or the crunching of leaves underfoot. Hmmm… that stile.

Then Fay, overcome by curiosity, sat up to take a look. When she unzipped the tent's window, the moonlight hit my eyes like a searchlight. The bush around us was bathed in so much light it felt more like an overcast day than the middle of the night. I rolled over and covered my eyes, while Fay sat at the window and peered around.

Suddenly, she gasped and whispered loudly: 'It's not a hyaena, it's a lion!'

I muttered something in my half-sleep, but she leaned over and shook me and said it again, with more urgency this time.

'There's a lion! Inside the camp!' she said, swallowing hard. 'And it's just outside our tent!'

I bolted up and peered through the window's fly-screen gauze. True enough, standing right there in front of me, with its huge yellow eyes boring holes straight through mine, was a full-grown male lion looking rather agitated. It grunted and paced and stopped, then paced and stopped and grunted again – just metres away from the thin nylon walls of our tent.

If you're unsure how the body responds to unexpected lion exposure, I can tell you that adrenaline pumps liberally, and then, just when you think it will stop, it pumps some more.

We had heard that lions see a tent as an impenetrable object. But then again we had also very recently been told that animals don't like to get close to human habitat and won't enter the campsite! Here was this very agitated lion that had somehow found itself inside the camp, presumably unable to get out again, no doubt feeling the confines of the enclosure, and evidently not liking it at all.

It grunted and paced and grunted and paced some more but never once ventured more than a few steps from our tent.

So we quietly discussed what the plan of action should be. Our car was about 10 metres away – too far away to get to in time. The only 'weapons' that we had to hand were a can of mosquito spray and a frying pan. That may work in a cartoon, but in reality they would prove pretty ineffectual against a full-grown adult lion. So instead we quietly put some clothes on, thinking that if we were going to go down, it was probably better to be found mauled with some dignity intact. And we waited.

I had first been awoken by the crunching sounds at around one o'clock in the morning. We sweated it out until around five o'clock when the first signs of daylight appeared. We had been greatly concerned for our fellow campers, because anyone could, at any time, have got up to go to the bathroom. In those hours that had passed, we had genuinely anticipated hearing gruesome screams from out of the darkness, but thankfully that hadn't happened. Not yet anyway – the morning ablution rush had yet to start.

Our camp neighbour – a very large Afrikaans man; large in both height and width – was in a caravan, and he and his wife appeared to be the types to rise with precision every morning and complete their ablutions in time to get to the camp gates just before they opened. We listened for their stirrings, and at five o'clock on the dot, we heard the guy yawn and stretch.

Fay shouted across to the caravan, '*Daar's a leeu in die kamp!*' (There's a lion in the camp!)

He opened his caravan door, immediately spotted the lion right in front of him and, with his big, sonorous voice, echoed Fay's call in a loud and explosive declaration: '*Haai! Daar's 'n leeu in die kamp!*'

The lion, already wary and still agitated, had clearly not expected to hear such immense booming so early in the morning. It bolted down the fence line and out of sight of our tent's window. Fay grabbed my arm and shouted: 'Now! It's gone – let's get to the car!' But I had not seen where the lion had run to. For all I knew, it might have just run around to the back end of our tent – which incidentally was precisely where the car was parked.

I hesitated and looked out the net window. Not seeing anything, I hesitated some more, until Fay assured me that she had definitely seen it run off some distance from us.

With shaky hands, I unzipped the tent door and we ran to the car, which seemed to be parked about 100 miles away. Then, with those same shaky hands, I eventually managed to slide the key into the keyhole and turn the lock, open the door, then open the passenger door for Fay – with the lion, in my mind's eye, breathing down the back of my spine the entire time.

We had made it. Four intense hours had come to a close, and there was palpable relief in finding ourselves safe in this little metal enclosure called our car. What about the other campers, though? We couldn't just leave them out in the cold with a big lion wandering around. So we decided to drive in the direction of the tented camping area, which is roughly where Lower Sabie's swimming pool is today.

We soon came across four people dressed in khaki uniforms, walking up the road from the direction of the tented campsite. They were a group of student rangers being led by the gate guard, and they had just spent the last hour or so removing an elephant that had trampled the fence, strolled in and eaten its way through half of the camp's aloe plants. Apparently, some campers from Greytown had opened the flap of their little bubble tent and discovered the elephant's trunk uprooting big clumps of grass just inches in front of them.

We stopped and blurted out to the group that there was a lion in the camp. Frustratingly, they seemed a little disbelieving of our story, and the guy who appeared to be in charge of the group asked us quite casually, 'Where is this lion now?'

As he asked and before I could answer, the lion thundered right past us and ran to the fence just behind the ablution block. With the whites of his eyes bulging and some shrieks from the others, the group scattered in all directions. One of the student rangers knocked frantically on the nearest chalet door and was quickly let in. The young lady in the group ran with the other male student to the safety of the ablutions, where the lion, we were later told, had made some aggressive attempts to jump up against the windows while they were in there. The gate guard, meanwhile, performed a miraculous disappearing act, which left only us to warn the other campers about the lion.

As we continued down towards the campsite, we met a young lady walking along casually. When we told her what was happening, she turned white, jumped into the back seat of our car and pleaded with us to drive her to her parents' bungalow a short distance away – which we did.

Returning to the campsite, we began warning the tourists. Some nervously ran back into their tents and huts, some carried on as if we were talking nonsense, while others pulled out their cameras and camcorders and, on foot, began to look for the lion; thus proving that bravery and stupidity are indeed first cousins.

They didn't have to look far. With its tail whipping agitatedly, the lion appeared from behind the ablution block, somewhere near hut 102. Unperturbed, the onlookers stood around filming.

At last a ranger arrived in his vehicle. The disappearing gate guard had found him and they began to usher the lion towards the gate. Fay said that she wanted to be at the gate to see it go out, because there was no way that she could relax without personally seeing it leave. I fully agreed with her.

We waited at the gate as the ranger managed to direct the lion towards the cattle grid, but the architecture was throwing up problems. The old gate wall at Lower Sabie had 'wings' jutting inward, and every time the lion came towards the gate, it got jammed in the corner of the wing and started walking back to the campsite.

While we couldn't quite see it, the ranger told us afterwards that the lion had become quite aggressive at that point and had tried to bite the tyres of his vehicle. He told us that he had come very close to having to shoot it, as its increasingly aggressive behaviour was making an attack on a tourist very likely. Perhaps the tourists should not have agitated it further by coming so close to it, then.

Eventually, and with huge sighs all round, the lion found its exit and duly trotted down the road towards its freedom – and ours.

With our adrenaline supplies drained and our excitement levels spent, Fay and I decided to take a slow drive up to the 'city' of Skukuza, where we could visit the museum or browse around the large shop. Not too long after leaving the gates of Lower Sabie, we came across a large group of cars. They stopped us and pointed to somewhere in the bush. 'Look – lion!' they told us excitedly. We both shook our heads and decided that we had had enough of 'lion' for a long while. Well, at least for a few hours anyway.

55

A MATTER OF KNIFE AND DEATH
Dr Pieter & Mrs Patricia Fourie

WHEN I FIRST GOT A PERSONALISED number plate for my Nissan Sani 4x4, I never imagined it would come in handy the day I was compelled to perform some unofficial veterinary duty in the middle of the Kruger National Park.

It was November of 2000 when my wife and I stopped behind some other cars at Olifantdrinkgat waterhole, north of Skukuza rest camp. All eyes were on a furious contest between two magnificent impala rams on the left side of the road. These two were so involved in their tussle that they paid no attention to the cars or people, at times almost bumping into the parked vehicles, as they struggled backwards and forwards. Eventually, they crossed the road in front of us and continued down the right-hand side of the car and back into the road again behind us.

By this time the cars in front had moved on, and I told my wife – who was driving – to do the same. Just as she pulled off, there was a tremendous bump at the back of the car, literally shifting its back side. Chauvinistic me immediately accused my wife of driving over a rock, which she flatly denied. We peered around, and on glancing back on my side, I saw a beautiful impala ram lying motionless behind the car. When we reversed alongside the animal, I saw that it was breathing heavily but showed no other sign of movement. As a veterinarian with many years of experience, I realised that the loser of the fight had suddenly taken off and, coming round a bush at full speed, had crashed head-first into my back wheel with a force strong enough to shift a two-and-a-half tonne 4x4 – breaking its neck in the process and rendering it a quadriplegic.

I also realised that in that state, the animal could remain lying there for a very long time before eventually dying or being killed by a predator coming close enough to the constant stream of cars. This left me, as a vet, facing an extremely difficult decision between leaving a suffering animal for hours, or doing something totally against the rules. Finally, the vet won and, having studied the surroundings very closely for predators, I stepped out of the car, pulled the buck away from the road and cut its throat with my pocket knife.

'*Wat de donder doen jy nou?*' was the horrified reaction of the man in the car behind. My car registration, OOI VET FS, was the only way I could try to convince him of my profession and explain the situation – which he only reluctantly seemed to accept.

Being a dead-end road, the cars in front had by this time all turned around and stopped on the way back, demanding an explanation for my bloodied hands. My wife worked very hard at convincing everybody. The driver of a car just like mine asked if he could load the carcass; I never quite worked out whether he was serious.

Realising that someone would surely report the incident, I drove straight back to Skukuza, about 20 kilometres south, and went to find a ranger, where I reported that I had killed one of their impalas. His reply was that accidents did sometimes happen when impala ran into the roads, especially when people drove too fast. His face was a picture when I said: 'I did not run over your impala, I cut its throat with my pocket knife.'

After explaining, he thanked me for not just leaving it there, as it would have taken them at least another hour to get to it. But, at the same time, he gave me a serious talk for getting out of my car – albeit with a smile on his face.

So, if anyone ever wondered why there was an impala ram next to the road at Olifantdrinkgat with what looked like its throat cut, you were right all the time. It *did* have its throat cut – by a Free State vet, with a Swiss army knife. I do not have the knife any more but I do still have the Nissan, and there is still a cracked rubber trim around the left back mudguard as a memento of the day I did it.

56

LIONS ARE FASTER THAN LAWN MOWERS
Dianne Henderson

IF I HAD TO LINE UP all the modes of transport that I would least like to use to escape a pride of lions, only rollerskates and a bicycle would come before a small lawn mower tractor. I say this because I have seen first-hand that a lawn mower tractor is simply not up to the task.

Having spent a peaceful afternoon enjoying the splendour of one of Kruger's most beautiful spots – the lookout over Orpen Dam near Tshokwane – my friend Rupert and I left in our separate cars to return to Skukuza rest camp. Little did we know the timing of our exit may just have saved a man's life.

We were getting close to the low concrete causeway that crosses the Sabie River near Skukuza when I rounded a bend and saw, up ahead of me, tearing along the road at speed, one of the small lawn mower tractors used by the maintenance crews to cut the grass on the verges of some of the Park's busier roads. My heart sank when I realised that the poor driver was fleeing for his life – well, fleeing as fast as his lawn mower could go – with a pride of lions chasing behind him, and closing in fast.

Sitting totally exposed on the little lawn mower's seat, and with a top speed that was clearly failing to outgun the lions – which were now both behind and alongside him – it was clear that this chap was in very serious trouble. It was only a matter of seconds, surely, before one of the lions launched itself at him and took him down like a buffalo. Distressingly, there was nothing at all we could do to prevent it. Even driving up beside him and pulling him off of his mower and into the car would not have been possible; the lions were way too close – they'd have snapped him up before he had moved an inch.

But Rupert had a plan, and incredibly it worked. He pulled up next to me and furiously indicated for me to go to the left while he darted to the right. Gradually, by weaving in and out, going forwards and falling back we managed to keep the pride at bay, while the poor maintenance man raced along with his head down, shoulders hunched and his hands gripping the steering wheel so hard he must have left imprints in the leather. I often wonder what terror he must have been feeling as he hurtled along, although I suspect the fact that he was shimmering with sweat is perhaps a clue.

As we reached the steep slope leading down to the causeway over the river, it was like the tractor had sprouted wings. It hit the downward slope and, suddenly assisted by gravity, tore off down the incline like a rollercoaster in freefall – leaving us and the pride of lions way behind. We watched as he sped across the bridge, flicking up stones and dust behind him, shoulders still hunched, head still firmly down and not once looking back. Reaching the far end, he rocketed up the opposing incline and, almost rolling his lawn mower, cut a sharp right turn towards the safety of Skukuza.

It was a terrifying experience – not least for the poor lawn mower man, I'm sure – but once back at camp we had a few chuckles over the way he just put his head down, gritted his teeth and disappeared into the distance. Whether he now chuckles about it, I don't know. But what would have happened had we not appeared behind him at that exact moment really doesn't bear thinking about.

57

BATTLE BEFORE THE GATES OF SKUKUZA
Kerri Bowie

THERE IS A TENDENCY IN KRUGER to think that the best sightings are to be found the furthest away from camp, or are saved for those who visit the Park regularly. This is nonsense, of course. In fact, the most incredible sighting of my life happened on only my second ever visit – and with the gates of Skukuza just about in sight.

Ironically, my mother and I weren't even staying at Skukuza that Sunday. We were in Pretoriuskop rest camp about two hours to the south-west. But it being our final full day in the Park before heading back to Cape Town, we had decided to do a large loop – along the Napi Road, bypassing Skukuza, then down to Lower Sabie before heading west back to Pretoriuskop.

It had been a quiet drive until we got near Skukuza. As we turned right at the four-way junction where the road leading into the camp dissects the road heading east towards Lower Sabie, I spotted a traffic jam up towards the camp gates. Anyone who has been to the Park will know that traffic jams usually mean there are cats about. This was no exception; we were in the process of turning the car around to go and investigate when a ranger slowed down alongside us and told us there were lions in the bush.

We soon joined the line of cars and, peering into the bush, saw three male lions quietly filing through the grass, with an intense, focused look on their faces. Pulling the car slightly forward, we discovered why: a herd of buffalo were standing around grazing just in front of them.

My mother, being the wildlife enthusiast she is, quickly realised what was going to happen and manoeuvred the car into a better position up ahead. We waited there for a good five minutes, never taking our eyes off the lions who, in turn, never took their eyes off the buffalo. Suddenly, one of the buffalo caught wind of the lions and grunted a warning. Moments later, a herd of about 25 of them came thundering through the bush right next to us, before breaking cover and charging across the road. My mother's calculations had been correct; despite having arrived late to the party, we were now in prime position.

The three lions were hot on the buffaloes' hooves. They didn't seem to have a particular target picked out – their quarry only became prey for the simple reason that it turned around to charge what I imagine it thought was a single lion pursuing the herd. As it did so, it discovered that it was in fact surrounded by three lions. Realising its blunder, the buffalo turned around again to run back into the bush, but unfortunately it lost its footing on the tar. As it slipped, one of the lions leapt onto its back. The second lion jumped in to help, while the third seemed a bit unsure of what to do and hung back.

Stupefied, we watched as the scuffle advanced slightly off the road and about five metres into the bush. One lion had the buffalo by the throat, suffocating it. The second lion was helping the first. The third lion, a little more sure of its role now, jumped onto the buffalo's back, as if to weigh the beast down and tire it out. The buffalo was bellowing and gurgling, but that was the only sound – apart from the adrenaline-filled rasping coming from my mother and me.

While I clicked away with my camera from the passenger seat, my mother was capturing the entire episode – rather shakily – on video. To my smug delight, I was later to discover that her shocked swearing had been picked up gloriously by the camera's microphone, for the whole world to hear. My mother never curses.

Ten minutes later and the grisly scene was still unfolding. This was one tough buffalo, but against three big male lions the endgame was near. When the second lion moved around to put its mouth over the buffalo's muzzle, I began to worry about being boxed in by the other cars. In an attempt to get pictures, everyone had closed in around the action, and I was concerned that if the buffalo somehow managed to escape, it would break free and simply stampede over everything in its path – our car included. Because of this – but perhaps more because the drawn-out battle was becoming too painful to watch – we decided to leave the throng and drive into Skukuza to refresh ourselves.

When we returned 10 minutes later, the lions had killed the buffalo, but the traffic had intensified so much it was impossible to get close enough to get any photos of the lions feeding – not that we had a stomach for that anyway.

The reality of what we had seen, not 20 metres in front of our eyes, began to sink in. For hours afterwards, my mother and I would both state, at random: 'I can't believe it.' One dreams of seeing something like a kill with one's own eyes, yet it had not been an easy thing to watch. I had been on the verge of tears for a good part of the latter stages of the battle. Still, the strength of the buffalo and the tactical skill of the lions made the whole drama unmissable. It was incredible to see it all unfold.

The video of what we saw, replete with my mother's foul language, was put online the next day. Within hours it went viral and was soon picked up by a number of newspapers too. The comments from viewers were particularly amusing, especially with regard to my mother's colourful language.

I might add that this was not the end of our once-in-a-lifetime day. Luck at Kruger is a funny old thing. You would think that what we had just witnessed would have emptied our quota of luck for years to come. By all rights, we should have been relegated to a lifetime of impala sightings, with perhaps an occasional stationary wildebeest thrown in. Instead, our buffalo kill seemed to just kick-start our good fortune, as a most remarkable sighting still lay ahead of us.

We had made it back to Pretoriuskop late that afternoon, just in time to go out with a guide on an organised sunset drive. As we headed east along the Napi Road, a guide in a safari vehicle heading the other way stopped and told our guide that he had just seen *skankanka* and *ingwe* near Transport Dam. In Kruger, guides will often use Shangaan words as a type of code when sharing sightings within earshot of their guests. That way, nobody has their hopes dashed if the animal has already moved on. But I knew that *skankanka* and *ingwe* are Shangaan for 'cheetah' and 'leopard', so naturally I was anxious to get there. But to my frustration, our guide seemed in no hurry, stopping every time our Spanish safari-mates yelled out that they had seen a buck. They clearly didn't understand the significance of hearing the words *ingwe* and *skankanka* in the same sentence. It was dark by the time we neared Transport Dam and, admittedly, I was grumbling in irritation. But I needn't have been – lady luck was evidently on our side that day.

My mother was in control of one of the spotlights and, in her best Shangaan, yelled, '*Nghala!*' In the beam of the spotlight, a male lion strolled through the bush. Our guide did a bit of bundu-bashing to get a better view of it, but the lion was kind enough to walk out into the road for us and crossed to the other side. Suddenly, another pair of yellow eyes emerged from the darkness some way behind the lion – and they appeared to belong to a noticeably smaller cat body.

The guide could barely contain his disbelief. 'Cheetah!' he gasped, before telling us to quickly lower our lights away from the animals. As he said this, the lion quietly sank down into the grass beside the road.

We watched as the cheetah, completely oblivious to the ambush awaiting it, walked along the tarred road in front of us. As it drew level with the lion, we all held our breaths, unsure of what would happen next. Then, in a sudden explosion, the lion jumped up and launched itself at the cheetah. We all gasped. The lion got a good shot at the cheetah's hind legs, but the cheetah, with speed as its trump card, managed to slip from the lion's grip and raced off into the bush. The lion made a half-hearted attempt to go after it, but this was no lumbering buffalo like earlier and the cheetah was already off and away before the lion could shift into second gear.

If Kruger does dish out its good luck in even doses, I am afraid that we really did use up a lifetime's good fortune that day. I'm yet to return to the Park, but I'm under no illusion that a day like that comes around but once in a lifetime. I fear it's going to be endless sightings of impala and wildebeest for me for many, many years to come.

58

SKUKUZA LEOPARD KILLS
Raymond Hewson

ON THE STEEP BANK in front of the restaurant at Skukuza rest camp stands an enormous sycamore fig. The position of the tree on the slope, just on the other side of the fence, means that its boughs branch out at eye level for anyone standing near the benches overlooking the river. I wonder who hasn't stared at this tree from that spot and pictured a leopard taking to its branches, providing what would probably amount to Kruger's greatest ever leopard sighting?

Believe it or not, it has happened. More studious Kruger visitors may even have read about it in Wilf Nussey and David Paynter's *Kruger: Portrait of a National Park*, where in their chapter on Skukuza they briefly mention how, in the eighties, a leopard once dragged its kill into the boughs of that very tree.

When you stand at that spot on a busy day, it hardly seems possible. But it did happen and, incredibly, I was there at the time.

On that particular trip – June of 1985 – I would rise early each morning and walk along the boundary fence between Monis Cottage and the restaurant and, each morning, would always see two bushbuck rams at the same spot on the other side of the fence, waiting for sunrise. One morning I could only find one. But as I approached the restaurant, I saw people looking into the branches of that sycamore fig, and there was the other – killed by a leopard during the night and dragged into the tree.

The dead bushbuck attracted a lot of attention that day, what with it being slung in the branches of a tree just metres from, and at eye level to, the benches in its shade. Some people who sat up to see if the leopard would return for its prey that night were rewarded. First it snarled at them, they said, because they were standing too close to the fence. But when they retreated, it climbed up, grabbed the carcass and disappeared down the tree and into the bush to enjoy its meal in peace.

That was not my only brush with a leopard in Skukuza. In January of 1977 my wife, my son and I were staying in a rondavel in the front row of huts nearest to Monis Cottage. There was a shallow ravine about 40 metres to the east of the huts, where a small herd of impala would come to spend the night, having entered the camp before the gate closed. And very wise they were too, we thought, being away from the 'ghosts of the night'.

After the usual drinks and *braai*, my wife was taking a shower while my son and I relaxed on our beds, reflecting on the day's sightings. From the shower room my wife called out urgently that she had heard a very strange noise outside. My son and I grabbed a torch and went outside to investigate. We shone the torch around and stood quietly for a bit, listening closely, but there was nothing more than the usual night sounds. Eventually we turned around and went back inside.

The next day, returning from our morning drive and calling at the shop for provisions, my wife met the camp manager, who shared with her something that she refused to reveal until we had parked up outside our rondavel and got out of the car.

She frog-marched us over to the impala's 'safe haven' beyond the rondavel, where the imprints in the sand made it clear what had happened. We followed the drag marks from the point of capture to the boundary fence – which wasn't electrified in those days – and there, in the fork of a tree just on the other side, lay the limp carcass of an impala ram. My son and I looked at each other and, remembering our nonchalant investigations in the dark the previous night, both shuddered at the thought of how easily it could have been one of us now slung up in those branches.

59

MAULING ON THE HILLSIDE
Helene von Wielligh

A FEW YEARS HAVE PASSED NOW and everybody still has different opinions of how things should have played out on that day – Paul Kruger's birthday, of all days – in 2008. What should have been done differently? What wasn't done? What should never have been done in the first place?

But ifs and buts won't change anything – the fact is, it happened. And while the newspapers and magazines have done their spreads and moved on; and the documentary crews have recreated the drama and entertained an audience for half an hour; for the guide who was attacked, the assistant guide with him and the eight of us guests on the walk that day, it is never going to be forgotten.

In the days and months that follow any calamity, your mind is inclined to work backwards through all the decisions and forks in the road that led you unwittingly towards that fate. You can usually whittle it down to some small choice made way back; for me, it started with an invite from the only other girl in the group that day. We had met at a church camp years previously and were both strangers in the same new city when a mutual friend put us in touch again. That was how I came to be invited, along with her family and their friends, on Kruger's Metsi Metsi wilderness trails – three nights in a secluded bush camp some way east of Tshokwane, with the days spent exploring the area on foot under the guidance of two experienced, armed guides. I had jumped at the chance, and indeed, by the end of the first day of the trip, I had been delighted with my decision.

On the second morning we were crunching through the bush long before the sun had peeked over the Lebombo mountains to the east.

When we stopped to rest on a rock outcrop a short while later, one of the guys asked the lead guide whether he had ever been in a situation where he'd had to shoot an animal on one of these trails. The ranger took a deep breath and replied: 'It isn't something that I'm proud of, and I don't like to talk about it, but yes, there have been singular incidents.

'But they're usually scared off with warning shots,' he added.

The fact that he said 'usually' rather than 'always' shook me a little. What had I got myself into? The desire to feel like a character in a Wilbur Smith novel had overpowered my judgement, and there I was, on foot, in the middle of the Kruger National Park. The only question remaining was what type of character would I be in that novel?

We did not get far before the two guides stopped us and had a whispered conversation between them. You didn't have to be a body language expert to tell that something serious was afoot. They shared the news with us in a hushed tone: they'd spotted a lioness some distance away – and she had some cubs with her.

There was an audible ripple of excitement through the group. We had already encountered elephant, buffalo and rhino on the trail, which were exciting, but here was a lioness. Well, somewhere was a lioness. They showed us where to look, but when I say over the hill and yonder, I'm not exaggerating. How those guides spotted her with the naked eye I will never know. Even looking through some powerful binoculars it took me quite some time to find her, and even then she was only a pale white blip lying prone in the unhelpfully pale white grass. We slowly went a little closer, and still, no matter how I squinted, I could see little more than a dot.

We moved a few steps closer – about 70 metres from the lioness – to a few small, leafless trees clumped together. At this distance I could just make out her features from between the tall grass. All I could see were her ears, eyes and nose. I never caught a glimpse of the cubs, but that was fine; I was already unfamiliarly close to a lioness on foot and that was good enough for me. My heart was racing and I could feel her eyes on us. It was clear that she had been watching us for quite some time and was no doubt busy measuring us up, deciding whether she was going to play with these new toys or just enjoy basking in the sun some more.

Despite the distance, we quietly snapped some photos while she lay staring at us with an almost amused look on her face. Some of the braver lads changed lenses for something with a bit more zoom and clicked away a little longer. I just wanted to get away from there. But we soon found out that retreating was not going to be easy. The lioness had indulged us in our fun, allowed us to take pictures and gawk, but now it was time to show who was boss. With every few steps backwards that we took, the lioness began growling – a deep, low-octave rumble that came straight from the depths of her belly and reverberated straight through mine. When we stopped dead, so did the growling, but as soon as we moved a few steps back, it started up again. And so began our slow retreat from the lioness's domain. Inching backwards, stopping, waiting for the growling to stop, then moving backwards again slowly. Finally, the guides felt we had edged away far enough for us to turn and resume our trek out of there.

And then all hell broke loose.

I usually walked close to the back of the group. And so, while waiting for my turn to fall in, I made sure I kept my eyes locked firmly on the lioness. I'd barely taken five steps when she launched herself from the grass and, in full sprint, began rapidly closing the gap between us, her ferocious feline muscles working hard.

I remember that I uttered a cry of 'She's coming!' I have no idea whether it was a whisper or a full-blown war cry, but either way it could not stop those yellow eyes growing bigger and bigger by the millisecond. Stepping to the side, the guides yelled at the lioness and fired a couple of warning shots, but she just kept coming, totally unfazed. I braced myself for the impact – but it never came. The lead guide's yelling and shooting had shifted the lioness's focus from us onto him instead.

The lioness was about three metres from the guide when she leapt through the air. Quick as anything, the guide jumped to his left and the lioness glanced off his leg and careered into a bush behind him. Immediately, she spun around and launched herself at him for a second go. With his rifle loaded, the guide took aim. The shot went off with the lioness in midair.

The impact of the bullet jerked the lioness's head back, but with momentum behind her, she piled straight into the guide, sending them both crashing into the dust. I expected the lioness to just sag limply onto him, but to no avail. She was still very much alive and, unluckily for the guide, was now fighting tooth-and-nail to remain that way.

The blood all over the lioness' coat was in stark contrast to the bleached winter grass they were tussling in. She was huge – so huge that I could not even see the guide from under her body. I was just hoping with all that was within me that it was only the lioness's blood that I could see, and not the guide's. The lioness was hard at work over him, ripping into his arm and his sides with her teeth, and pummelling this tall, strong man around like a rag doll.

The rest of us were in full panic; there is no other way to put it. Remembering what we'd been told in our briefing on the first day, I kept screaming to myself in my mind: 'Don't run, whatever you do, don't run!' Some of us were frozen to the spot. Others – seemingly forgetting that rule – were running, no matter where to, just away from there. Most tried to get behind the second guide who had moved off to the side.

Concluding swiftly that there was strength in numbers, I reached for the guy closest to me, but I imagine he was just thinking, 'Don't drag me down, woman!' – and I couldn't blame him at all. He took off towards the rest of the group in a wide arc. I started taking some hurried steps towards them too, keeping the lioness in the corner of my eye the whole time, fully aware that I was the closest to the battle and she would almost certainly be cognisant of my movements. I was not wrong. In the next moment, our eyes locked. I knew what that meant: I was next.

The lioness raised herself up off the motionless ranger, and time slowed down to a bare trickle. My legs had stopped working, and all background sound – the screaming, the yelling, the screeching growls – had disappeared. There was only the sudden crack of the second guide's rifle and I watched as the lioness turned and ran off over the ridge.

We all stood there, frozen in the silence after the chaos, waiting for the lioness to regather her senses and come roaring into attack from another angle. I turned round and round in circles scanning the *veld* for her, whimpering to myself, and trying hard not to lose focus through the clouds of dust where I believed the guide had just been killed.

And then, a miracle. A voice, very soft and weak at first, called from where the grass was trampled and smeared with blood. Just two words over and over, growing stronger every time: 'Help me… Help me!'

I had been convinced that no man could have survived a brutal mauling like that. But there he was, stumbling towards us with outstretched arms, blood dripping from the rags that were once his shirt.

He fell to his knees in front of us and that was when we snapped out of it. The intern doctor got to put her trauma training to good use – she moved him to the shade of a nearby tree and, after examining his wounds, used what was available in the limited first aid kit to take care of the worst of them. The bulk of the damage was on his arms, made when the lioness's teeth tore into them as he tried to cover his face. These weren't just bite marks – his arms were torn wide open as if they had been sliced with a butcher's knife. It was quite a sight. I felt I needed to do something, so I rinsed the blood off every puncture wound, nick and scratch that I could find. They were mainly on his face, back and head, but chillingly there were some on his neck too.

We later learned that the bullet from the shot he had taken at the lioness when she leapt for him the second time had knocked one of her canines clean out, broken her jaw and exited her body by the shoulder – which accounted for all of the blood that I saw on her coat. The shot missed her brain by less than an inch.

That her jaw had been broken by the bullet – and, to a lesser extent, that she had one less canine – was clearly the pivot that skewed the outcome of the battle in favour of the guide. In an interview some time later, he explained that if it wasn't for that shot, the lioness would have had full use of her jaw and thus would have crushed the bones of his arms, and as he had bite marks on his neck, she would have definitely killed him.

At the time, though, all that mattered was that the guide was alive. The ordeal, however, was far from over. As quickly as the previous 10 minutes had passed, the next few hours felt like they would never end.

While we were cleaning his wounds, he valiantly tried to call for help on the two-way radio, but to no avail. It was heart-wrenching to watch. He pressed the button and pleaded, 'Somebody, anybody, can you hear me?' All he got in reply was static. He tried different frequencies, but after a while he had to make peace with the fact that nobody was coming – we had to go to them, or at least walk until we could reach someone by radio.

Not only that, we were worried that the lioness, now injured and surely not far away, was even more of a danger. We had to get out of that valley as fast as we could.

We started talking about what we could use as a stretcher, but he stopped us and said: 'There is nothing wrong with my legs. I'll walk.'

As we prepared to start moving, we realised that his rifle and hat were still lying where they had tussled. Somebody had to retrieve the rifle, at least. I made sure that I was busy with something, just to make sure that the task didn't fall to me. One of the younger guys volunteered and crept anxiously over to the spot as though he was walking across a minefield, while the other ranger followed a few steps behind him in similar fashion, with his rifle cocked. They retrieved the rifle – and the blood-stained hat – and repeated the same jittery walk back to where we were huddling.

Whether the lioness was there or not, I could feel her eyes on me the whole time. And I am sure I wasn't the only one who felt that.

With his arms dressed and his rain jacket around him – as his shirt was now little more than bloody rags – we hoisted the injured ranger up. He ordered us back in line as if nothing had happened, even cracked a few jokes, and we started walking. There was just one problem though: he could no longer carry his rifle.

We cleared the ridge and got together to discuss the problem. We all looked at each other, waiting for someone with hunting experience to step up, but there were just blank faces. I realised that these were nature-loving people – none of them had ever hunted before. I almost stepped up to carry the .458 caliber rifle, my only experience being the times I shot an air rifle at empty tins as a little girl, with my brothers giggling in the background after convincing me to aim with the wrong eye. The task eventually fell to one of the older men who had done military training in his youth. He took the rifle and loaded it nervously, but in the process accidentally brushed the trigger. A shot exploded out of the barrel and cracked through the air. Thankfully, he was standing off to the side and nobody was hit, but it left little doubt about the seriousness of the situation we were in.

The injured guide took the lead, as usual, but it wasn't long before he also realised that with the best will in the world, he had just been savaged by a lion and was not up to it. The other guide took over the responsibility. The new 'second rifle', determined not to brush the trigger by mistake again, fell in behind him, with the injured guide and the rest of us following after. I was no longer walking at the back; I hovered as close as I could to the patient. Taking care of him was all that mattered to me.

It always interests me how people react differently in stressful situations. For me, I need a purpose and I have to keep busy, so I took on the motherly role: forcing some of my sweets on him to keep his blood sugar up, offering him water, wiping the blood from his face. When he asked for a cigarette, however, I was quite relieved – given my inexperience with smoking – to hear one of the other guys offer to light one for him. That was his way of doing something to help (and he later confessed that that was the first time he had ever drawn on a cigarette in front of his father).

It was a good five kilometres through pretty tough terrain back to the vehicle we had left earlier that morning. Every few minutes we stopped for water, sweets or cigarettes and tried again to make contact with the outside world. But each time we received nothing back but the hiss of static. And so, we slogged on. The injured ranger, despite his mauling, bravely continued to make jokes, as if to reassure us that everything was fine. Admirably, he even glanced back every now and then to make sure we were all okay.

We had walked a long, long way when we finally made radio contact. I almost cried with relief when I heard the crackly voice of the field ranger at N'wanetsi answer back. After some back and forth, he assured the guides that a team were on their way to meet us at the vehicle and that he had informed Skukuza, the Park's epicentre, of what had happened. A short while later the radio crackled back into life – a different voice this time – and after a quick verbal assessment of the guide's injuries, the man on the other end said a helicopter with a doctor on board was preparing to take off.

We started moving again, but with the promise of help on its way it was clear that the injured guide's adrenaline supply had hit empty. He was dragging his feet along the dirt, and every now and again he would stumble over a stubborn clump of grass or an obscured stick or rock. I couldn't help but notice he was walking with his eyes closed at times too – this man was clearly moving forward on bullheaded willpower alone.

Just shy of two hours after setting out from that cursed valley, we eventually made it back to the vehicle – thankfully with no animal following the faint scent of the guide's blood, or the doubtless stench of my anxiety.

We made our patient as comfortable as we could, propped up against the wheel, and waited for the helicopter to arrive. As we scanned the skies in silence and cocked our ears waiting for the *pft-pft-pft* of the helicopter, there was a sudden hubbub from behind us. We all spun around to see the injured ranger jump up and start dancing and jiggling about like a loon. Seeing us all staring at him with open mouths, he looked back with mild embarrassment before exclaiming, 'Bloody ants!' That was the reassurance we needed – if he can jiggle around to get the ants out of his pants, the chances were good that he would survive the lion attack.

This time he opted to sit on the front seat of the vehicle instead, away from any ants. We all gathered around him for a photo, and professional to the very end, he served up the biggest smile he could manage as the other guide took the picture.

I didn't realise it at the time, but that photo – scarcely hiding the sweat and the dust and the blood and the fear and the bravery behind a lineup of smiles – was the curtain call to this misadventure. In a few minutes the helicopter would be there, and the rest of us would all be ushered into the vehicle and driven away, while the injured guide would be stabilised and put on a drip before being choppered out behind us in a cloud of dust and dry grass.

Nothing bonds quite like adversity, so it seemed strange and disjointed to be separated from the man who had saved our lives and nearly lost his in doing so. We still had another night at the Metsi Metsi trails camp, and despite a new guide being shipped in and him trying his best to make everything seem normal, it all felt flat. We were in shock for one thing, but worst of all we could not shake the discord that while we were supposedly enjoying ourselves listening to folk tales of giant snails and fever trees, our guide lay in agony in a hospital bed a few hundred kilometres away.

Leaving the gates of Kruger the next day felt strange and seemed oddly disrespectful. The world outside was abiding as though nothing had happened – cars whizzed along the roads, workmen dug their trenches lazily while foremen watched, hawkers stacked their avocados and *naartjies* in piles on the side of road. But I felt different – I wanted those people to stop and have a moment of silence or, at the very least, acknowledge what had happened on that hillside. Instead, the world just turned. Did they not know that a man had battled a lioness to save the lives of the party he led? That he had somehow trekked out of the bush and now lay with open wounds in a hospital bed? Did they not know that that same day a party of rangers, accompanied by our other guide, had tracked down and found the lioness not far from where it all happened and, with her wounds so extensive, had had no choice but to put her out of her misery? Did they not know that the cubs were never found and had probably fallen prey to hyaenas in the night?

But time is a healer and, in time, we all moved on – to some degree or another anyway. The guide made a remarkable recovery despite the horrific wounds to his arms, and he now sports a series of impressive scars that his children are no doubt fascinated by. Only he would be in a position to talk about the mental scars, though. He has stated that he wants other guides to learn from the incident – that lion behaviour is ultimately unreadable, no matter what they may or may not do most of the time, and no matter how well we believe we understand their behaviour. We should not put ourselves or the animals in situations like this, he has said, as it will end up being fatal for at least one of the parties – just as it was for our lioness on that hillside. And for her cubs.

PART TWO

TALES FROM CENTRAL KRUGER

FOR MANY PEOPLE, KRUGER'S glorious central region offers the best of all worlds: as beautiful and varied a landscape as anywhere in the Park, not nearly as busy as the south, yet more game-rich than the north. For the purposes of this book, the central region stretches from Tshokwane picnic spot in the south, over the acacia-studded plains between Satara and Olifants, right up to the Letaba River.

In central Kruger, cheetah, wild dog, sable antelope and white rhino are all frequently encountered; the woody banks of the Timbavati River are home to countless leopards; and as you approach the mopane *veld* north of the Olifants River, you enter true elephant and buffalo country. But most famously, the area between Orpen Gate in the west, Satara rest camp in the east and Letaba further north is possibly Kruger's densest lion country. So it is unsurprising that so many of the stories that follow revolve around lion encounters of varying levels of terror …

60

A FINE PLACE TO BATH
Darran Myers

A SIGHTING OF the species *Homo Stupidus* is not uncommon in Kruger. Anyone who has driven around the Park long enough will have seen all sorts of terrible behaviour from people doing their level best to exit the gene pool. But there are varying degrees of stupidity and recklessness, and the spectacle we stumbled upon while on a night drive one warm February evening must surely rank up there as the stupidest thing ever undertaken by tourists in the Park.

The night drive had taken us to the predator-rich area around Muzandzeni picnic spot, and as we were turning around to make our way back to camp, the guide decided to swing past Shimangwaneni Dam to see if any hippos had come out of the water.

As we approached the dam, the lights of our game drive vehicle picked up a reflection in the distance that looked like red eyes. As we drove closer, though, we realised we were looking at the front reflectors of a Mitsubishi Pajero parked up at the edge of the dam.

To say that we were all surprised would be an understatement, but nobody was more surprised than the guide. He called out loudly, asking if anyone was there. A voice answered from the rear of the Pajero, and a scrawny man wearing nothing but a towel appeared from the darkness and approached us.

Less than impressed, the guide asked him what he was doing there. In a strong German accent, the man explained matter-of-factly that when he realised he wasn't going to make the gate in time, he figured he would stop and camp next to the dam for the night instead.

Clearly irked by the interrogation, he then explained why he was naked: we had rudely interrupted his shower – and would we mind if he continued and left him in peace? The guide was dumbstruck, and for a moment it sounded as if he had lost the power of speech. But he gathered himself and explained – surprisingly diplomatically – that what this chap was doing was both illegal and dangerous, and that he would have to accompany us back to Orpen rest camp.

'I shall do so when I have finished showering,' was the man's response.

There was a sharp intake of breath from one or two of the guests in the back. But what was the guide to do? He couldn't drag the man away naked or force him to drive in just a towel. So, reluctantly the guide agreed, and the semi-naked man toddled off behind his vehicle, where I suppose he had set up a portable shower from the low branches of a tree.

A few minutes later – fully dressed and looking more presentable – he sidled up to the vehicle and asked where he was to sit.

'No, no, no,' said the guide, clearly fighting the urge to bang his head against the steering wheel. 'You must follow behind us in your vehicle and we will escort you back to Orpen.'

The man looked disturbed by this suggestion and shook his head. 'But my wife needs the car,' he protested.

'Your wife?' spluttered the guide, now losing his powers of diplomacy. 'Where is your wife?'

'She is taking a bath.'

There was a brief pause. I think every one of us on that game drive vehicle knew where this was going.

'Where is your wife taking a bath?' asked the guide, suspiciously.

'In the big dam,' replied the German.

If you've ever been to Shimangwaneni Dam, especially in the summer months when it is deep and full of water – as it was that night – you will know that it boasts a very healthy population of both hippo and crocodile.

At the man's reply, the guide hurriedly switched on every light in the vehicle and, shouting at us to keep the spotlights on him, jumped out of the truck and ran to the edge of the dam. There in the depths, several metres from the shore, we could just make out the silhouette of what appeared to be a very attractive blonde woman splashing away like she was in her bathroom at home in Germany.

At the top of his voice the guide shouted for her to come out immediately. She stopped her splashing and looked at him as if he was mad. Surmising that she probably didn't understand English, he began gesticulating wildly with his arms instead. She glared at him some more before slowly wading towards the shore. In the light of the headlights, she emerged from the water like Ursula Andress in *Dr No*, with the sole exception of that famous white bikini. For there was no bikini here – the woman was stark naked!

Dripping wet, and without the slightest hint of modesty, she walked up to the guide and looked him square in the eye. Then, quite unexpectedly, she erupted in a fit of rage and unleashed all hell on him for ruining her bath. We had tried to stay quiet in the truck while the guide was dealing with this, but it was just too much. When someone snorted a disguised laugh behind his hand, the result was contagious and we all erupted with laughter.

The guide somehow remained diplomatic, despite the tirade in front of him and the uproar behind him. He calmly let her finish her rant, then took hold of her shoulders and turned her around so that she could see the multitude of eyes in the water, all glinting back at us from the lights of the truck. She went very, very quiet.

Slowly, she walked to her vehicle and returned a few minutes later, fully clothed. She apologised for her behaviour and thanked the guide, then spun around to face her husband – who was standing meekly behind her – and delivered a cracking flat-hand to the side of his head.

'You told me it was safe!' she screamed.

We didn't see much on the way back to camp, the Germans following closely behind in their Pajero. But the utterly bizarre shenanigans at the dam – and the sight of that attractive blonde woman emerging naked from the depths of the water – more than constituted a successful night's sightings.

61

AT THE MERCY OF THE RISING TIMBAVATI
Marion Vlaming

FOR ALMOST ALL OF ITS 32 KILOMETRES, the gravel road to the Timbavati picnic spot tightly hugs the contours of the Timbavati River, as it winds its way north through pockets of bushwillow and thick acacia bushveld teeming with game. It is some of the Park's best leopard country too and is statistically the most likely place you'll ever see a white lion in Kruger, given its proximity to the adjoining Timbavati reserve. If you drive this road in winter, though, you will find my story of our 30-hour ordeal at the mercy of the Timbavati River almost impossible to believe.

In the thirsty months, the Timbavati River is just a wide expanse of spoor-littered river sand, so dry it is hard to believe it has seen water for millennia – let alone months. But in the summertime, depending on the rains, the river flows again. When it floods – as it did in January 2013 – that river is a terrifying beast; fed angrily by a string of tributaries that dissect the road, it crashes and froths downstream with alarming ferocity, plucking fever trees and sycamore figs from the banks like daisies.

My grown-up son and daughter, Darren and Shireen, were with me on that trip, and the rain had been building and building the entire time. At Shingwedzi rest camp a few days earlier, we had seen with our own eyes how fast the rivers in the Park can turn from trickles to floods. In the space of a few hours, the river in front of the camp had swelled from a little stream to a frothing torrent, lapping just a couple of metres from the restaurant's veranda. Tragically, just days later Shingwedzi would be entirely submerged, with the water levels topping out just below the eaves of the camp's thatched roofs. We weren't in Shingwedzi to see that, though. We were already suffering our own ordeal some way further south by then.

It was raining intermittently on the morning we wound our way up the gravel road towards Timbavati picnic spot. We didn't know it, but we were the last car that morning to venture up that road before it was closed off by Park officials, which explains why nobody pulled up behind us when we came across two lionesses lying in the wet grass alongside the road. Further on, the causeways along the road were already submerged by straits of water flowing steadily across them and down into the river. At each one we reached, Darren checked around for predators before jumping out of the car and wading into it to make sure it was neither too deep nor too strong for the car to drive through. Eventually, we reached the last causeway before the picnic spot. But with the rain falling steadily, the water levels were rising, and we could tell as soon as he stepped into it that there was no way our car – a BMW sedan – would make it across. So we turned around and headed back.

Despite having safely driven through all the causeways on our way in, Darren still jumped out to check each stream as we headed back south, just in case the levels had risen in the meantime. When we reached one particularly shallow looking causeway, we didn't think it necessary to test it and drove straight in. What peanuts we were. As soon as we hit the water we understood how deceptive these causeways can be; it was far too deep to cross, and the water splashed up against the front window of the car before the engine spluttered and died. Seemingly untroubled by our lack of foresight in driving into the water in first place, we compounded our problems by making the second bad decision of the day: we opened the door to get out and push. As the door opened, the water rushed in and flooded the inside of the car. The insurers were not going to like this.

In the pouring rain we pushed the car out of the water. With the engine soaked, we were going nowhere, so we sat in the car and waited, naïvely assuming that someone in a bigger car would come trundling along the road soon enough and exact a rescue. But with the road closed off on the southern entrance and the causeway at the northern end flooded, we were, in fact, the only car on the entire s39 – and nobody would be driving along there for many days to come.

But ignorance is bliss, and despite being drenched through and ankle deep in water inside the car, we were not yet overly concerned. The rain was falling harder, though, and we were entranced by the sight of the river to our right getting angrier and angrier as it swelled. It seemed to be rising by the minute. Just then, through the misted windows, Shireen spotted something unnerving. Barely four metres from us, a panicked hippo came crashing up onto the low ridge between the car and the river, fleeing the rising waters. For a few moments it just stood there, staring at us, unsure whether more danger lay behind it in the flooding river or in front of it in the parked car. Erring on the side of caution, it turned 90 degrees instead and rumbled off along the ridge before disappearing into the thick bush.

The river, meanwhile, was rising alarmingly fast and gradually inching closer and closer to the car. I had my eye on a rock not far from my window, and when I looked back not a few minutes later, I was horrified to see the rock completely submerged. With the stream across the causeway behind us swelling too, it was clear that very soon we'd be washed away one way or another. Fleeing off into the bush like the hippo was not an option – we had no choice but to push the car to higher ground.

Pushing a one-and-a-half tonne car up a hill is one thing, but pushing it up a muddy, corrugated, rocky incline in torrential rain is quite another. When your party consists of just one strong man, a dainty 30-year-old and an arthritic woman in her sixties, the task becomes herculean. Make them all barefoot and what we managed hardly seems feasible. Somehow, though, we pushed that car a full kilometer up the hill to slightly higher ground.

We did it in tiny increments – 50 centimetres at a time – and it took most of the afternoon. Darren pushed and steered from alongside the front door on the driver's side, while my daughter positioned herself at the left-hand front wheel, where she literally pulled the car by its wheel arch. I pushed from behind, egging everyone on like a coxswain, with screams of 'Push! Push! Push!' With each heave, Darren and Shireen held the weight of the car from the front, while I hurriedly jammed rocks behind the wheels to prevent it rolling back. We'd rest for a bit, then push again – half a metre each time. By the time we were done, my son's back and arms and shoulder were cut and bruised, and all our feet were cut to shreds.

Our efforts to move to higher ground may have staved off immediate disaster, but when we finally came to a stop we were still only 10 or 12 metres from the river, which was showing no signs of abating. On the contrary, with the rain still pouring down, it seemed to be getting worse.

Our efforts had at least bought us time. Drenched and exhausted, we took off our wet clothes – bar our underwear – and piled into the car. By that stage I was not embarrassed to be sitting in my bra and panties in front of my 40-year-old son – but I was concerned about warmth and food. We had a large bottle of water, though, as well as two flasks of boiling water to make some coffee, which we immediately drank to warm ourselves up. Under the front seat we discovered a first aid kit containing a space blanket, which was quickly unravelled and turned out to be big enough to cover us all; Shireen and I on the back seat and Darren in the front.

My biggest worry was Shireen, who suffers low blood sugar. After the tremendous effort of hauling the car up the hill, she was in a bad way. Fortunately, we found a sachet of brown sugar in the basket with the coffee, and every now and then she would pour a couple of grains onto her tongue, which did just enough to stave off hypoglycaemia. The rest of the time she sat quietly under the space blanket, drifting in and out of sleep, trying to conserve her energy.

There was little we could do but watch the rain and wait. A couple of ground hornbills paid us a visit, but strangely that was the only sign of life we saw the entire time. Everything else had clearly had the good sense to get as far from the flooding river as possible. For us, that would have meant abandoning the car, and although I mooted the idea of attempting to walk back to the main tarred road from Orpen to Satara, it was quickly slapped down by Darren as being crazy. We weren't that desperate – yet.

Using a cloth and a couple of plastic mugs we passed the time by scooping the water out of the car. Darren had meanwhile commandeered the tool kit from the boot and continually got out of the car and buried himself beneath the bonnet, trying his best to dry the plugs and get the engine working. But with the best will in the world, that engine was spent.

Still the rain came down and still the river, rushing past us in a deafening roar, continued to rise. But we were out of options: there was no higher ground to where we could push the car, as the road ran parallel to the river and steering it off into the thick bush to our left was impossible. With the raging waters creeping closer and closer, we began to plan for the worst and scanned the bush to the east for any large trees we could seek refuge in – not so much from the water, but to escape predators.

By five o'clock, the river had swelled to within just a few metres from the side of our car, and we were terrified. I have never ever experienced such a mighty mass of water; the torrents roared and frothed past us furiously, carrying along massive trees which bobbed and bounced around like toothpicks. My daughter and I are both terrified of water, and this seemed to be the cruellest dilemma: succumb to the floods, or flee the car and pit ourselves against the wild animals of Kruger. I am not prone to hysteria, but in my prayers I asked if this was how I was to die.

Nervously, we monitored the height of the river by checking it against prominent trees and plants. Eventually, just before it got dark, the rising water met one of our markers and rose no further. Was it just a lull? We waited and waited as the light faded, our eyes locked on the marker, but the level remained steady; the river had finally stopped rising. It was just two metres from the car.

Darren hardly slept at all that night. I just nodded off every now and then, waking each time thinking it was all just a dream. Shireen had the worst night; her blood sugar was at rock bottom and she was hallucinating. At one point she woke up fitfully, imagining that hyaenas were chewing the tyres of the car.

Finally morning dawned. It was drizzling on and off, the river was still rushing past us not far from the car, and we were still damp and cold. Twenty-four hours had passed since we left Satara rest camp. We imagined that our hut attendant would soon discover that we had not returned the night before, as the beds would have remained untouched – or so we hoped. But what if she didn't put two and two together and simply moved on to the next hut?

It had been light for a while when Shireen heard the faint hum of a helicopter. It was like a fire alarm had been set off. We all jumped out of the car, Shireen and I still in our underwear, hoping it was coming our way. But as we cocked our heads, all we could hear was the sound of the chopper receding into the distance. With this, Shireen convinced herself that nobody was coming to find us and became quite hysterical. Gradually she calmed down again, recognising sensibly that things could have been much worse. However, that was before she tried putting on her clothes again.

Darren had wisely worn his wet clothes all night, which had eventually dried from his body heat. I pulled my trousers back on even though they were still very wet, but I was unable get my wet top on. I reconciled with the fact that if I was going to get rescued, it would have to be in my bra. Shireen, on the other hand, had been wearing jeans, and when denim gets wet it is an impossible fabric; she tried and tried but simply could not get back into them. Horrified at the thought of having to be rescued in just her underwear, she tied together two thin triangular bandages from the first aid kit and fashioned them around her waist for a bit of modesty.

The rain had set in again, and there was nothing we could do but sit. The day passed slowly. Shireen kept her door slightly open for the sound of any activity in the skies above us, but all we could hear was the patter of rain on the roof of the car. Eventually, at around five o'clock, she asked me if I could hear the sound of the helicopter. I listened closely but couldn't hear anything – she must have been hallucinating again, I thought. A few seconds passed, then suddenly we all heard it very clearly.

There was no way we were going to be missed again this time. We jumped out of the car, me still in my bra and my daughter in her underwear with her makeshift apron, and began waving the space blanket wildly. It worked – the pilots spotted us. I cannot describe our elation as the helicopter circled overhead, slowly manoeuvred into position and landed on the road behind us. It had been 30 hours since we had first driven into the causeway.

Who knows why we do what we do in these sorts of situations, but I grabbed whatever I could from the car – my camera and handbag, my sandals, my daughter's wet ID book and, inexplicably, a sopping wet roadmap – and ran hysterically towards the chopper, terrified that they would leave without us. The co-pilot ran towards me and, seeing my desperation, gave me a reassuring hug. He promised me that they were there to take us back to camp, but I still scrambled into that helicopter with such haste, I am sure they chuckled about it later.

Flying over the plains back towards Satara was fascinating. There was just so much water everywhere. I could not contain my nervous excitement at being rescued and chatted through the headsets to the pilots for the entire 20-minute flight. But I couldn't keep my eyes off the land beneath us; the ground was drenched and covered in vast pools of water as far as I could see in any direction. We flew over countless impala, and I will never forget the sight of a herd of elephants trudging through the green bush below.

The helicopter landed on the grass just outside the gates at Satara, attracting a crowd of tourists on the inside of the fence, who began snapping away with their cameras. The co-pilot told us to stay in the helicopter – which is just as well for Shireen who was suddenly feeling very naked – while he ran into camp to alert the office that we had been found and that one of the party had on very few clothes. A few minutes later, a double-cab *bakkie* driven by the section ranger and the assistant camp manager came rushing out the gates and pulled up alongside the helicopter. We filed out of the chopper and hopped into the car, where we were greeted with relief and driven back to our hut. Behind us, the helicopter took off again immediately. We were probably not the only ones missing, and those two heroic pilots must have had their work cut out for them that day.

The heartwarming way we were treated by the staff at Satara was almost overwhelming. Soon after we had showered and cleaned up, there was a knock at the door. It was the smiling assistant camp manager with some coffee, sugar, milk and rusks for us, as she had heard that ours had all been left in the abandoned car. Word of our safe return spread quickly and the young man who drives the golf cart delivering linen to the huts pulled up to welcome us back. He could barely contain his joy at our being alive and well. Soon, all the other hut attendants in the circle came by to show how happy they were that we were safe, as it had been one of them who had noticed that our beds had not been slept in and had reported it straight away. Our clothes were taken to be laundered, and we were driven by the assistant camp manager to the restaurant, where we were treated to dinner. We were particularly grateful for this, as a rogue troop of vervet monkeys had, in our lengthy absence, managed to open the latches of our food storage box on the veranda and cleaned out our food supplies.

At dinner we were told that we would be taken to collect our car as soon as it was safe to do so. The next day, the roads were still flooded. But on the morning that followed, we headed out with a ranger in an open-topped game viewing vehicle and promptly got stuck in the first causeway south of the Timbavati picnic spot – the exact same causeway we had been forced to turn around at a few days earlier. This time, though, it was a beautiful sunny morning and, with the ranger easily able to call for some back-up on his VHF radio, we could relax. We spent the next couple of hours wading around in the water, sharing stories and enjoying the sunshine.

When the other vehicle arrived, one of the rangers was holding a number plate which they had found lying in a causeway further south. Incredibly, it was the number plate from our car.

The rangers immediately set about digging out the sand around the wheels of the stricken game drive vehicle before towing it out. Very soon we were back on the road, heading south towards our abandoned car. Despite having had a few days to dry out, the car would not start, so it was towed back to Satara. The mechanic from Letaba rest camp drove all the way down to look at the car the following day and worked on it for a number of hours but, in the end, declared what we had suspected: the engine was shot. All of Darren's efforts under the bonnet in the pouring rain that day had been in vain. It wasn't until Friday – a full week after becoming stranded – that my brother, who lives in Nelspruit, was able to drive up to Satara and tow us away.

Thankfully, the insurance company covered the enormous cost of the engine damage and the damage to the car's bodywork. Despite being flooded, the interior dried out nicely in Nelspruit's high temperatures, and there is no lingering damp smell to remind us of our ordeal on the road to Timbavati picnic spot. The images in our minds' eyes of the raging water rising closer and closer to the car will be harder to shift. But I like to think that it will be the memories of the heroic pilots who skilfully plucked us up from alongside the flooding river, and the smiling Satara camp staff rallying around us like returned prodigal sons, that will linger with us the longest.

62

HERDING WARTHOGS
Riël du Toit

I HAD ALWAYS WANTED A CAR with an old-fashioned 'Tin Lizzie' horn – one that rang out with a loud and powerful *a-oe-a-oe-a!* For years I searched high and low for such a thing, but horns like that are as scarce as secondhand coffins. Then, one year I was inspecting an air force unit and stumbled across one, installed on the veranda of the Sergeant Major's office. He would use it, he told me, to summon the troops or to announce teatime.

The first time I got to hear it was just as the unit was breaking for tea. I was sitting in his office when the Sergeant Major pressed a button, and the horn blared from the veranda outside. I nearly jumped out of my skin. Its unearthly blast was easily the ugliest, hardest, most grating sound I had ever heard. Henry Ford must have been terribly cruel. When I had recovered my senses, I mentioned to the Sergeant Major that I would love to own such a contraption and install it in my car for fun.

On a follow-up visit, I found the horn on the Sergeant Major's desk along with a note bequeathing the horn to me as a gift from the unit. It was a big surprise and a very welcome gesture. I installed the horn under the bonnet of my Mercedes Benz, to the great amusement of my children and even greater bemusement to the pedestrians in town who must have thought it odd for a new car to have such an ugly, old horn.

During a stay at Satara rest camp some time later, we discovered a sounder of eight or nine resident warthogs roaming the camp, destroying the plants with their large teeth. Each day, the staff would try and round them up and herd them out of the camp; in addition to being destructive to the landscaping, they're still wild animals and can be dangerous, particularly to small children. The most practical way to do this, they found, was on foot, shepherding them along the road to the main gate before shooing them out into the bush. But herding warthogs is a bit like herding cats, and I could see that rounding them up and coaxing them out was by no means a simple task. Warthogs are reluctant and suspicious creatures. If one of them gets even a whiff that its freedom is being interfered with, or it feels in the tiniest way threatened, it'll simply disperse and flee – with the others following immediately behind it. Now, Satara is a big camp, and once that group dispersed between the huts, the entire operation had to be cancelled and started again from scratch.

It was late afternoon, and my son and I had to quickly go and buy something from the camp's shop. We drove my car from the hut to the shop, which sits about 100 metres from the main gate. On our way there we came across six staff members in the middle of a careful operation to slowly and calmly shepherd the warthogs towards the gate. As we approached, one of the assistants motioned to us to stop, asking us to be patient and not drive past at such a crucial stage of their efforts. They clearly had the situation well under control as they gingerly ushered the warthogs along. They were already not far from the gate, and a group of staff had formed a funnel on either side of the road leading all the way to the exit, with the plan to gradually close in behind the pigs and encourage them straight out through the gates. It must have taken the staff hours to get the warthogs this far. Behind us, a few other cars had stopped too, appreciating the sensitivity of the operation. With the gate – and thus the positive outcome – in sight, nobody dared breathe.

Everybody sat patiently until I, on the spur of the moment, pressed my *a-oe-a-oe-a!* horn. Don't ask me why I did something so irresponsible because I don't know, but I immediately regretted it. Even for me, the horn sounded unforgivably loud and ugly.

On the road in front of us, there was suddenly total chaos: the terror-stricken warthogs burst off in a blur of dust and tails, snorting away in nine different directions and knocking two of the helpers clean off their feet.

And so, the warthogs were back to digging up the plants around the camp. The hours-long operation was scrapped. The funnel of helpers lining the road shook their heads and filed away. The disappointed staff dusted themselves off and glared furiously at me. The *a-oe-a-oe-a!* of the horn still echoed around the camp, and it felt like the whole of Satara's attention was focused squarely on me. I truly felt like a louse.

'Dad,' said my seven-year-old son, turning to me, 'this time you've really blown it.'

Nothing could have been closer to the truth.

63

A KILL FROM OUR VERANDA
Mario Fazekas

MANY PEOPLE IN KRUGER will spend the entire day driving around hot, dusty roads looking for animals. Indeed, when the camp gates open each morning, there is always a queue of cars, their engines idling, waiting to get out – even in summer when the camp gates open at 4.30 AM. From then on there is a steady flow of cars, and by 8 AM, ninety-nine per cent of visitors have left and the camps feel like ghost towns. The few that stay behind, however, could witness a once-in-a-lifetime-sighting – just as we did one morning in April at Olifants rest camp.

Olifants is famous for its aspect. Nestled on top of a steep hill overlooking a bend in the 300-metre-wide Olifants River below, the views from the camp down to the river and across the plains to the south towards Satara are spectacular to the point of breathtaking. From this eagle's-eye-view you can spend hours with a pair of binoculars watching game make its way to the water to drink.

That morning, we decided to stay in camp as we had been allocated a rondavel right on the precipice of the hill, with an uninterrupted view of the upstream bend in the Olifants. With a vista like that, driving around in the heat seemed a foolish choice.

From our vantage point high up above the river, we could see a herd of waterbuck plodding around peacefully in the shallows below. Suddenly, something startled them and they began to run. We scanned the river banks for what had scared them and quickly found the culprit: a lioness ambling lazily along the bank. Moments later a second lioness joined her, and together they crouched down on the bank and drank some water.

It is unclear how lions communicate their hunting strategies, but these two clearly had a plan. The first lioness wandered nonchalantly over to a bush and sat down in the shade, attracting the attention of the waterbuck, which were keeping a nervy eye on proceedings from a sandbar a short distance from the bank. Meanwhile, the second lioness, out of view of the buck, crouched down beside a rock and waited in anticipation for one of them to move close enough for her to pounce.

We too were waiting in anticipation. But just as a watched pot never boils, a watched lioness never hunts. In fact, in this case, watched lionesses apparently just go to sleep.

And so, with the action halted and the temperature beginning to rise, my wife got up and went into the rondavel to fetch us some Cokes. Her parting words were: 'Just make sure you keep watching the lions!' I had said yes but I could see that nothing was happening, so I rested my eyes for a few minutes – until my wife shoved a Coke into my hand and yelled: 'Wake up, the lioness is chasing an impala!'

The lionesses' faux-sleeping had been a ruse. One of them had burst from the bush in pursuit of an impala ewe which must have been on its way to the river to drink. Fortunately our cameras were set up on tripods, so I jumped up and began shooting. The impala was too fast for the lioness and escaped by fleeing straight into the shallows of the river. I snapped away with the camera until I lost sight of it behind the branches of a tree just below me.

It appeared to be a lucky escape for the impala – or so we thought. Another three lions appeared from nowhere and joined the first two lionesses as they began to cross the river, jumping from island to island and using the rocks as stepping stones, clearly looking for something. Eventually we saw what they were after: the escaped impala had ended up as a crocodile kill.

The crocodile had emerged from the water onto a sandbank and had the impala's head firmly in its mouth. The lions attempted to intimidate the crocodile into releasing its catch, but this croc was large and not one for being bullied. It simply flicked its tail at the lions a few times before disappearing back into the river with its meal.

This type of sighting would be very difficult to see or photograph from a car. But from our comfortable vantage point high above the river below, the conditions were ideal. All of this happened between the hours of seven and eleven in the morning; so the light was very good for photography, the sun was behind us and we had had plenty of time to set up our cameras on tripods in anticipation of something happening. This proves that patience in Kruger always pays off – even from within the confines of the rest camps.

In the years that followed, every time we returned to Olifants we would request the very same rondavel. One day the duty manager at the time asked us why we always wanted the same unit. So we told him the story. Delighted by the anecdote, he would often retell the tale with relish to arriving guests – but they were always sceptical, he said. So we framed the photograph of the lioness chasing the impala into the river, and it now hangs proudly in Olifants reception as evidence to support the duty manager's story.

Needless to say, when visitors who have seen the photograph in reception make their bookings for Olifants, they request the same rondavel in the hope that some of our luck may rub off on them. But rondavel number 16 has no magical properties and is not much different from any of the other rondavels on the perimeter; we just enjoy having a view of both the river and far-reaching bushveld from that particular corner of Olifants hill. No, any of our neighbours would have seen this action from their verandas too – had they also just stayed in camp that day.

64

AND THE LEOPARD WILL LIE DOWN WITH THE KID
Anton Kruger

THERE IS A PASSAGE IN THE OLD TESTAMENT that foretells of a time where there will be paradise on earth and everything will be in harmony: predators and prey will be at peace, and 'the leopard will lie down with the kid'. Well, in Kruger's lush summer months when the bush is thick and green, the rivers are in full flow and the mopane trees are bubbling over with birds, the northern parts of the Park don't feel at all far from paradise. So imagine how our jaws dropped when, against that idyllic backdrop, a leopard really did lie down with a 'kid'.

It was early December and my wife and I were staying at Shimuwini Bushveld Camp in the northern region of the Park. We weren't expecting great sightings on the trip because, as most South Africans know, the bush is impenetrably thick in the summer, particularly in the mopane *veld* of that area, which makes game spotting very difficult.

We had decided to take a leisurely morning drive from Shimuwini down to Letaba rest camp, following the gravel roads, past Mingerhout Dam and onto the tarred road that heads south towards Letaba.

Passing a small clearing, we saw a single impala ewe lying all alone on the open patch of ground. There was something odd about this, so we pulled up alongside her. The car had barely stopped when, to our amazement, she started giving birth. We switched off the engine and settled in to watch this extraordinary spectacle.

After about 10 painful-looking minutes, the baby impala had its first glimpse of the world as it slid out behind her in a wet bundle and shook its head, flapping its big ears. The mother wasted no time stretching around, eating the birth sac and licking the newborn clean – clearly conscious of their exposure to predators and no doubt in a hurry to get the calf up and moving to rejoin the herd, where there would be safety in numbers.

Suddenly, the mood changed dramatically; the mother started jerking her body and staring fixedly into the bush behind.

'Why does she look so scared?' asked my wife.

Before I could even respond, the ewe sprang up and, with parts of the afterbirth and birth sac still hanging out of her, crashed off into the bush, leaving the calf lying prone and confused in the middle of the open ground.

A large male leopard appeared from the bushes to the left and sauntered over to the calf. The leopard knew we were watching and kept its eyes firmly on us as it bent its knees and crouched down alongside the calf. Then, just as the Bible had prophesied, the leopard lay down alongside it. For a short while, both the calf and the leopard lay there and stared at us while we stared back. It was an extraordinary scene – this huge predator lying mildly alongside the newborn prey – and we did not dare breathe for fear of disturbing it. It was to be short-lived, though, and any notion that this was indeed heaven on earth as that Bible passage asserted was soon crushed; the leopard edged forward, steadied the calf with its paw, then wrapped its jaws around the calf's head and bit down. It was over.

With the young impala hanging from its mouth, still limply kicking its gangly legs, the leopard sat upright and stared at us again for a moment, before standing up and melting off into the bush with its prey between its teeth.

The clearing was empty again, and our ears tuned back into the bird-song and the insect chirps that we'd blocked out as this had all unfolded in front of us. Perhaps that prophecy in the Book of Isaiah hadn't quite come to pass; nature's predator and prey were clearly not at peace. But for those short minutes where the leopard and the 'kid' lay together, staring back at us… well, it certainly came close.

65

THE LIONESS THAT OPENED THE DOOR
Theuns & Elzet Hurter

I HAVE BEEN VISITING THE PARK since I was a young boy in the sixties. However, it wasn't until July 2000, while on a celebratory trip to the Park with my wife, that Kruger served up something we've been dining out on ever since – and which, ironically, involved something very nearly dining out on us.

It was our fourth wedding anniversary, and we were staying a few nights in a bungalow at Satara rest camp – famed for its high concentration of lions. Being mid-winter it was quite cold, misty and still dark when the camp gates swung open at six o'clock and we headed north along the tarred road up to Olifants. As always, we were eager to see what Kruger had in store for us, and with this area being 'predator central', lion sightings were high on our wishlist. We didn't have to travel far.

We had barely driven four kilometres when we came across two male lions and a lioness in the middle of the road. A few other cars that had been ahead of us at the gate had all stopped too, enjoying this early stroke of luck. It was a skin-tingling sight watching the lions moving around in the mist and darkness like ghosts in the headlights of the cars.

The lions were gradually padding along the road in a northerly direction. Anticipating a better view a little further on, I passed the lions and the other cars and stopped a short way ahead of them, before switching off the engine. With video camera ready, I prepared myself to record some close-up footage. I had no inkling of just how close-up that footage would eventually turn out to be.

From my new vantage point I was able to see the lions a lot clearer. It soon became clear that the lioness was in oestrus, and that she and one of the males were a mating pair. While the other male was idling around, keeping a relatively safe distance, the mating pair were weaving in and out between the cars, much to the delight of the occupants.

The lioness was clearly in a mischievous mood, licking the dew droplets from the sides of some of the vehicles and even nibbling on the wing mirrors of a couple of the others. Some of the drivers lost their nerve, or got worried about having to explain lion damage to their insurers, and left. But driving off was not on our agenda – we were all set to make the most of this sighting.

As traffic began to build up behind us, we again decided to move forward. But when I turned the key in the ignition, nothing happened: no dash lights blinked, no starter motor whirred – nothing. The car's battery was completely flat, it seemed. My wife and I shared a nervous chuckle as we realised simultaneously that we'd not be able to move should the lioness start nibbling on our side-mirrors or chewing on our tyres.

Within moments the male lion was next to my door. Up close, it was even bigger than I had thought and sported the most magnificent mane. I watched it through the viewfinder of the video camera and was getting some great close-up footage when my wife breathlessly suggested I record the action on her side, where the lioness was right next to her door, looking in through the closed window. It too was huge up close, and its yellow eyes, just inches from the glass, were focused chillingly on my wife. To this lioness, I don't think we were any longer a big metal object to be ignored – we were a meal in a tin can.

What happened next is the stuff of nightmares. Having eyeballed my wife and deciding it liked what was on the menu – or perhaps just through feline curiosity – the lioness shifted its focus to the door handle, opened its mouth, got a hold of the handle with its lower canines and, with a heart-stopping clunk, opened the door.

Although this all happened in just a couple of seconds, I still recall it playing out in slow motion.

Surprised that the door had given way, the lioness stepped backwards and the door swung open. Suddenly, my wife found herself 10 centimetres away from the jaws, and the rapidly refocusing yellow eyes, of Africa's apex predator.

I dropped the video camera onto my lap, reached over my frozen-stiff wife and pulled her car door closed. To this day, though, she still maintains it was her who closed the door – but, really, it was me. The lioness, meanwhile, looked in at us, half-puzzled and half-annoyed that the restaurant door had just been slammed in its face.

Frantically, I tried to lock all the doors – but they refused to engage. It is still beyond me why it was impossible to press my door button to lock all four doors. Perhaps it was stuck, or maybe the air-system was unable to operate without battery power. Whatever the reason, I knew we were in deep trouble; if that lioness could open the door once with such ease, it could open it again.

That was when the panic set in. It is difficult to explain the feeling of iciness that overcomes you when you're trapped in a car that won't start, with doors that won't lock, and an enormous lioness has just worked out the simple mechanism of a car door handle.

'Hold your door shut – the locks won't work!' I screamed.

We were terrified that the lioness may try to open the back door, which was difficult to hold shut while we were both trying to hold our own doors tight. I had visions of the lioness clambering onto the back seat, which would have flushed my wife and I out of the car – and straight into the mouths of the waiting males.

Fortunately the lioness soon tired of this game. As it sauntered off into the mist, we broke out into very nervous laughter. We couldn't quite believe what had just happened.

Visitors behind us saw the whole thing, and a couple of them drove up alongside us and asked whether the lioness had really opened the car door. They said they thought that their eyes were deceiving them.

When the mating couple had moved about 50 metres up the road, which we judged as a relatively safe distance, a good Samaritan alongside us offered us a jump-start. He and I both scrambled from our vehicles and quickly jump-started my car – all with our backs to the lions. My wife failed to videotape this procedure, as she was caught up in the surveillance of the area from inside the safety of the car. What happened to the second male lion remains a mystery. For all we know, it could have been watching me jump-start the car from the cover of the surrounding mists.

Fearful of a similar incident, we immediately turned the car around and returned to Satara to check the battery. Great was our surprise to find the battery fully functional and all systems operating perfectly.

Perhaps the problem was caused by a loose connection due to the cold, or perhaps the mist had played a part in shorting a vital connection somewhere – we just don't know. The only remaining evidence of the incident was some lion spit below the handle.

We enjoyed many problem-free kilometres in that car in the years that followed, and never once, up to the day we sold it, did anything similar happen with the battery or the locking mechanisms. How strange it was that the only time it ever happened was when we were parked up in the middle of a pride of lions.

Since then, we have shared this story around many campfires in Kruger. But, admittedly, it is always accompanied by a few nervous laughs from our side – as well as the inevitable disagreement over who *really* closed the car door in the end.

66

NEW YEAR'S EVE BIRTHDAY SUIT
Glenda Keys

IN ANY CAMP IN KRUGER, on any night of the year, you'd be foolish to think there weren't prowlers of one sort or another skulking around in the shadows: honey badgers, jackals, genets, African wild cats or even a leopard. But this story is about a different sort of night prowler altogether, and thankfully one you do not see often in Kruger – nor would you want to!

My husband, Rod, and I had decided to celebrate the New Year of 2007 in Satara. The camp was bustling, and on the veranda of the rondavel next door to us a Dutch couple, who were clearly first-timers to the Park, appeared befuddled about the whole setup from the get-go. That evening, while preparing dinner on the veranda, we couldn't help but notice the wife of the couple searching confusedly for the cutlery – of which there wasn't any – and, from her actions and muttering, she appeared not to know where to put anything. She would find her feet soon enough, we thought.

After supper the whole camp seemed to suddenly die; doors were closed, lights switched off and just the embers of a few *braai* fires remained the only sign that the camp was even inhabited. So much for a New Year's celebration. We'd envisaged an evening of jollity and old-fashioned Kruger camaraderie that night but had discovered that the promise of good sightings early on New Year's Day was more of a drawcard for our fellow guests than singing *Auld Lang Syne* in the middle of the camp at midnight.

With the camp in silence, we decided to investigate what was happening over at the restaurant block, but that too was dark and abandoned. So we just headed back, wished each other an early Happy New Year and went to bed.

Now, let me set the scene: it was a hot night and all the windows were open; the screen door of the rondavel didn't lock; there was a paraffin lamp on the tiled counter by the fridge outside; my bed was next to the door; and it was very, very dark.

I woke suddenly when I heard the paraffin lamp sliding across the tiles. Something was on the veranda. I held my breath and listened. I heard the fridge door open. Was it a baboon? Then I heard the wine bottle clink on the tiles. Then I heard the fridge door close. Then the scraping of the metal chairs along the tiled floor of the veranda.

'Rod!' I hissed. No response.

'Rod!' Just snoring.

Suddenly the door handle creaked and moved down. Whatever was outside was coming in. I dived off the bed, waking Rod, who shot up and grabbed the handle of the door. 'Who's there? Go away!' he shouted, but all we heard was '*Shhhuuu, shhhuuu, shhhuuu*' from the other side. Gingerly, Rod opened the door.

'Oh my gosh!' said Rod as his jaw dropped. I was desperately curious to see what was on the other side of the door, but Rod shouted, 'Lovie, get back!' Nevertheless, I squeezed next to him and peeked out.

There, standing in the doorway, was the Dutch woman from next door, as naked as the day she was born, staring straight back at us, equally astonished. Her confusion about the location of the cutlery appeared to have extended to confusion about precisely which rondavel she was staying in – and perhaps where her pyjamas were too! Realising she was probably in the wrong place, she spun around and disappeared off into the shadows, although worryingly in the exact opposite direction of her rondavel.

From out of the darkness, her husband breezed in from stage left – he too was stark naked – and darted past our rondavel in pursuit of his wife. Rod helpfully pointed in the direction she had run off, which the naked man acknowledged with a smile and a polite nod of the head.

For a while, we stood at the door in amazement. Then, just as we were about to go back to bed, the couple came back past our rondavel, arm in arm, still stark naked. Thankfully, they were now heading in the right direction.

'Sorry about that!' said the husband as they passed by.

We turned around back into our rondavel, closed the door and burst into a fit of teenage giggles. Despite it being two o'clock in the morning, we decided we'd leave at 4.30 AM for an early morning game drive – just to avoid the possibility of bumping into the night prowler face-to-face once again. And to think, a few hours earlier we had gone to bed believing there was no action in Satara on New Year's Eve.

67

PERILS OF THE CALL OF NATURE
Melissa Grib

IT IS A COMMON PROBLEM in Kruger: when you drive around all day in the heat, you end up drinking a lot, and with all that extra intake of fluids, the call of nature can come knocking quite abruptly – very often far from camp.

On one of our many visits some years ago, we were driving around in the Satara area, the predator capital of the Park, when my mother's urge to go became increasingly desperate. We were too far from any camp or picnic spot to make it to an established convenience in time, so we had little option but to stop on the side of the road and let my mother scurry a few metres into the grass while we all looked the other way.

The following day, we drove along the same stretch of road, and as we approached the precise spot in the grass where my mother had marked her territory less than 24 hours earlier, what did we see? A pride of eight lions feasting on a wildebeest carcass. My mother's blood ran cold and the colour drained from her face. But we all found it hilarious and thanked her immensely for attracting the lions to this spot right next to the road – a jest she didn't find the least bit funny.

And perhaps she was right not to laugh. Before she had answered nature's call the previous day, we had all scanned the bush carefully and felt reasonably certain that there were no predators in the immediate area. But in Kruger you can really never tell; apex predators haven't become successful hunters because they stand out like flies on a wedding cake. The drama of what happened next drummed that point home.

The huddle of cars at the kill was growing, and after a while the lions abandoned the carcass and moved further off into the bush, out of sight. However, from our vantage point behind the seven or eight cars that had arrived at the sighting before us, we could still see a large male lying in the grass some distance from the carcass, chewing on a bone. To our astonishment, the driver in the car closest to the kill opened his door, climbed out and strolled right up to the carcass to inspect the remains. Clearly, the big lion lying just a tennis court's length away from him was obscured – until, that is, it jumped up and revealed itself. That man shot back into his car like he had been fired from a cannon.

Some of the drivers in the other cars pulled up alongside him and made their feelings about his foolish behaviour very clear. But we sat silently, chastened by just how dangerous it is in Kruger to get out of your car anywhere you're not supposed to – full bladder or not!

68

LIONESS JOINS THE PICNIC
Marijke Arends

HEADING SOUTH from Letaba rest camp down to Orpen with my family one October day, we decided to detour off the tarred road and head west towards the Timbavati picnic spot, as it was fast approaching lunch time. It's strange how in Kruger, a tiny decision like that – Shall we do this quick loop? Shall we linger a minute longer at this sighting? Shall we go left rather than right? – can flap its wings and become a hurricane further on down the road.

We'd barely gone a few kilometres along the gravel when an approaching car signalled us to stop and excitedly told us about some lions they'd seen at the Ratelpan waterhole, just north of the picnic spot. A good lion sighting is always worth putting aside hunger for, so we rattled along to the waterhole. Sure enough, lying flat on the sand near the hide were three handsome male lions.

Sitting safely inside our air-conditioned Nissan X-Trail, the lions seemed so benign as they snoozed away the heat of the day. Just quite how naive that impression was wouldn't be revealed for a good half an hour yet.

So, leaving the lions to sleep out the rest of the afternoon, we moved on to Timbavati picnic spot for our marginally postponed lunch. In the shade of the trees and thatched umbrellas, *skottel braais* were hissing, as families and children enjoyed the quiet of the picnic area. Kruger's picnic spots are famously not fenced, so we were pleased to see two attendants on duty sitting in the shade – just in case.

While I made the sandwiches, my two boys went exploring the site with some other youngsters, and before long they had found a small bushbuck roaming around between the picnic tables, quite tame and oblivious to the humans.

The sandwiches were soon ready. But just as the kids came to sit down, the rapid cracking of branches halfway up the slope behind the washing-up facilities caught my attention. A bushbuck, its eyes bulging with terror, was bolting down the hill straight towards the picnic spot. For a moment I was puzzled, as I had never seen a bushbuck run that fast. But I soon understood why: something was hot on its tail, crashing through the bush behind it. At first I couldn't see what it was as it graciously tore between the bushes. My first thought was 'Leopard!'

I abandoned my sandwich and grabbed hold of one of my sons, pulling him up against me. At the same time, one of the attendants jumped up and screamed, 'Lion!'

True enough, it was a lioness. And how perfectly we had chosen that exact spot to enjoy our lunch – the hunter and her quarry were on a direct collision course with us!

My first instinct was to run for the car with my husband and kids, but my legs didn't move and instead we just stood there dumbstruck. The bushbuck and its bulging eyes tore right past me, while the guards ran forward to intercept the lioness, shouting and waving their arms wildly. It wasn't until that moment, with the two grown men jumping around and the lioness bearing down on them, that I realised quite how big a lioness is.

It all happened in a matter of seconds, but as with all extraordinary fleeting things in life, it felt like an age. The lioness and the screaming guards ran towards each other. Suddenly, realising she had stumbled into a situation she hadn't quite envisaged, the lioness skidded to a halt and stopped dead. A dust cloud hung in the air behind her. And there she remained, comfortably inside the picnic area, staring at us. Everyone stood in shocked silence. I doubt there was a single eyeball at the Timbavati picnic spot not staring straight back into the eyes of that lioness. Eventually, she dropped her gaze, turned around and padded away as if nothing had happened.

I looked around to see where the bushbuck was. It was still running, kicking up dust and twigs as it hurtled off into the riverbed on the other side of the picnic spot, apparently unaware that its pursuer had given up. That was one lucky little buck.

Once the lioness had disappeared, the visitors at the picnic spot all came together, talking and laughing nervously about what had just happened. Despite the chuckles, not a single person there seemed unshaken by the event – except perhaps for the two attendants, who just sat back down in the shade and grinned widely. Clearly, this was just another day at the office for them.

69

THE ELEPHANT AND THE DROWNING CALF
Mariana de Klerk

ALONGSIDE THE TARRED ROAD between Letaba rest camp and Phalaborwa Gate lies a series of natural rock pools in the river bed. You'd probably never notice them, as they're little more than dry hollows for most of the year, but during the rainy season – and for a while after – they're filled with water. It was at these pools where I captured that now very well-known footage of the elephant and its drowning calf.

It was the spring of 2011, and as I pulled up alongside the pools a herd of elephants came down from the bush to drink. They must have been very thirsty because most of them came running and were soon fanned out, drinking from the various pools. The herd consisted of about 20 elephants, ranging in age from sizeable young females with very small babies to some youngsters and even a few older bulls.

There is something so tranquil about watching elephants; perhaps it's because they are so enormous, yet they remain so incongruously silent and gentle as they slowly go about their lives. And so it was with this herd too. There was a real sense of quiet as they quenched their thirst – but that was suddenly broken when one mother elephant started trumpeting, tramping up and down, and flapping her ears. All hell seemed to have broken loose, and it was clear that something was very wrong.

Up to its ears in the water was her tiny calf, trapped in the rock pool, desperately trying not to drown. I hadn't seen how the calf had ended up in the water, but I suspect curiosity had led it in, and now it was in deep trouble. The poor thing was scrabbling against the slippery edges of the pool, but the water was too deep for it to get any purchase with its hind legs, while the edges of the pool were too steep to allow it to haul its body weight out with its clumsy front legs. As much as it tried, gravity always won, and it would slide, spluttering, back into the pool.

The calf's mother was in a state of panic: shaking her head in despair, pacing up and down and back and forth alongside the pool, lunging forward and dipping her trunk in the water, then retreating with more shakes of the head.

One shouldn't project human emotions onto animals. But elephants are enormously intelligent creatures that hold a deep family bond, and this mother's actions so closely mirrored those of a human mother in a similar predicament that I could just imagine the distress she must have been feeling at seeing her offspring drowning.

My heart was thumping because even I, with all the advantage of an apparently developed human brain, couldn't think of any way the situation could be resolved. The edges of the pool were wet and uniformly angled, with steep inclines – a metre or two in height – rising from the water on all but the front side of the pool, facing me. But even there, where the mother was flapping and pacing, the rock sloped downwards at such an angle from the lip of the pool that the calf stood as little chance of hauling itself out as the mother stood of effecting a rescue from that spot.

How this was going to play out, I had no idea, but I knew it would be consequential either way. So I reached for my video camera from the seat next to me and started filming. I had no idea I was about to capture on film one of the most riveting and touching scenes of elephant behaviour; footage that would eventually touch the hearts of countless South African nature lovers, as well as hundreds of thousands of other people around the world.

I am uncertain at precisely what point the idea entered the mother elephant's head, but through my camera lens I watched as she stopped her flapping and stepped towards the calf, which was gripping the lip of the pool with its two front legs. Using her trunk, she nudged the youngster away from the edge, sending it splashing back into the pool with a snort. Then she dropped to her knees right there on the side of the rock pool. What was she doing? Was she about to get into the pool too?

From her kneeling position she lowered her front feet into the pit, then dragged her belly along the wet edge and heaved herself in. There was a gentle splash – far gentler than you would imagine from an elephant entering a pool – and there she stood, up to her belly in water, alongside the calf. I could sense straight away that the calf seemed calmer knowing its mother was now alongside it in the water.

There was nothing random about her entering the pool; she had a plan and she wasted no time kicking it into action. Turning immediately towards the calf, she slipped her trunk underneath its body to keep it above the water, then gently moved it towards the left-hand edge of the pool, where she began pushing and nudging it up the incline and out of the water. With each push, the calf's little legs would scramble and flounder and slide around awkwardly on the slope, its floppy trunk proving useless too, getting in the way more than helping. But the calf could gain no purchase on the slippery edge, and each time would slide gawkily back into the water with a big splash.

The steep exit point that the mother had chosen was the problem. Remarkably, she quickly realised this and changed tack. Despite the incline at the back end of the pool, there was a less steep furrow leading up through it and off to the right, where over the years water had worn away the rock as it flowed down from the higher pools above. That route was the key to getting out, so she repositioned herself with her back to me – and pushed. I could just make out the form of the calf being heaved up over the edge, its legs folded up beneath it and its face squashed flat into the rock, sliding up the wet surface. With a final nudge it was out and trotted comfortably up the furrow to the higher ridge above.

I felt so relieved the calf was out that I caught myself cheering from where I sat in my still-idling car. But my jubilation was short-lived. In her single-minded efforts to rescue her offspring, the mother elephant had given no thought to how she would get out of the pool herself.

At the exact same spot where the calf had emerged seconds earlier, the mother now floundered on the edge. With no larger elephant to push her from behind in the way she had done with her baby, she did not have the purchase to pull all that body weight out of the pit. Suddenly, the desperation I had felt in watching the calf struggle to pull itself from the water was now replicated in watching the mother try to do the same.

She dropped her knees onto the edge and somehow even got her left rear knee up too. But as with the calf, gravity was having none of it, and she slipped back with ten times the splash the calf had made. All around the steep edges, the rock was glistening wet and my heart broke as the elephant looked around helplessly. In the meantime, the rest of the herd were hurrying up the slopes of the rock towards the little one to comfort it.

While the mother may have been able to stand in the water without the fear of drowning – the water only came up to just above her belly – this was of little consolation. If she couldn't clamber out, she would die there anyway; it would just be a lot slower than drowning.

She tried again, but no luck. It just seemed impossible – the pit was just that bit too deep and the edges just that bit too steep. She flapped her ears and trumpeted and swayed back and forth, looking for perhaps another spot where exit may be easier. But her options were strictly limited and she returned to the same spot. This time there was a determination, and she began to rock herself back and forth to build some kind of momentum. The surface of the water frothed and bubbled around her. Then, with a heave, she lifted her front feet up and out, wobbled a bit, counterbalanced herself by leaning to the side and pressing her trunk against a dry portion of rock, and suddenly her left knee was up and out too. With a big stretch and a great pull, she rocked forward and her last remaining leg emerged from the water. She was out!

She quickly made her way up the furrow and over to her baby, holding her trunk out to it, and was soon surrounded by the rest of the herd, who appeared to comfort and congratulate her. Their rumbling communications were so loud, my camera recorded it from 150 metres away.

The touching and loving interaction between the herd and the mother and calf made me realise that this is indeed an amazing species, with feelings and intelligence and compassion nothing short of that of humans. Even the young ones in the herd walked closer to the sodden pair and held their trunks out in solace.

I have watched my video of this incident a thousand times, but it is the magical last few seconds of the footage that still shoots me straight through the heart every time. As the rest of the herd gather around, flapping their ears in support, the mother turns to another female, which in turn stretches out its trunk and, just for a second, touches her gently on the nose in a way that says, 'Well done, girl'.

I sat in my vehicle trying to work out what I had just seen. Having been behind the camera the entire time made me feel as if I had just watched a film. I was shaking – not only because of what I had just watched, but because the camera and lens had got so heavy in my arm that I felt I could barely hold it any longer.

Just then, to my surprise, the mother walked the calf back towards the top end of the rock pool, and they both stood there for some time, staring down at the pit. I imagine she was telling her calf: 'I hope you have learnt a lesson. Be careful next time.'

A few days later, my husband suggested that I send the video to a popular South African wildlife television show in the hope that they would use the footage in their regular segment of viewer-submitted content. Not only did they show the video, I was later told that I was a finalist in their annual viewer competition and that I was invited to attend the prize giving function at Golden Gate National Park in the eastern Free State.

My finalist position became the winning position and I became the lucky owner of a brand new 4x4 double-cab *bakkie*. Meanwhile, on the internet, the video continues to delight hundreds of thousands of animal lovers all over the world, where I hope it shows, to those who didn't already know, just how intelligent, caring and sensitive these gentle giants of the bush really are.

70

LEAVING MY CHILD TO THE LIONS
Ewoud Duvenage

IN KRUGER, IT'S A RARE PLEASURE to find yourselves the only people in a hide – especially one like Ratelpan, which stands just a few kilometres north of the popular Timbavati picnic spot and is particularly rewarding with its views over the Piet Grobler reservoir. So it was only when we eventually heard the rumble of another car approaching, that my family and I decided to leave the hide and head back to our car.

As we walked out, though, we were met by the sight of an Isuzu *bakkie* that had turned off the gravel road and was belting straight towards us at some pace. Our first reaction to this obnoxious bit of driving was annoyance, but the reason for it was soon clear.

The driver skidded up alongside us, rolled down his window, and said breathlessly: 'Be careful, there is a male and female lion approaching just behind me!'

Disbelievingly, we looked up the road – and our jaws hit the floor. As clear as day, there was a large lioness, not 20 metres from us, jogging down the road in the direction of Timbavati. More worryingly, though, the male lion that was supposedly accompanying the lioness was no longer anywhere to be seen. If the lioness was just 20 metres away from us, the male was probably even closer, somewhere in the grass around us. We all scrambled for my double-cab *bakkie*, jumped in, slammed the doors tight, hit the central locking (one can never be too careful!) and sat there out of breath – terrified but excited.

Just as I started the vehicle to follow the lioness, there was this little knock on the right rear window, and a small voice filtered through the glass: 'Please open the door, I want to get in…'

There was my 12-year-old daughter standing outside, close to tears, and as scared as a mouse in a snake tank – we had totally forgotten about her! We still had no idea what had happened to the male lion, but in my mind's eye I imagine it was slunk low in the grass, licking its lips at the tasty treat tapping on the window of my double-cab.

After opening the door and dragging her in, we apologised profusely and eventually calmed her down. Of course, I used the excuse that we'd only jumped into the car so that we could follow the lioness to see where it was heading. But that wasn't really true – we'd jumped in because we were terrified. Forgetting your daughter is a terrible thing for a father to do, but we still all chuckle about it every so often.

71

ALMOST LEOPARD BREAKFAST
Petro Nel

OF ALL THE BIG FIVE – buffalo, elephant, leopard, lion and rhino – the leopard is by far the most elusive. So for some Kruger visitors, especially those having an unlucky time, just the sniff of a leopard sighting is enough to make them lose their heads and forget the Park's rules altogether. I am afraid I was one of those people.

Back in 1975, in the days before Venter trailers had replaced roof racks as the preferred method of luggage stowage, we were driving along the gravel road that runs westwards along the elevated bank of the Letaba River towards Mingerhoud Dam. It was early morning and the sightings had been scarce. So when we saw a green Mercedes parked up under a massive *rooiels* tree ahead of us, we hoped that they might be looking at something exciting. We were right – the four elderly occupants excitedly ushered us alongside them and told us that they had just seen a leopard in the dry riverbed.

Luck had not been with us on that trip, so I was not prepared to lose out on this sighting. We scanned the riverbed and as much of the nearby bush as we could, but there was no leopard. After several minutes of fruitless searching, I decided that a bit of elevation might help. I opened my door, stood up on the seat, and with one hand awkwardly grabbing the roof rack behind me and the other holding my binoculars, I was able to command a far better view of the riverbank – so good, in fact, that I spotted the leopard almost immediately.

To my surprise, it was considerably closer to us than we had thought, crouching down in the grass just 35 metres from the car. It was close enough for me to see clearly that it had spotted me too – and it did not look at all pleased. It stood up and with blistering speed stormed straight towards me. If it had been the Olympics, I would have comfortably won the gold medal for my diving attempt back into the station wagon.

Thankfully, the screams of the senior citizens in the other car stopped the leopard in its tracks, just metres from my door. It growled savagely, turned around and disappeared off into the bush. If the leopard's behaviour left everyone stunned, it left me horrified and weak; I could barely turn the keys to start the Peugeot 404.

A few hours later we returned to the spot and stopped again under the tree, scanning the area for the leopard – this time keeping well inside our car. To our surprise we found it in the low branches of the tree directly above us, tucking into its breakfast. It was so close I could have pulled the carcass out of the tree with my hand. That explained the leopard's aggressive behaviour earlier: it had thought that when I stood up on the side of the car, I was trying to steal its kill from the boughs of the tree. Of course, I had not intended that at all – I hadn't even seen the carcass, such was my desire to find the elusive leopard.

The Park's rules, it turns out, are in place for a reason. That leopard sighting was so nearly disastrous; I came within a whisker of my story becoming a grisly headline in a newspaper somewhere. Thankfully, it's now only a cautionary tale in a book like this.

72

WALKING TOWARDS THE LIONS
Keith Griffiths

MY LATE FATHER loved visiting the Kruger National Park, especially during the off-season when not only could he enjoy a sizeable pensioners' discount at all the camps, but he could explore some of the quieter areas of the Park almost all to himself.

On one such visit in the late winter of 2003, while driving in his old Mazda 323 from Olifants up to Letaba along the gravel road that skirts the river, he passed four lions striding purposefully along the roadside. It had been a dry winter, and the lions were lean and appeared to him to be on the hunt, looking for a bit of *padkos*.

Unfortunately, the sun was dipping towards the horizon, and with a fair distance still to cover, he couldn't spend too much time admiring them as they strode along. So off he drove, leaving the lions in his rear-view mirror and keeping his eyes open for whatever unsuspecting creature in their path would soon fall prey to them.

He didn't have to wait long to discover what it would be: just 500 metres further on, he rounded a bend and almost drove slap-bang into a petite and well-dressed young woman walking briskly along the road – straight towards the lions.

When my exasperated father rolled down his window and explained that there were four lions on the hunt approaching fast, she didn't hesitate to accept his offer of help and jumped into the car.

She was a French tourist named Marie, and it turned out that her fiancé, Jean-Paul, had foolishly taken a wrong turn down a no-entry road in their hired Renault and had got them stuck while attempting to cross a riverbed. With no phone, and realising they were off-route and that nobody would be coming along to rescue them, she had set off alone to seek help.

Having explained all this, Marie directed my father to the turn-off –
marked with a prominent no-entry sign – where she and her fiancé had
taken their wrong turn. My father parked up on the side of the main
road and, taking Marie with him, hurried along the rough dirt track to
where her husband-to-be was waiting.

Mindful of the approaching lions, my father and Marie were able
to push the small car out of its sand-trap. But to their dismay, Jean-
Paul sped off in a cloud of dust back to the road, leaving them to
follow behind on foot. By then it was dusk, and walking back through
the mopane bush was not a pleasant experience, my father told me
afterwards. Particularly as he knew those lions would have covered that
half a kilometre by then and were probably within sniffing distance of
them as they hurried towards the road.

Marie could be heard berating her man heatedly, in French, for some
distance, as my father drove away, mildly stunned by the preceding
sequence of events and hoping to get to camp before the gates closed.

Later that evening, while he was enjoying a meal at the restaurant,
the two young tourists thanked my father most profusely for helping
them out of their predicament. He was pleased to note that they were
holding hands and wished them well for the rest of their stay in the
Park – but not before warning them, in his fatherly way, to stick to the
proper roads in future.

73

THE CROCODILE THAT STOOD UP
Piet Grobler

YOU USUALLY KNOCK MONEY OFF for this sort of damage, but I am told that if I ever come to sell my beloved Mercedes Benz, I should add an extra two thousand rand just for the story that accompanies the deep scratches on the car's rear-door handle.

It was early autumn and I had been driving my Dutch friend along the gravel road from Letaba towards Olifants when, not far downstream from Olifants, we stopped beside a large pool of water on the right-hand side of the road. Regular visitors to this part of the Park will be familiar with this pool, as it is often full of terrapins – particularly after a rainy summer – and provides the ideal opportunity to photograph them up close.

That day was no different. The pool was alive with terrapins and, excitingly, they were not alone; a healthy-sized crocodile, a good one-and-a-half metres long or more, was making up the numbers.

As soon as we stopped, despite being pretty much in the middle of the road, the terrapins emerged from the water like trained dogs. With the crocodile following them, they scuttled over to the car and peered up at us with their beady eyes. Clearly, visitors had been feeding them as they all seemed keenly aware that a stationary car offered the promise of treats.

My passenger moved behind me into the back so that we could both enjoy a window seat to the action. But after only a minute the terrapins realised they were doing too much posing for too little reward and turned around and headed back to the water. The crocodile, however, was far more optimistic. It settled itself closer to the car, roughly a metre away and equidistant to the front and rear doors, and stared at us with begging eyes.

We were both clicking away through the open windows with cameras in hand when suddenly – and completely unexpectedly – the crocodile raised the entire front part of its body and stood up on its hind legs. Using its tail as counterbalance, it lurched forward, jaws open, towards the camera in my friend's hands, having perhaps mistaken it for a piece of food.

With just fractions of a second to react, I swung my door open hoping it would clip the upright crocodile and knock it off course – but my calculations were marginally out and the door missed it by an inch. Mercifully, it did the job anyway. Startled by the door swinging millimetres past its face, the croc dropped away to its left and, in the process, dragged the claws of its front feet across the car's rear-door handle.

Sensing there was clearly little to be gained here but a concussion, it returned to the water, turned around, put its head on the side of the pool and stared back at us as though nothing had just happened.

When we came to look at the photos later, we were disappointed to see that neither of us had actually captured the most extraordinary sight of the crocodile standing upright on its hind legs, having both chosen to abandon camera-snapping duties to deal with an entirely different type of snapping. In fact, were it not for the deep scratches in the door handle of my white Mercedes Benz, I fear that very few people would ever believe it had even happened at all.

74

A KILL UNDER SPOTLIGHTS
Nicole Meiring

KRUGER HAS A STRANGE WAY of dealing out luck. We certainly all felt a little unlucky as we drove back into Satara rest camp late one September afternoon without a single predator sighting all day. Not even the small herd of buffalo grazing just outside the gates could do much to excite us. But, while the day's game viewing was over, the best sighting of our lives was still just brewing – and it involved one of those buffalo we'd only just barely acknowledged.

After our *braai* that evening, we sat on the veranda of our hut listening to the usual night sounds. A honey badger ran across the circle of huts looking for a snack and disappeared into the shadows on the far side. With the kids already fast asleep, my brother-in-law, his wife and I decided to take a walk to see if we could find it again, while my husband stayed behind.

As we wandered towards the perimeter fence, each with a torch in one hand (the other protecting our genitalia – the honey badger's supposed target of choice when attacking), we heard the cackle of hyaenas and the snorting of a buffalo in distress. Prickling with excitement, we followed the source of the noises to the Stanley Guest House, which overlooks a waterhole just beyond the fence. The people staying there beckoned us over. And there, in the brightness of the spotlight that washes over the waterhole, I saw my very first kill.

About 14 or 15 hyaenas had the buffalo cornered. In trying to escape, it had become trapped in the waterhole and the hyaenas were surging forward relentlessly, biting into its flanks. The buffalo's throaty moans were almost drowned out by the whoops and cackles of the hyaenas. They knew dinner was about to be served.

I couldn't believe it: we had spent the entire day in the car searching for excitement, and here it was just on the other side of the camp fence. I desperately wanted my husband to see this too, but he was back at the hut on the other side of the camp. We couldn't just leave the sleeping kids unattended – but I had a plan.

My Cape Town lungs almost burst as I sprinted the half kilometre or so back to our hut where I breathlessly explained what was going on – and how we could both go and watch it while still ensuring the children were okay. The solution was simple: I put a call through to my husband's cell phone and, with the line open, rested his phone on the bedside table next to our sleeping kids. My phone would come with us. It was a makeshift child monitor, Kruger-style.

In the meantime the hyaenas had managed to exhaust the buffalo. We arrived back to see it lying collapsed in the waterhole with at least seven of the hyaenas ripping into it, and more arriving by the minute. I cannot describe the noises that were filling the air, nor our sense of disbelief as we watched this all play out, under lights, right in front of us.

But the show had just begun, and the lead actors had yet to make their appearance.

Twenty minutes later a huge lion, followed closely by a lioness, stepped onto the stage from out of the darkness. Despite its swagger, the lion's attempts to reach the carcass were quashed by the hyaenas. They surged at the lions and forced them both to retreat. This band of sisters was determined to feast on their kill, and no lion was going to play scavenger at their table.

With the lions around, the hyaenas' behaviour at the carcass was fascinating. While there were well over 10 hyaenas around the buffalo, never more than five of them would feed on it at any one time – the remainder all took up positions to guard against the interlopers. They worked in a very organised rotation, and their battle strategy every time the lion moved in was quite something: the lion would make a go for the carcass and the hyaenas would all back off, but then just as the lion put its mouth to the kill, they'd swarm the intruder like bees and force it into a hasty retreat. Eventually, the lion realised that it was onto a loser and melted away to a safe distance, from where we could hear it roaring grumpily.

The hyaenas' impressive organisation didn't extend to all areas, however. When they tried to drag the carcass out of the waterhole a while later their co-ordination left a lot to be desired; there didn't seem to be much consensus on who was to do the pulling and who was to do the pushing. All the while more and more hyaenas appeared, and the cackling and whooping became almost deafening.

Just then, the lion – perhaps feeling humiliated in front of its concubine – made a final roaring surge towards the kill. But the numbers were stacked against it even more than before, and it had to retreat at least 100 metres this time, with a gang of hyaenas snapping at its tail.

The feeding continued for a long time. Every now and again a hyaena would steal off into the darkness with a different body part between its jaws, until eventually very little remained of the kill, and the usual night sounds returned.

Getting back to our hut, with the kids still fast asleep and our cell phone bill in the stratosphere, we were in total awe. Having visited the Park so many times in the past, we knew just how incredibly lucky we were to have seen something like this – and on a day when we felt we'd not seen much at all. Kruger does indeed have a strange way of dealing out its luck.

75

BREAKING DOWN THE DOOR
Kevin Bouwer

IT IS PROBABLY KRUGER'S WORST KEPT SECRET that despite electric fences, hyaenas are found within many, if not all, of the Park's rest camps. I knew that, though, having already seen them at both Pretoriuskop and Skukuza earlier on in our honeymoon trip. But it was on the final morning of our stay at Satara in one of the little thatched rondavel huts, when I discovered that hyaenas are not the cowards many believe them to be. I also discovered a few truths about marital bonds – and the relative weakness of a rondavel's door hinges!

I was up early that morning – probably 4.30 AM or so – and had started ferrying our luggage to the car while my wife busied herself in the rondavel. The car was parked about 40 metres from the hut. On my second journey, I heard the crash of a dustbin falling over somewhere to my left, in the direction of the camping area. I reached the car, put the luggage in and had just begun my walk back when I saw four hyaenas standing around a tipped-up bin, staring at me. I ignored them and continued walking, but after a few steps I noticed they had abandoned the scattered rubbish and were moving in my direction.

At that point I was equidistant between the car and hut, so I decided my best bet was to continue straight to the hut. I increased my pace – and so did the hyaenas. About 15 metres from the hut, I decided maybe I should jog quickly to the door, which was open. But to my horror, as I started to jog, the hyaenas' awkward loping pace suddenly developed into a surprisingly swift gallop. I had heard all the stories about hyaenas being cowards, but there was nothing cowardly about this lot as they rapidly closed in on me.

Just then, my wife appeared in the doorway and was greeted with the ungainly sight of me, in full sprint, shouting, 'Hyaenas! Chasing! Me!'

With those spluttered words, and no more than a couple of strides away from safety, my wife's initial bemusement turned to self preservation as she first exclaimed, 'What? Where?' before promptly slamming the door and locking it – with me on the outside! Now, I am six foot two and weigh over 90 kilograms, so I ran that wooden door flat, clean off its hinges. But just as quick as I had smashed it down I had it up again, like a great big, green shield.

What happened to the hyaenas, I do not know. When I had caught my breath and regained my composure, I pulled the door aside a crack and peeked out, but they were nowhere to be seen. We left for Olifants rest camp a little later than expected that morning, as I had to repair the door before leaving.

Whenever we go to the Park and stay in a rondavel, we remember that morning in 1976 and have a good laugh. But my wife has never been able to offer me a satisfactory answer to why she slammed the door on me. 'I wanted to keep the hyaenas out!' is her stock reply.

76

THE HYAENA, THE FENCE AND MY LITTLE BOY'S HAND
Johan Armstrong

TO THIS DAY, reading the stats about hyaenas still gives me the chills. Relative to their size, they're said to have the strongest bite of any animal alive. With the ability to exert almost a ton of pressure, their jaws can bite through giraffe bones as thick as gutter pipes – so they must be able to rip through flesh like wet paper towel. What's more, with a diet of rotting meat and scant regard for dental hygiene, the hyaena's mouth practically hums with bacteria.

Back in May 2010 I didn't really know much about hyaenas; in fact I had never even been to Kruger before. My wife, on the other hand, had been visiting the Park since she was a child and so, along with our young son, Johan – who was just 20 months old at the time – we took our first family camping holiday in the Park.

My wife and I were both very excited – not just for ourselves but for little Johan too, who had never seen wild animals before. To add to the excitement, we had planned to camp at Balule, a small rest camp just south of Olifants, famous – and popular – for having no electricity and offering a purer bush experience.

That evening, we set up our caravan and tent in the corner of the campsite, alongside the fence. While *braaing* a little while later, we noticed the sloping shadows of a hyaena patrolling up and down the fence, attracted by the smell of the cooking meat. With no lights in the camp, it was unfortunately too dark to show Johan the hyaena, so we settled down for the night instead. We drifted off to the sounds of the bush outside the caravan, blissfully unaware of the horror awaiting us the following day.

The next morning I was sitting back and enjoying a cup of coffee while watching Johan toddling around near the fence. It was my first morning in Kruger, and what a perfect day it seemed. As I turned around to put my cup on the table, I heard a noise and a loud wail from my son. I shot around and froze on the spot. Just metres in front of me, a hyaena on the other side of the fence had my son's hand firmly in its jaws – and was tugging on it violently.

Could this really be happening? It felt like I was in a film – suddenly everything had been slowed right down and all sounds evaporated. For those who say there is nothing like a mother's instinct to protect her offspring, they've never been a father watching a hyaena try to bite his son's hand off. I leapt up and dived over to Johan. In a single motion, I wrapped my left arm around him and, with my right fist, punched the wire mesh so hard I thought my hand would rip right through it. Shocked, the hyaena let go of Johan's hand, and I pulled him safely away from the fence.

The scene was horrific; there was blood everywhere, the skin on top of his hand had peeled over his fingers like a glove coming off, and I could see that one of the hyaena's canines had pierced clean through the palm. Every bone in his hand must surely be broken, I thought, as I pulled the skin back and screamed for help. A thousand things rushed through my mind: How did this happen? What must I do? Will my boy be okay? Where can I find a doctor?

At the time, my wife was in the caravan, but hearing the screams she came rushing out to see what was going on. I remember shouting across to her that we must get help as a hyaena had bitten Johan's hand and thinking to myself how surreal it felt to say those words. She ran to my father-in-law, who was in the camp too and, thankfully, had a medical kit in his caravan. He covered the wound with bandages from the kit and, with no cell phone signal and little idea about what to do next, dashed off to get help from the camp manager. The camp manager was able to use his bush radio to get in touch with Skukuza and relay to them what had happened. They directed us to the nearest hospital in Phalaborwa.

And so began a frantic race through the Park. We jumped in the car, and despite clocking speeds well in excess of the strict Park limits, it still felt like we were crawling. We weren't crawling at all of course – quite the opposite – and the entire drive I was terrified that an animal would dash out in front of us and make the whole situation even more of a catastrophe. Whether it was the speed we were driving or whether it was just a quiet day in Kruger, I don't know, but I don't recall seeing a single animal the entire 90-kilometre journey.

Meanwhile, I was breaking more rules: I was on the phone while driving, frantically trying to make arrangements to get my son to a local doctor rather than to the only hospital in Phalaborwa, which, I had just found out from the operator there, had long queues of patients waiting to be seen.

Poor Johan, not even two years old, was in agony. My wife was holding his hand upright to hopefully ease the pain a little, but how can you ease pain like that for anyone, let alone a toddler? At one stage he fell asleep – probably exhausted from the shock – but was still crying and whimpering even as he slept. Meanwhile, the blood was starting to seep through the thick bandages, despite my wife's best efforts to apply pressure to the wound to stem the bleeding.

My efforts on the phone to find a doctor were paying off. I had managed to get in touch with a friend in Tzaneen who in turn had arranged for a friend of his to meet us at Phalaborwa Gate and lead us to a doctor in the town.

Forty minutes after setting out, the top of a radio tower and the apex of a thatched roof finally came into view. We had made it to the gate. As we approached, I flashed my car's lights and the guards at the gate lifted the boom and waved us through without a question asked.

The town of Phalaborwa lies just a few hundred metres from the Park gates, so it wasn't long before we were at the doctor's rooms. They had been expecting us, as my friend had called ahead and briefed them on exactly what had happened. Just as well too, as they almost certainly wouldn't have been able to make sense of what I was saying, such was my desperation to have my son seen to.

The doctor himself was busy with another patient when we arrived, but as soon as we burst through the doors, he ushered the patient out and let us in.

My wife waited outside, sobbing; she couldn't face seeing her little boy's shredded hand as the bandage was removed. The doctor immediately administered a local anaesthetic to ease the pain while I held Johan tight, talking to him and trying to calm him down as the doctor tended to the wounds. He was given a very strong antibiotic, and the doctor told us to come back for a checkup every day.

As our own shock wore off, we realised how much worse things could have been. The hyaena would almost certainly have severed Johan's hand, or even his whole arm, had I not been able to get there so quickly. But what if it had clamped down with its jaws, rather than let go, when I had punched the fence?

That night, back in the caravan, Johan slept fitfully. I don't know if he was having nightmares or whether the pain was so bad, but he didn't sleep well. And neither did we.

The next day we moved to Letaba rest camp to be closer to the doctor, as the camp lies just an hour and a half from Phalaborwa. Johan was in a lot of pain and he wasn't himself; whereas before he loved tottering around, now he just wanted to be carried. His hand had become very swollen, and his arm was red and warm to touch. Back at the doctor's we were advised not to take any chances and to go back home and get him to hospital to get intravenous antibiotics, as there was clearly infection in the wound. The lustre of our holiday had long since faded anyway.

The next day we packed up, made our way home to Pretoria and went directly to our paediatrician, who revealed that Johan's hand was severely infected. The doctor phoned a specialist who was in theatre at that stage, but instructed us to wait for him just outside the operating room. As we got there, the specialist emerged in his scrubs, took one look at the hand and hurried Johan into theatre to clean the wound. Afterwards, we were relieved to hear that there were no broken bones, and miraculously the hyaena's canines had missed the most vulnerable part on the inside of his hand.

Johan spent the next three days in hospital, going into theatre every day to have his wound cleaned. After that, we were in and out of hospital for another six weeks or so, with a series of rabies injections administered, before the infection finally cleared up. Due to a new method of cell renewal used by the surgeons, the wound healed miraculously.

My son can still use his fingers, but despite much occupational therapy he can no longer properly make a fist, as the nerves were rotted by the infection. Today, though, he is a bouncy young boy with an extraordinary story to tell anyone who asks about the large scar on his hand. In fact, this has become his 'pick-up line' to make new friends. Most kids don't believe him, of course, and come running to my wife and I to ask us whether it is true. When we tell them that he really was bitten by a hyaena they are most impressed. I imagine that line will be used more than a few times to impress the girls when he is a bit older.

Johan now also has a younger brother, over whom he is most protective. When we visited Kruger again in 2012 – our first trip back since the incident – Johan showed no signs of any psychological scars of the incident. Rather, he seemed to want to pass on his knowledge, and it was so sweet to overhear him warning his little brother to stay away from the fence – 'because the hyaenas will bite you!'

77

HIDING UNDER THE HIDE
Kathleen Stevens

IT IS STRANGE how I would never entertain stopping my car in the middle of Kruger, casually getting out and wandering around on foot near a waterhole – yet this is exactly what we all do when we arrive at any of the hides dotted around the Park. I suppose the presence of a man-made structure and a neat clearing for parking makes the place seem less untamed somehow. But why should it? After all, if we humans enjoy watching game amble down to drink from the shade of a hide, it stands to reason that predators would, too.

One dusty July afternoon I pulled up to the Ratelpan hide with my French boss and her two teenage sons. The hide is a wooden, thatched structure, set in the shade beneath a large tamboti tree and raised a metre or so on stilts above the bank leading down to the Piet Grobler reservoir.

Those who know the area – just north of the Timbavati picnic site – wouldn't disagree that it is some of Kruger's densest lion country. In fact on that trip alone we were treated to a total of 45 lions in the space of just nine days.

Regardless, out we all jumped. But as the others trotted towards the walkway that leads into the hide, I noticed that we'd foolishly left the car windows open. Not wanting to risk any unwanted creatures sneaking into the shade of the car while we were in the hide, I turned back and went to close them. As I leaned through the driver's window to turn the key to operate the electric windows, a commotion broke out behind me.

I spun around to see my boss and her sons belting back towards the car; arms flailing, faces white, mouths hanging open, screaming, 'Get in, get in – lions!'

We were back in that car with the doors slammed shut in seconds. They'd barely sputtered out the rough location of the lions when, from the shade beneath the hide, four enormous male lions charged out, roaring and growling and kicking up a whole lot of dust.

Satisfied that they'd seen off their unwelcome guests, the lions turned around and ambled back towards the hide; this time they settled in the long grass and bushes alongside it, where they continued to grunt and grumble like old men.

When the dust clouds dispersed and our blood pressures returned to a relatively safe level, we noticed something we had been oblivious to before: there had been three other cars parked up at the hide, with their occupants all safely ensconced. Clearly, they had all been aware of the lions before we arrived – which I suppose would go some way towards explaining why they were all now staring at us with shocked faces. We had pulled up to the hide, got out of the car and then hastily returned again so quickly that there'd been no time for anyone to warn us of the danger.

My boss and her sons were pretty shaken up, so we didn't hang around for much longer. We did however drive past on the way back. It was perhaps two hours later and we could still hear the lions grumbling in the long grass – and to my dismay, there were people in the hide!

78

WATER!
Trevor Lagerwall

MY FATHER-IN-LAW had visited Kruger his entire life and knew the Park intimately. So when we arrived at Letaba rest camp and discovered the Letaba River completely dry, he was more astounded than the rest of us. Never in his life had he seen the river bone dry like that. Indeed, the drought of 1992 had a lot to answer for – there wasn't a sniff of water in the riverbed; not the smallest trickle nor the shallowest pool for as far north or south as our eyes could see.

Just then, a commotion in front of the restaurant caught our attention. Game rangers, waiters, cleaning staff and visitors were all suddenly clambering over each other to get a better view. Some were pressed up against the fence while others stood on the low wall at the edge of the restaurant's veranda and peered in the same direction upstream. Whatever it was in the riverbed was causing quite a stir.

Intrigued, we hurried over and scanned the area everyone seemed to be looking at, but we must have been blind because all we could see was sand, sand and more dry sand. What on earth was everyone getting so excited about? Eventually my mother-in-law, feeling slightly embarrassed by peering at nothing, tentatively asked one of the cleaners what everyone was looking at. 'The water!' came the reply.

The water? As far upstream as we could see, there was only sand and the occasional tufts of dry grass sticking up here and there from the riverbed. The severe drought must have caused everyone to go a bit loony, we thought, so we left them and went and sat on a bench further back to have a picnic lunch.

About 20 minutes later there was a sudden chorus of cheers from the crowd and some joyous dancing from a few of the staff. Getting up to investigate again, we sidled over to the fence and that was when we saw it – it was indeed water. In the distance, a wall of muddy water bubbled its way around the bend and snaked along the course of the riverbed before eventually rushing right past us in front of the restaurant.

Unbeknown to us, a major storm had broken outside the Park a few hours earlier and word had got round that the river would finally come to life at lunch time. It was only from the reaction of the staff when they had heard the news that we realised quite how bad the drought that year had been.

Curiously, it was only the humans who reacted so jubilantly. The small herd of waterbuck lying in the riverbed seemed far less impressed by the breaking of the drought. As the water rushed past, they slowly got up and made their way over for a drink without much fuss and as if it had been there all along. Not for us. Over the years we had seen some amazing things in Kruger, but that rushing torrent of water, and the outbreak of joy when it arrived, still ranks as one of the most extraordinary things we've ever seen.

79

BETWEEN A LIONESS AND HER CUBS
Caroline Evans

MY FAMILY AND I have been trekking up to the Park from the Eastern Cape every year since I was two years old. Each visit has been a thrilling adventure, but one visit in particular proved a little more thrilling than we were comfortable with.

It was September 1994 and we were staying at Talamati Bushveld Camp, tucked away on the southern bank of the N'Waswitsontso River, about an hour's drive south-west of Satara. We decided that a guided night drive from the camp was an absolute necessity and that this particular evening would be perfect for it.

It was a still but muggy evening, framed by one of those amber sunsets you only seem to see in Kruger. With great excitement we left the camp with our checklists, bird books, binoculars, cameras and a guide who reminded us of a typical Eastern Cape farmer – a man who is perfectly suited to wearing khaki, enjoys more than the occasional cigarette, has a dry sense of humour, and displays a stupefyingly laid-back approach to life.

We made ourselves comfortable at the front of the game drive vehicle while a group of five other guests, sounding like a flock of arrow-marked babblers, piled in behind us. In those days the guides would ask guests if any smokers were on board so that the necessary smoke breaks could be made along the way. Much to the guide's delight, a show of hands – including my father's – confirmed we were harbouring a fair few nicotine addicts. Smoke breaks there would be. The boozed up bunch at the back could barely contain their delight at this development.

As the last light was fading, we found a spot on a straight stretch of gravel road to stop for a smoke and drinks break. Not being allowed to smoke on the vehicle, we all climbed out for a good leg stretch. The babblers were chatting to the guide, while my father and I stood a few metres away, quietly enjoying the emerging chorus of night sounds. After about five minutes an eerie silence descended and the calls and cricks and trills seemed to stop in unison. Then, from somewhere no more than a few metres from us, we heard a soft but deep chesty sound.

Now, my father is a very observant man and knows wildlife sounds and behaviour like nobody I have ever met, so I have learnt to gauge his reactions to nervous situations and react accordingly. I peered up to him as if to say: 'I think I know what that was – what must I do?'

He grabbed my hand and we slowly walked towards the others, who were still engaged in deep conversation. He politely interrupted the guide and quietly, so as not to alarm anyone, suggested that he tell the guests to get back onto the vehicle. The guide looked at my father as though he was daft, and replied with a laid-back: 'In a few minutes, sir. There's still some leg stretching time left.' Then, drawing casually on his cigarette, he added: 'I haven't heard anything that should cause alarm.'

He had barely closed his mouth when pandemonium broke out. The lioness that we had heard gently trying to call her cubs had tired of our nonsense and let out a blood-chilling roar. I have never seen people pile into a vehicle so quickly in my life: half-smoked cigarettes were dropped, drinks went flying and any need for a bathroom break was quickly forgotten – or inadvertently performed en route into the vehicle!

Seconds later – and it really was just seconds – we were all safely in the truck. The guide scrambled for the spotlight and swung the beam in the direction of the roar. There alongside the vehicle, within spitting distance, was the lioness, glaring back at us with piercing eyes. We always say that when an angry lion looks at you, it is as though they are staring straight into your soul, judging your every wrongdoing. Well, this lioness was burning a hole through our souls that night, as we had inadvertently parked between her and her young cubs. We were all still trembling as the ranger started the vehicle and slowly edged forward out of the way. With a last look of disgust, the lioness trotted across the road to her cubs. The ranger sheepishly turned around and whispered to my father, 'Thank you. Sorry about that.'

Meanwhile, the babblers in the back had been shocked stone-cold sober – and no one asked for another smoke break for the rest of the drive.

80

YES, ALL CARS HAVE COILS
Winston Floquet

BACK IN 1977, Nwanedzi was a small rest camp east of Satara at the foot of the Lebombo mountains, near Kruger's eastern border with Mozambique. Sadly, it no longer exists, having been demolished to make way for one of the private concession lodges. But at the time, it was quite primitive and had a limited capacity – so limited, in fact, that our party of six adults plus our two small sons had the entire camp to ourselves that September.

On the first morning, we set out in chilly but clear weather for an early game drive. Our friends Mike and Bea and Bob and Shirley were all in the Peugeot station wagon in front, while my wife, Wendy, and I followed with our two young sons a few minutes behind.

As we rounded a bend not far from the camp, we saw that Mike had stopped his car alongside what appeared, at first sight, to be a crocodile lying in the road. As we got nearer, however, the 'sleeping crocodile' turned out to be nothing of the sort. It was a python – an extremely large python – sunning itself on the gravel road, and the rumble of our cars pulling up towards it had evidently woken it up. Its body firmed up, and we watched as it swelled to the diameter of a slim lady's waist before it gathered its senses and began to gradually slither off the road.

With my head out of the window, trying to fit the length of this most unusual sighting into the viewfinder of my camera, I shouted to Mike in the car in front: 'Hey, call it back – its head is going into the grass.' Mike, for whom rules were often of only minor concern, opened his door and gave the snake's tail a quick tug. It immediately spun round and curled up on the side of the road, glaring angrily back in the direction of Mike's car.

Now apparently snakes are drawn to the warmth of car engines, or perhaps it was peeved at having his tail yanked, but after a minute or two it slithered forward and moved purposefully under Mike's car. Mike, of course, opened his door to get a better view. Bob, who was in the front passenger seat, opened his window to view it come out from under the car on the other side. But, after a short while, he announced worryingly: 'It's not coming out. It's still under the car!'

This announcement caused some considerable consternation in the back as Shirley and Bea sprung up onto the back seat – their backs pressing flat against the roof – in anticipation of the python appearing through the gaps around the car's pedals. It did, after all, owe them one, having had its tail rudely tweaked by one occupant of the vehicle.

Mike yelled to me that I should look under the car, as he was not going to drive off in case he injured the blighter. Not forgetting that this was bang in the middle of Kruger's – if not Africa's – densest lion country, I got out gingerly and peered under the vehicle. To my great surprise the python was gone. Well, it was almost gone. Hanging from the bottom of the engine was the tip of its tail.

I relayed the bad news to Mike, who got out, walked to the front of the car and opened the bonnet using his camera tripod to release the catch. All the while he was shouting: 'It's got a bite like a dog!' – as much to explain why he was not using his fingers as to make sure I wasn't going to do anything silly, like give him a playful shove, while he was focussing on the task at hand. Believe me, my thoughts were centered exclusively on the gigantic snake in his car, not on playing pranks.

Having been squashed flat up against the underside of the bonnet, the python swelled up again as soon as the lid was lifted. It looked quite relaxed, clearly over its earlier irritation at having its tail pulled, and allowed us to take numerous pictures while it enjoyed the warmth of the engine.

But what now? We had thought it would be funny to drive to the nearest petrol station and tell the attendant: 'Yes, please check the oil and water…' but in reality the python's now enlarged body prevented us from closing the bonnet at all. To coax it to depart in peace, we persevered with the camera tripod – without which we'd have had a serious dilemma. All the 'kitty, kitty, psst, psst' in the world would have had little effect on an enormous python.

As it started to slide out, coaxed by the tripod, it became clear just how big this snake actually was. Using the width of the car as a yardstick, about three-and-a-half metres would have been a conservative estimate. Fully stretched out, it may well have been significantly longer than that.

It slithered quietly off into the bush without any sign of ill feeling. But, with all that bother, I do wonder whether it ever took a nap in the road again?

Once developed a few weeks later, our photographs of the encounter enjoyed quite a lot of publicity, appearing in several local and overseas magazines. I remember *Scope*, a popular men's magazine at the time, featured a three-page spread about it and combined the photographs with witty captions like 'Never mind a tiger in your tank…' – a parody of an the old Esso advertising slogan 'Put a tiger in your tank!' – and then, my personal favourite, which still tickles me today: 'Yes, all cars have coils'.

81

THE CALCULATING LEOPARD
Janet Wills

EXPERTS TELL US that animals in Kruger think of cars as just another noisy species. So long as we keep our body parts inside the cabin, the animals are apparently unable to distinguish between the vehicle and its occupants, even with the windows open. This is why, in the Park, you have good reason to scold anyone you see leaning right out of their car window or standing up through their sunroof – they're effectively giving the game away.

But one sunny morning in 2009, while our son was out on a fleeting visit from London, we discovered to our horror that the secret may be out – and some animals are onto us.

We were only in the Park for a single night on that trip, and we had spent it at Tamboti Tented Camp on the banks of the dry Timbavati River. The following morning we left the camp at about 8.30 AM. With our windows wide open to take in the smells and sounds of the bush, we headed east along the tarred road towards Satara. About five kilometres along that road, on the right, there is an inconspicuous turn-off that leads you along a gravel road to the N'wamatsatsa waterhole. As we had the whole day to explore, we decided to take the short detour. It turned out to be a great decision because as we rounded the very first bend, two tiny leopard cubs scampered across the road ahead of us, closely followed by their mother.

The cubs soon disappeared in the long grass to the right, but as we pulled parallel to where they had disappeared, the mother's spotted back and tail were still clearly visible about 10 metres in from the road. We expected her to disappear into the thick bush after her cubs, but without warning she turned around and, snarling loudly, tore through the grass straight towards us – and our open windows!

A leopard can cover 10 metres breathtakingly fast, so thankfully she stopped abruptly at the edge of the road, which gave us just enough time to furiously close all the windows.

We switched off the engine and kept very still. But the leopard was irked. She rushed up to the car; first to my husband at the driver's window, then around the bonnet to my front passenger window, snarling all the while and glaring at us with what I can only describe as murderous intent. She glanced at the window behind me and, seeing it closed, paced back around the front of the car and glared at us again. Then, just as she appeared to be heading off towards her cubs, she turned suddenly, charged towards us and launched herself at my son's window. There was a collective intake of breath as she swiped wildly with her paw and struck the glass with such ferocity, the whole car shook. With that, she turned and ran off into the bush after her cubs.

We were left with thumping hearts but several questions: What would have happened if we had not closed our windows in time? What if we had been in an open safari vehicle? Would first-time visitors have reacted so quickly?

It was chilling to see how calculating that leopard was – and how thoroughly she checked for a way into the car. There is no doubt that she could not only distinguish between the car and the humans inside, but would have attacked us if she could have got through a window. I still shudder when I think how quickly the situation could have turned to tragedy, and it's a reminder of just how wild Kruger can be.

Some days are diamonds, and that was most definitely a blue chip leopard day. Incredibly, we saw seven leopards in all that day; this family of three, plus two mating pairs. We saw the last pair just before leaving the Park at Phabeni Gate late that afternoon. There were several cars parked on the bridge a few kilometres before the exit, and as we had not seen lions on that trip, we hoped they were the reason for all the attention. While we waited for a viewing opportunity, we asked the occupants of another car what there was to see. They excitedly told us that a male and female leopard were in the river bed. Imagine their surprise when my son groaned and said, 'Oh no, not more leopards!'

82

THE GIRAFFE THAT COMMITTED SUICIDE
Jeff Gordon

'DO YOU KNOW HOW THAT GIRAFFE DIED?' asked the red-faced man through the open window of his *bakkie*. I shook my head. 'It committed suicide,' he said gravely.

It was the early spring of 2009 and my first full morning in the Park after an absence of 20 years. We had set off early that morning from Letaba rest camp, heading due south along the gravel road that follows the Letaba River, hoping to spot something interesting. It didn't take long – barely a kilometre or two from the camp, we came across a dead giraffe lying untouched in the dry bush, just a few metres from the side of the road.

A man and his wife in an old *bakkie* pulled up alongside us and rolled down the window. The dust was clearly getting to the man, as his face was red and he was wheezing a little. That was when he came out with his extraordinary declaration about the suicide – which he then followed with a coughing fit.

'I don't understand,' I said, through his coughs.

Finding breath, he explained that he had been on his way back to camp just before gate closing time the previous evening and had come across two giraffes sparring violently at the very spot where the dead giraffe now lay.

He watched them battle it out, before one of the giraffes swung its head in a wide, low arc and snapped the leg of the other, sending it collapsing to the ground in a cloud of dust.

The injured giraffe tried numerous times to get up, he said, but its attempts were futile. A giraffe is an ungainly animal even when fully intact. With a broken leg and an inordinately high centre of gravity, it was clear to the man that the giraffe would lie there struggling until hunger, thirst or scavengers finished it off. Yet still the giraffe persisted, hauling itself as far up as it could, grappling to gain a foothold with its functioning legs, before collapsing back down again.

Time ticked on and gate closing time loomed, but the man and his wife couldn't tear themselves away from the heartbreaking scene.

Eventually, the giraffe seemed to acknowledge that it was never going to get up. It lay there for a while, he said, as if gathering its thoughts. Then, with a changed demeanour, it lifted its head up really high and smashed it back down onto the ground with a mighty thud. Again and again, it lifted its head as high as its neck could hold it then brought it crashing back down onto the hard ground, until eventually it died.

'It was *not* trying to get up,' said the man adamantly, staring me straight in the eye. 'I had already seen it try and get up. This was different.'

He began to cough again.

'It was trying to kill itself.'

We left him and his wife and his coughing and drove on quietly, deeply unsettled by what we had just heard. I didn't believe it for a second, though. A giraffe, wonderful and graceful creature that it is, could surely not be cognisant of life and death to the degree where it could solve the problem of an inevitable slow death by willingly ending its own life, could it? And then do so by smashing its head against the ground?

The strange encounter with the emphysemic man and the dead giraffe lingered in my mind for the remainder of that trip – and long after too. Back at home, I set about trying to find out more and was unnerved to discover that this was not the first report of a giraffe apparently committing suicide. An incident at the Paris zoo left me wondering whether the man was somehow right. It is reported that the giraffe at the zoo had been showing signs of depression for days, before it eventually killed itself by repeatedly slamming its head against the concrete wall of its enclosure.

83

EMPTY SPOOL HEARTBREAK
Gavin Selfe

IT WAS A HOT MORNING in the days before digital cameras when a friend and I left Olifants rest camp for a leisurely drive along the river road that meanders up towards Letaba.

The previous night in the restaurant had been somewhat convivial in terms of red wine, so we were moving and talking with the slow, rehearsed movements one reserves for survival at times such as these. The biltong was in its usual greasy paper bag between the seats, the freshly-packed cool box was on the back seat, and I had my trusty Canon AE1 at the ready on my lap.

It was one of those special, low-light bushveld mornings where everything seems to glow. There was a light haze in the air, and the scents of dew, elephant dung and dry earth were wafting in through the open windows. It was paradise.

At a small opening in the acacia woodland some way up the road, we were greeted by a large flock of guinea fowl rustling around in the dirt, wriggling themselves into small depressions and fluffing out their feathers whilst dust-bathing. Like many photographers, I love guinea fowl, and with the sun's rays at a low angle and clouds of dust hanging like halos around their heads, I knew that this was a great photo opportunity. I checked the film counter.

'Only got 3 shots left,' I mumbled to myself. 'Wonder if I should use 'em? Need to get more film in Letaba.'

'Don't be crazy,' said my friend from the driver's seat beside me. 'If you shoot them all off we're definitely going to see a kill, or something spectacular.'

Maybe that's a good reason to do it then, I chortled, and proceeded to shoot off the last remaining frames. We drove on happily, looking slowly left and right, taking in the cheerful song of a scrub robin and the occasional whiff of a purple-pod cluster-leaf on the breeze.

Not 10 minutes later, as we rounded a bend in a heavily vegetated area, we drove straight into the middle of the most amazing scene I had ever encountered in 25 years of visiting game reserves all over South Africa. In the middle of the road was a leopard crouched low over a large impala ram, its teeth sunk deep into the ram's neck, its eyes flaming angrily at us.

'Back off, back off!' I hissed, but my friend was already ahead of me; the car was in reverse before we'd even stopped, and we shot backwards as if catapulted. Sadly it was too late; we had got too close. Spitting and hissing, the leopard crept backwards into the bushes, its laser eyes never leaving us.

'Damnation,' I cursed.

'Told you,' whispered my friend triumphantly. 'Where are your last photos now?'

I moaned quietly as I viewed the scene through the viewfinder, the camera now about as useful as an empty beer can.

But there was more to this sighting to come. As we sat there, the impala ram started to cough and rattle – a hoarse, hacking sound like a child with croup. Steadily, it started to come to life. It dragged its horns noisily over the gravel and kicked its legs feebly, while those unnerving, watchful eyes of the leopard deep in the guarrie bush never wavered for an instant. Stunned into complete silence, we gawked at the ram as, after five minutes of uncontrollable jerking and coughing, it rose unsteadily to its feet.

The sight of its hard-earned meal getting up and walking away was too much for the leopard. Instinct took over and it began to edge forward through the bush, crouching so low that only the top of its head showed.

'Ooohooh,' I groaned unhappily, as I imagined what we were just about to witness. We were the only car present, and we had not a photon of useable film between us. My friend shook his head slowly and steadily in disbelief.

The ram, apparently overwhelmed by fear-conquering endorphins, looked around calmly, seemingly unaware of what had just happened and totally unafraid. Its flight instinct had left it. It took a few tentative steps towards the leopard. Involuntarily, we both held our breaths. The leopard was barely two metres away, but it did not pounce. The bewildered ram turned and started to walk away, painstakingly slowly. It tottered a few metres down the road and then turned randomly into the bush, weaving its way unsteadily along a narrow trail. At last, the leopard burst out of hiding, shot across the road like an arrow and disappeared into the thick grass on the far side. The last we saw of it was its low spotted back, white tail-tip twitching, stalking the still oblivious impala as it wandered unhurriedly out of sight into some thick scrub. There was no doubt what the final outcome was going to be.

My breath whistled as my chest deflated and I slowly exhaled. I had no idea how long it had been since I had sucked on fresh air. I recall an emerald-spotted wood dove calling dolefully from the nearby thickets, and my left arm was burning in the strong sunlight. I looked at my friend. He was pale and shaken.

'Well then,' I croaked, 'should we maybe go to Letaba and get some film?'

'Maybe,' he said quietly. 'Yes, I think maybe we should do that.'

84

SPOTTING A DIFFERENT KIND OF MAMMAL
Ian & Melanie Smith

THERE ARE, I HAVE BEEN TOLD, 147 species of mammal in Kruger. And while very few people get to see every one of them in a lifetime of trips to the Park, it's always a delight to spot one you've never seen before.

However, this delight doesn't extend to spotting the unofficial 148th species of Kruger mammal – one that migrates regularly east-to-west through the Park, trudging along game trails, in the thickest of bush and usually far from the tourist roads. Every day, human beings pit their chances against Kruger's terrain, its predators and its soaring temperatures as they run the 60-kilometre gauntlet between Mozambique and the chance of a better life in South Africa.

It was the last day of our trip to the Park and we were heading out towards the Phalaborwa Gate by way of the Letaba River loop gravel road past Mingerhout Dam. Not far from where it cuts across the Mahudzi River we saw, some way in front of us, a flash of blue dart across the road. Knowing that there are no blue animals in Kruger, we rolled slowly to the spot where we had seen the movement. Before long we found what we had seen: lying flat on his back in a shallow furrow on the side of the road was a tall, young boy staring back up at us.

'What are you doing here?' I asked through the open window of the car. His response still rings in my ears whenever I think of it.

'I am lying here dying,' he said.

He had been crossing the Park with his family, he told us through cracked lips, but he had become ill and they had left him behind, as he was slowing them down. Looking at the state of him, there was clearly no way he would have made it out of the Park alive.

We were close enough to Letaba to receive a cell phone signal, so I phoned the camp and told them I had found someone in the bush. They thanked me and said they would send along a ranger to pick him up as soon as they could. But we couldn't just leave him there – nor could we wait around, as gate closing time was not far off and we still had a fair distance to go.

So, rightly or wrongly, we decided we'd take him to Letaba ourselves.

We got out of the vehicle – a 4x4 double-cab *bakkie* with a canopy – and opened the back door for him to get in, but he was so weak he was unable to make the short hop up into the back without us lifting him up and pushing him in. Once he was comfortable, we gave him some chocolate biscuits and cold water and headed off to Letaba as quickly as we could.

Arriving in Letaba, we were surrounded by a crowd of people who had either figured out by the dishevelled appearance of our passenger, or heard via the 'bush telegraph', that we were transporting a refugee plucked from the mopane *veld*. Among the crowd were some Kruger staff, so we explained to them where we had found him and what he had told us of being abandoned. They helped the refugee from the back of the vehicle and took him off to the staff quarters, where they said he would be able to wash, eat and rest before being dealt with by the police.

Amazingly, this was not our first encounter with refugees in Kruger. Just less than a year earlier, we were enjoying an early morning drive not far from Punda Maria in the north of the Park. As we followed the dirt road along the Mandlati River, near the power lines that bisect the Park and carry electricity to South Africa from the Cahora Bassa hydroelectric facility in Mozambique, we saw, coming towards us from around a bend, two women and two young men carrying dirty old jerry cans and large bundles on their backs. They were dishevelled and dusty, and it was immediately obvious that these people were not supposed to be there.

We pulled up alongside them and asked them what they were doing, but they didn't reply. Up close it was obvious that they had been walking for a long time. They were covered in dust, their lips were dry and cracked, and they were clearly exhausted. One of the women's feet looked in a particularly bad state – so much so that she could no longer wear shoes and was battling to walk.

It's strange how one behaves when first confronted by a situation like this. Unsure what we could or should do, we slowly pulled away from them. But not far down the road, we decided we couldn't in good conscience turn our backs on them and, quite literally, leave them to the lions. We reversed back and told them they could get into the back of the vehicle. The little water they had with them in their bottles looked foul, so we gave them a large bottle of fresh water, which they passed between themselves and drank in thirsty gulps.

This being our first encounter with refugees, we were curious to find out more and asked where they had come from and where they were going. Their response came in Portuguese.

At first their hand actions mimicked eating, and we figured they were telling us they were hungry. Then the chilling story of what had happened to them was played out. From what we could make out, they had started out their journey across the Park with their husbands. But, through a series of harrowing hand gestures, we understood that the men had been killed by elephants. Shocked to our cores we made our way to Punda Maria with our tragic passengers sitting quietly in the back.

Back at camp we went straight to the offices to let the staff know what we had discovered and what we understood to have happened to part of their party. Meanwhile, my son rushed to the shop and bought a loaf of bread, which they tucked into ravenously.

What became of these refugees and the young man at Letaba, I do not know. I assume they were all eventually repatriated to Mozambique. But such is the hunger of these people to forge a way out of the grinding poverty in their own country, I would not be surprised to hear that they all attempted the crossing again – despite the questionable odds of making it across alive.

85

THE STRANGE TALE OF THE DOG IN THE NIGHT
Jacky Le Roux

IN THE 1950s, when the Kruger National Park was still referred to by everyone as just 'the game reserve', things seemed simpler. Bookings were seldom needed nor made back then; one would just turn up at the camp and see what accommodation was available. This didn't always go without a hitch, though. One year my sister and brother and I arrived at Skukuza to find the camp completely full, so all three of us just slept in the car. Luckily cars were fairly large in those days, but sleeping on the floor at the back was not at all comfortable.

On a trip in 1950, we arrived at Letaba rest camp and were allocated a couple of the temporary canvas bell tents that were erected en masse in the camp each winter to supplement the existing rondavels. The tents were set out in long rows, like a military camp, and although bitterly cold at night they were remarkably comfortable.

It was on that particular trip that my mother had a curious encounter in the middle of the night which still makes me smile all these years later.

Back in those days, neither the tents nor the rondavels had any ensuite facilities; everybody used the communal ablution blocks. And so, as those of a certain age will appreciate, in the middle of the night my mother got up from the old iron bed in the tent and stumbled her way through the semi-darkness to the ablution block some distance away to answer a call of nature.

The next morning she breezily told us that on the way to the ablutions in the night she had met a large and seemingly friendly dog that walked along with her for part of the way. When we mentioned this to the camp manager later that day, he assured us there were definitely no dogs allowed in the camp – but a rather large hyaena had been scrounging around the bins that morning…

My mother dined out on this story many times, always adding that she was grateful that she'd been too groggy to stop and give it a pat and a couple of strokes under the chin!

86

BABOON BULLIES AND THE LEOPARD CUB
Johan van der Merwe

THERE IS ONE ANIMAL IN THE PARK for which I can no longer muster any love at all: the baboon. My cup of goodwill towards them had never been very full anyway. But after an incident in the Park early one spring – which left grown men in tears – the cup was rapidly drained and my hatred for them was sealed.

My father and I were camping at Satara, and one morning we decided to head down to Skukuza for brunch. Just past the southernmost baobab tree we came across a cluster of cars parked up ahead of us – which, on that road, is always a sure sign of a good sighting. As we drew closer we spotted what was causing the traffic jam: in the bough of a tree alongside the road, a female leopard sat with an impala kill. But that wasn't all – the leopard's young cub, perhaps just three or four months old at most, was lying in the grass on the other side of the road.

You could tell that the cub was full and contented given how unruffled it was by the cars alongside it, only picking up its head when a vehicle rumbled past a little too closely.

Not much happened for half an hour. Then suddenly, the mother leopard in the tree pricked up her ears, slunk quickly down the trunk to the ground and disappeared into the bush. Seconds later she reappeared on the opposite side – I assume via a storm drain under the road – close to her cub.

Out of the corner of my eye I saw the cause of her sudden panic: a baboon was heading straight towards the cub. The leopard's maternal instincts kicked in and she charged the baboon, which spun around and retreated. But the next moment all hell broke loose – and with it began my passionate loathing for baboons.

The baboon's approach had just been a sortie; the full offensive was about to begin. There were about 30 baboons in all – young, old, juveniles, females with babies and, of course, the alpha male. They all stormed the leopard mother with such ferocity and in such numbers that she really had no option but to turn around and run, leaving her cub behind.

The poor cub, realising it was no longer being protected, tried to outrun the attackers but its legs couldn't carry it fast enough. With escape impossible, it tried to hide under a bush between two trees, but the baboons flushed it out into the open and formed a circle around it like a gang of schoolyard bullies. It was unclear what the baboons wanted from the cub. They weren't going to eat it, surely, and it was certainly no threat to them. So their antics just seemed, from where we sat, to be nothing more than persecution simply for the heck of it.

The cub hissed and tried to lash out at the baboons, but it was desperately outnumbered – and what damage could a leopard cub deal out to a bunch of nimble baboons many times its size? One baboon swatted the cub from behind and sent it rolling onto its back into a defensive position, where it stayed, hissing and jabbing up at them with its paws.

For the next 10 minutes it felt like time had slowed right down as the baboons callously smacked, prodded and harassed the cub, which continued to squeal in terror. It was agonising to watch, and it felt like only a matter of time before the stress would take its toll on the cub – or before one of the baboons would tire of tormenting it and administer a death blow. Looking around, I saw that we weren't the only ones unsettled by this. Small children in some of the other cars were sobbing, a few women were wiping away tears, and there weren't many men who didn't look visibly upset either.

Mercifully, after what seemed like an age, some of the baboons started to lose interest in the cub and made their way down to the dry river nearby until, eventually, the alpha male was the only baboon left. The cub had quietened down. All hissed out and exhausted, it lay on its back with its paws up, padding weakly at the air.

The alpha male dropped down from the bush he had been sitting on and sauntered towards the cub like an alleyway thug. We all held our breath. The baboon stared at the cub for a moment, but then, distracted by one of the troop, turned his head towards the riverbed. The cub lifted its head and, noticing the baboon preoccupied, grabbed the moment and sprang up, wobbled a bit, then bolted off into the long grass.

There had been silence as the whole drama had unfolded. But as soon as the cub disappeared out of sight, the hooters, the whistles and the cheering from the onlookers could have been heard from Tshokwane.

Since that day I hold the same contempt for baboons as I do for all bullies, and I suspect that young leopard feels the same way too. I imagine also, with a wry smile on my face, that it has grown up to become Kruger's most indomitable baboon slayer.

87

THE KING CHEETAH
Klaus Kreft

WHEN YOU CONSIDER that Kruger's entire road network covers around just two percent of the Park's total landmass, stumbling across a rare animal – a roan, a pangolin, a caracal, a suni or one of the many other seldom-seen inhabitants – is a bit like a lottery win. So quite how you would describe what we spotted I do not know, for it was only first ever photographed anywhere on earth in 1974 (incidentally also in Kruger) and some sources claim there have been only six confirmed sightings of the creature in the wild, ever. Well, they can notch that figure up to seven now.

Early in January 1992 I decided to drag the entire family, including our American in-laws to be, on a tour of Kruger and the surrounds in our Kombi Syncro with a heavily-laden trailer in tow.

Over several days we had some interesting sightings. But on this particular morning, we left Talamati Bush Camp after breakfast, and barely four kilometres east of the camp, just after taking the turn-off that leads to the thicket of trees near the river, we saw a cat in the high grass on the left drinking from a pool of water.

'Look at that leopard!'

Everybody bustled over to the left-hand side of the vehicle and craned to get a closer look. But this was a strange looking leopard.

'No, that's not a leopard. It looks more like a cheetah – but it's huge… and what about those spots?'

The speculation was rampant. It couldn't be – could it?

This was not like a Sasquatch sighting, where the beast bolts through the forest so fast it leaves nothing but a vague imprint in the mind's eye and a blurry photograph as evidence – this cat was going nowhere fast and gave us plenty of time to examine its features and the extraordinary pattern on its coat. Where there should have been spots there were heavy blotches, and running the length of the hackles on its back were the distinct thick stripes, like a tyre track, of none other than the king cheetah. We were indeed face to face with that rarest of rare animals.

Oblivious to the excitement it was causing inside the Kombi, the king cheetah walked along through the grass for a while and then sat down to survey the surroundings. Eventually, it stood up again and came towards us to cross over, before suddenly engaging in a full sprint across the road. On the other side it slowed to a saunter again and finally disappeared into the grass.

Incredibly, we had been able to watch it for a good quarter of an hour before it disappeared, and in that entire time we'd not seen a single other car. With so much time to watch it, I had been able to get my video camera rolling very early on and captured some extraordinary – and apparently very rare – footage. Just as well too, as without evidence it is unlikely we would ever have been believed.

The adventure, however, was not yet over. As I started the engine, there was a hissing noise from the rear (where, if you remember the vw Kombi, the engine was located) and we decided this needed investigation. But where was the king cheetah?

Determined to not be the first person ever killed by a king cheetah – which would surely count as the rarest of all deaths – my son decided to worm over into the boot and inspect the problem from the safety of the interior of the Kombi. We were in stitches as he contorted himself and lifted the engine cover. The laughter stopped, however, when he discovered the source of the problem: the one coolant pipe from the aircon had sprung a leak and needed fixing – and there was no way to do it from the inside.

And so Eric found himself under the car with a roll of duct tape in his teeth while everybody else carefully scanned the surrounding bushes for the cat. Cheetahs are of course timid creatures, and by then it was probably halfway to Satara anyway, but in Eric's mind I imagine all he could think of was the inevitable bizarre conversation that would follow his demise: 'How did Eric die?' 'Oh, you didn't hear? King cheetah!'

88

BOOMSLANG BITE AND A LONG DRIVE HOME
Geoff Lockwood

DESPITE SPENDING A LOT OF TIME in the bush, the idea of snakebite had, for me, never been much more than an occasional mental game of 'What if…' Certainly, it was the last thing on my mind as we prepared to wrap up a very successful group birding weekend based at Kruger's Talamati Bushveld Camp.

We had seen the snake – a stunning apple-green male – on a bird walk through the camp the previous evening, and ironically I had corrected someone who had spouted the conventional wisdom that being back-fanged, a boomslang could only inflict a bite on an extremity such as a finger or an ear. Little did I realise at the time that the very next morning I would be offering a real-life demonstration to prove the contrary.

My wife and I were standing outside bungalow number 2 chatting to friends from the birding group when I noticed, perched in a low bush next to the hut, the African barred owlet which we had been seeing around camp over the previous few days.

I raised my camera and moved into the best position for a photograph when I suddenly felt a sharp pricking on the front of my right shin. Thinking it was a thorn, I continued taking pictures until, a short while later, the sensation changed to what felt like a gummy, toothless bite. I can remember thinking: 'What on earth is a chameleon doing trying to bite my shin?' – but when I looked down and saw a two-metre long boomslang clamped onto my lower leg and chewing away, I knew that I was in trouble.

I brushed off the snake with a swift backhand and sat down on the steps of the bungalow to check for fang puncture wounds. Three beads of blood confirmed the bad news: I had been bitten. Our plans for the rest of the day had just taken a radical left turn. A burning at the bite site suggested that this had not been a 'dry' bite either; venom had been injected.

As my wife ran back to our bungalow to fetch the car, I noticed that the owlet had moved into an even better position, so I took advantage of the situation by taking some more photos – much to the horror of the growing group of shocked onlookers. I reassured them that the venom was slow-acting, that we had time, and that we would leave as soon as my wife returned with the car.

It was amazing – I had always pictured total panic in the event of being bitten by a venomous snake and had even laughed out loud during first aid training at the instruction to 'keep the patient calm'. Now that it had happened to me, I was perfectly calm and thinking clearly and coolly while everyone around me was going frantic. It certainly helped that I had identified the culprit and also knew a little about the effects of boomslang venom and how it would need to be treated.

Boomslang venom is potently haemotoxic and affects the blood's ability to clot, so untreated patients usually die from severe internal and external bleeding. However, these snakes are typically found in trees and are also very shy, so bites are mercifully rare. Treatment requires the administration of a monovalent antivenom specifically developed for this species, as the more common and widely available polyvalent antivenom used to treat the bites of other dangerous snakes is totally ineffective. Because of the rarity of human bites by boomslangs – as infrequent as once every five years or so – antivenom is not typically kept at hospitals but rather ordered from the producers once a boomslang bite has been confirmed.

My first decision therefore needed to be where to go for treatment.

The two best options appeared to be Nelspruit or Johannesburg. Although Nelspruit is significantly closer – less than a couple of hours from Orpen Gate, as opposed to Jo'burg, which is a good seven hours away – I felt that it may not be the best choice. We would first have had to convince the doctors there that I had indeed been bitten by a boomslang, and they would then have to order the antivenom – which would have to come from Johannesburg anyway. Furthermore, the weather in the Lowveld that day was appalling, with low cloud and heavy rain squalls, which I calculated would make delivering the antivenom by air difficult, or even impossible. With all this in mind, I settled on the long drive to Johannesburg.

When we reached Orpen Gate, I set about contacting my family in Johannesburg so that they could initiate delivery of the anti-venom to our destination: a private clinic in the city.

My first attempt at reaching my sister was a disaster. I had only got as far as 'Hi Trish, I've been bitten by a snake and…' when we lost signal – for nearly 10 minutes! By the time I got through again my sister was frantic. But, in a series of interrupted calls, I was finally able to give her all the details and tell her to contact the clinic and get them to order the antivenom.

By that point I had developed a bad headache and was starting to feel nauseous, but at least the cellphone network coverage was more reliable and I was being regularly updated on progress.

After some initial misunderstandings with a casualty doctor who insisted that they had antivenom – they did, but only the polyvalent antivenom – my sister was put through to the pharmacy, and they contacted the National Health Laboratory Services to order the antivenom.

My nausea soon developed into regular vomiting. I had to convince my wife repeatedly that I was okay – and to stop speeding, as it would only delay us if we were pulled over. As we drove, we continually updated our fall-back options should my condition suddenly deteriorate. It wasn't until we finally passed Witbank – about 90 minutes from Johannesburg – that we felt sure that we would make it to the clinic in time. It was also about there that my sister called again to say that the antivenom had been dispatched. So, having done all we could at that stage, I lay back in the passenger seat and tried to relax.

We reached the clinic seven-and-a-half hours after the bite. Initially, the doctor on duty in the casualty ward was sceptical about my claims (with some justification: boomslang bites are very uncommon, particularly on a leg. What's more, there was no bleeding from the fang puncture wounds, and my ankle was quite swollen – both atypical symptoms). However, after drawing some blood and leaving it to stand in a test tube for 20 minutes, it was clear that my clotting factors had already been badly affected – in fact, the blood wasn't clotting at all! With that, a boomslang bite was confirmed. Before the doctor could dash off to order the antivenom, I told him that there was no need – we had already had some delivered to the pharmacy.

I was admitted to the high care ward, hooked up to all sorts of monitors and an IV drip, and after first administering adrenalin and Phenergan (to counteract any possible allergic reactions) I was finally given the antivenom.

From the beginning I had complete confidence in the team assigned to me and was able to totally hand over responsibility for my treatment. I am considered to be a bit of a control freak and this hands-off attitude surprised many who knew me. I had fully expected a 'miracle cure', however, and believed that I would be discharged the following day – but things were worse than I thought. Instead it took another eight days in the high care ward and two nights in a general ward before I finally made it home.

Boomslang venom has a far-reaching effect on the body. My blood only began clotting again three days after the bite, and some of the blood markers were only back in the normal range more than a month after the incident. The breakdown of the red blood cells had also caused the tubules in my kidneys to become clogged, and I needed four sessions of renal dialysis before they were able to resume their critical filtration function.

But ignorance is bliss, and at the time I had no idea of how ill I really was. I felt okay and never doubted that all would end well; I was going to the bathroom under my own steam and even showering – much to the puzzlement of the nursing staff who could not reconcile what they were seeing with what they were reading on my chart. Finally, one of the nursing sisters explained that normally when they see blood test results similar to mine, they know that they are dealing with a seriously ill patient. The sight of me eating well, walking around and cracking jokes with them and the other patients simply did not gel with their experience or their training. I laughed and pointed out that those patients were usually chronically ill and that, at least up until 7.29 AM on Sunday morning, I had been pretty healthy.

Several years on now, I am happy to say there have been no lasting side effects from the bite, nor have I been left with any mental scars. I still enjoy walking in the bush, I still often wear sandals and I don't find that I am constantly looking on the ground for snakes.

I have even been back to Talamati on two subsequent birding weekends – but I did not see my 'friend'. The relief camp manager, however, did proudly show me a photograph he had taken of the snake inside the bird hide a few days before our first return. I think he wanted to reassure me that my plea to not kill the snake – implored to him as I dashed out of camp on my way to hospital – had been heard.

89

HOW MY SPORTS CAR GOT ITS SCARS
Kevin Bouwer

BACK IN 1976, my wife and I spent our honeymoon in Kruger, visiting four camps over 10 days in my three-week-old Toyota 2000 coupé sports car – replete with the large, low-angled rear window characteristic of that sought-after model.

My story begins as we left Satara rest camp early one morning, as I believed that the 'early bird catches the worm': first out, first to see the lion on the road. After all, with it being winter, lions would often come out and draw warmth from tar after a cold night.

As was our usual practice, I drove while my wife sat in the back so that we could both move left and right to view game. About 10 kilometres out of Satara, on the tarred road leading north towards Olifants, we came across a pride of about 10 lions. With no other cars in sight, and the sun barely rising, we were able to get very close to them.

After a good 20 minutes, a large black-maned lion heaved itself up off the road and ambled towards the car. 'Great,' I thought, 'here's my chance to get a real close-up with my Kodak Instamatic *mik-en-druk*' when suddenly I felt the back of the car dip and, simultaneously, a great weight on my neck. I thought the roof had caved in – but it was my wife coming over the seat at a rate of knots. When I removed my face from the steering wheel, my wife was frantically pointing at the rear of the car and mouthing, or squeaking, the word 'lion'. I looked back and there, on the boot, was a full-grown lioness, her two gigantic front paws pressing down hard on the car's sloped rear window. My first thought was: 'Is the window going to hold? Because if she gets in, there is going to be sports!'

In a blur I started the car and pulled away. But as the lioness slid off, there was a disquieting scraping sound as she dragged her claws over the boot, etching a distinct trail deep into the paintwork of my brand new sports car.

My car wore those claw marks as a badge of honour for almost two decades. I eventually sold it in 1994 with the marks still on the boot – a reminder of the close encounter on our honeymoon in Kruger. I like to think that somewhere out there someone is still driving that Toyota 2000 coupé, totally oblivious to the provenance of the strange, deep scratches on the rear paintwork.

90

THE NHLANGANINI BABY SNATCHER
Johann Fankhauser

HAVING HAD THE PRIVILEGE of growing up in Phalaborwa – on the front *stoep* of the Kruger National Park's western border – it goes without saying that I've made more trips into the Park than I can remember. But there was one trip in particular, way back in the early 1970s, that I have never been able to forget.

It was a Sunday morning and my father suggested we take a drive through the Park down to Olifants rest camp for lunch, as the camp's hilltop restaurant was then – and remains to this day – surely one of the finest spots in the country to sit down and eat. After a few relatively uneventful hours on the dusty road to Letaba, my father turned right onto the short loop that hugs the dry Nhlanganini riverbed, which, from experience, often proved a rewarding detour for us.

After rounding the *kopje* on the right, we approached the first drift through the riverbed. A car was already parked in middle of the drift on a flattish rocky area just off the left edge of the road. So we approached slowly, with four pairs of eyes eagerly scanning the riverbed for whatever it was they had stopped for. But there was nothing. My father rolled down his window and asked the driver of the car what he had seen. Rather mysteriously, the man refused to be drawn on exactly what it was, but suggested we be patient as the subject of interest would hopefully soon be back.

My father immediately pulled up behind the parked car, switched off the engine and there we waited, barely able to stifle our curiosity. Sure enough, after about three minutes – although such was the anticipation that it felt considerably longer – an adolescent male baboon dropped down into the riverbed from the trees on the opposite bank with what appeared to be something under his arm. He swaggered slowly over to where we were parked and stopped about three metres from the cars. Then, like a sports captain holding aloft a trophy, he revealed in a most extravagant display the prize that he had been concealing: a tiny and very noisy leopard cub.

We couldn't believe our eyes. This harebrained baboon had got himself a toy, and boy, was he proud of himself.

We watched open-mouthed as the baboon nuzzled the cub and clumsily tried to mother it, squeezing it up against his chest so hard we thought the cub might burst. Then every now and again, with a big baboon-grin plastered across his face, up would come the arms, with the leopard held aloft.

Of course, we all immediately started formulating plans of how we could liberate the poor leopard from this thug; one idea being to sacrifice some of our *padkos* to attract him to the car with the hope that he would drop the cub in panic when we suddenly open the doors. No such luck – the baboon was onto us long before we could even think of putting such a plan into action. He must have known we were up to something, because he simply stood up, walked back a few paces and plonked himself down again, this time a good 10 metres away, and continued his showboating.

The leopard cub was clearly unhappy and increasingly began to make its feelings known to everyone within earshot. The squealing did not appear to be going down at all well with its captor, who was growing edgy and had begun making nervous glances in the direction of the nearby *kopje*.

After several minutes the baboon decided that the show could no longer go on with all this racket. He stood up, turned around and made off back to the safety of his troop in the trees, with the still screeching cub firmly under his arm. We stayed on for some considerable time hoping for a reappearance, but that was it – the baboon refused to come back for a curtain call.

There was probably no happy end for the leopard cub, but I suppose that's the way nature works.

There was no happy end for my father either. He had taken a number of photos of this extraordinary encounter with his old Pentax SLR and was pretty sure that he would soon be making a small killing when he sold them to the highest bidder. However, when he got the slides back after developing and mounting, he was hugely disappointed to find that in all the excitement he had forgotten to close the lens' aperture ring and had got the exposure horribly wrong. The photos were just passable enough to allow him to prove the authenticity of the sighting to everyone he had earlier bragged about it to, but his dreams of a financial windfall and international wildlife photography accolades were all but scuppered.

91

THE WATERBUCK AND THE *LAAGER*
Andy Maclaurin

THE GIRIVANA DAM near Satara rest camp is considered one of the single best places in the Park to see predators, particularly in late winter when the dam is dry and animals congregate in numbers around the shallow concrete drinking trough alongside it.

Over the years, that trough has occasionally produced some very worthwhile sightings for my family and me, but none more so than the time we took a quick detour past it on our way back to Satara late one September afternoon.

Approaching the dam on the gravel road from the south you get a view of it long before you arrive, and we were a good 500 metres away when one of us spotted something odd in the trough. We slowed right down so as not to frighten whatever it was and came quietly to a stop in a dusty clearing about 50 metres away. It turned out to be a hyaena sitting motionless in the water.

A minute or two later, one of our children spotted something the rest of us had completely missed: a wildebeest lying on the ground just a few metres from the edge of the trough. We guessed that it had been drinking and while doing so had been attacked by the hyaena. After what must have been a considerable struggle, given the state of it, the wildebeest was nine-tenths dead, and the hyaena, it seemed, had decided to cool off in the water before tucking into its meal.

We waited and watched for about a quarter of an hour, during which time half a dozen more cars had joined us. In their desire to get a good view, they had parked haphazardly around us, which ended up forming a small circle of cars. Beyond us, the hyaena still sat in the trough, and the dying wildebeest, one of its hind legs occasionally jerking, still lay on the ground.

Suddenly, the hyaena became alarmed and took off at great speed. A moment or two later, a waterbuck came crashing through the bush with about 20 wild dogs tearing after it. The terrified waterbuck made straight for the middle of our circle of cars and stopped right there in a cloud of dust. The wild dogs, highly agitated, rushed about on the outside of the *laager*, but for whatever reason would not venture in. How the waterbuck had known they wouldn't follow, I do not know, but there it stayed, surrounded by the dogs yet seemingly untouchable in the middle of the circle.

This commotion continued for what seemed like an age – but was probably only a couple of minutes – and just as we were beginning to wonder how this standoff was going to end, one of the dogs caught scent of the dying wildebeest, went over to it and sent message that dinner was over there instead. With this, the entire pack set about the wildebeest, which was torn apart and devoured in no time. But not before the waterbuck had timed its escape; it slunk quietly away, using the circle of cars as a screen.

It was a happy ending for that clever waterbuck, but I still wonder how it knew that the dogs wouldn't follow it into the circle of cars. Moreover, how would the episode have ended, I wonder, had the wild dogs not been distracted by the dying wildebeest?

92

BLACK MAMBA HITCHES A RIDE
Neil Taylor

HONESTLY, THE FOLLOWING STORY IS ALL TRUE. Okay, I may employ a tiny bit of poetic licence here and there, and I admit I can't help allowing my British sense of humour to tailor the storytelling a little – it's just the way we Brits are – but it really did happen like this. Oh, and to avoid any costly court battles, I should come clean right away and declare that throughout the ordeal my wife was in reality cool, calm and collected and that the Kruger staff were, for the most part, not quite as bumbling as I make out. They were, in fact, remarkably brave – way beyond their pay grade – even if their methods looked, to my eyes, a touch unorthodox. But then again, how orthodox would you be dealing with a large black mamba?

A few kilometres south of Olifants rest camp, a high-level bridge crosses the Olifants River. If you're feeling brave, you can get out of your car halfway across it, stretch your legs and have a peer over the edge into the pools and reed beds below. Anyone who's made the long drive up from Satara to Olifants would probably have made this stop and felt reasonably safe in doing so. After all, standing at the midpoint of the bridge offers a clear view of either side and plenty of time to hop back into your car should anything with sharp teeth approach from either end.

The last thing you'd expect is for something to come over the sides!

My wife and I had barely begun our first ever trip to the Park and were on our way up to Olifants when we decided to stop on the bridge for a leg stretch. No sooner had I yanked on my handbrake when, from over the edge of the bridge alongside me, emerged a two-metre long, olive-grey snake.

A quick mental risk assessment concluded that I should steer well clear and go to the far end of the bridge, out of the way. However, in the true spirit of the accredited Health and Safety professional that I am, I totally ignored the warning bells, grabbed my camera and jumped out of the vehicle to fire off a couple of quick photographs. That is, until the snake decided it was not happy with me poking this clicky thing in its face. It reared its head up to what seemed like about half its length and showed me the inside of its coal-black mouth. While I had had an inkling before, there was now no doubt that this was not just any old olive-grey snake; this was a real, live black mamba.

Now, there are a lot of myths surrounding the black mamba, but few experts would deny that with its extremely aggressive nature and its phenomenally toxic venom – which can kill a man in under 20 minutes and has even been recorded to have killed a full-grown elephant – it is probably the world's most lethal land snake.

Suddenly, getting the perfect photograph didn't seem quite as important. I slowly lowered my camera and gave the snake enough room to pass by and return to the safety of the bush on the southern end of the bridge. The snake, however, had other ideas and instead slithered onto the road to investigate the underside of my vehicle – possibly to check out the source of the hysterical screaming coming from the vicinity of the passenger seat.

A quick glance underneath revealed that things had just got serious as I glimpsed the last few centimetres of its tail disappearing up into my engine compartment. A rather nervous and furtive glance inside the vehicle confirmed that my wife did not appear at all happy. I studied my options, and despite finding many good reasons for leaving her there, I decided I had better get her out. Rather surprisingly, she jumped quite a long way for a large woman.

After sitting her down and giving her some water, I thought I had better check the inside of the car and close the vents. While I did this, another tourist, who had watched the mamba's disappearing act into my car's engine, phoned the rangers at Olifants and then kindly proceeded to explain to my wife what a 14-carat plonker she had married. While I was pleased to see our vehicle had wall-to-wall carpets and provided no way in for the snake, I wasn't too pleased to hear my wife agree wholeheartedly with her new friend.

Some 45 minutes later my wife's pulse was back to normal. But there was still no sign of any knights in shining khaki, so I made an executive decision to drive us on to Olifants. At least I could get a stiff whisky there.

I carefully explained the plan to the wife, who needed more than just a bit of gentle persuasion to get her back into the passenger seat. We'd barely driven for more than five minutes (with our feet on the dashboard) when a Park's vehicle came over the horizon and stopped alongside us. The two obviously knowledgeable but very cautious Park employees in the other vehicle slowly assessed the situation and decided that the salary they collected on a monthly basis in no way covered this task.

After a further 15 minutes of ducking and diving their responsibilities, my two new friends were relieved to see arrive on the scene a more senior ranger. Mr Senior Ranger claimed that he heard the commotion on the radio and came along to have a laugh. His initial Mickey-taking, British-style, turned to a gasp of terror when I showed him the size of the problem by way of the view-a-seven-feet-long-black-mamba-that's-just-gone-into-my-engine-compartment facility on the back of my digital camera.

A decision was made to take us to Letaba rest camp, about an hour further north, where a garage with a ramp was available and a suited-and-booted snake handler was on standby. I offered to swap vehicles with Mr Senior Ranger and said that I would leave the wife with him for company. Oddly, he didn't take up my offer. So, feet back on the dashboard, we were off to Letaba – in record time, I might add.

Upon arrival, the specially-trained snake-handling rangers took control impressively, immediately grabbing the uninvited guest by the neck and dragging it out of the vehicle. I felt duty-bound to intervene and explained that the uninvited guest was in fact in the engine compartment, not on the passenger seat, and my wife, as strange as it seemed at the time, was my travel companion and not the reason we were there. The rangers put the vehicle on the ramp and began to execute the eviction order.

The snake was spotted by a mechanic against a hole in the grill, and I was introduced to a secret weapon: carburettor oil! Apparently, snakes do not like being sprayed with carb oil. The mechanic sprayed what he could see of the snake, and when I say all hell broke loose, I mean all hell broke loose. The snake set off around the engine, and the rangers dived in and out from under the vehicle; one guy lost his goggles, the mechanic fell over a crate of empty bottles, brave Mr Senior Ranger took cover behind my wife, and the noise was cacophonous. After what seemed like a full-length feature of *Monty Python's Flying Circus*, the snake made a welcome mistake: it dropped its tail out the front of the vehicle. One of the little mechanics pounced, grabbed the tail and pulled the mamba backwards out of the grill.

Now, you might think that was that, but let me tell you that what followed in terms of sheer excitement was on another level. Realising the length of the snake, the mechanic sussed that his situation was tenuous, to say the least, and made the wise decision to keep the fang end as far from him as he could by swinging the snake around and around above his head. Now, I attend a fair few business meetings, and a black mamba tie would go down really well and do wonders for my street cred back in England, but a test fitting with this one – which I assumed was not a happy chappy – was pretty low on the agenda.

A quick glance around and another mental assessment of my situation exposed a rather startling fact: I was on my own in a garage with a madman swinging a seven-foot black mamba around his head. Mr Senior Ranger was running down the road in a cloud of dust, my wife was thirty yards in front of him, the mechanics had rapidly gone on an impromptu tea break, the snake-handling rangers were cowering in the engine compartment – and my life was flashing in front of my eyes. I did what anybody else would do in this situation and started penning my will, with the usual first line: 'To my much-loved daughter, I leave my debts...'

To my great relief, the cavalry arrived in the shape of one of the snake-handling rangers who was surprisingly possessed with a renewed vigour and astounding bravery and ordered the mechanic to release the mamba across the floor. To their credit and with great skill, they took control of the situation, emptied two cans of carb oil and eventually brought proceedings to a close by apprehending the traumatised snake on the end of a noose.

My wife and I were so upset at bringing all this upheaval to the snake that we insisted on going with the rangers to release it back into the wild, where we watched it melt back into the bush unharmed but somewhat dazed and confused. Which is pretty much what happens to most people who meet my wife!

PART THREE

TALES FROM NORTHERN KRUGER

THE GREAT UNSPOILT AND WILD northern region of Kruger, with its dense, baobab-studded landscape so rich in birdlife, is by far the quietest part of the Park. Patient visitors who venture north of Mopani rest camp through the seemingly infinite mopane *veld* are often rewarded with the most remarkable sightings all to themselves. A sense of Kruger-of-old still seems to pervade the winding dirt roads and the charming rest camps of the north, the Big Five spotters and weekend warriors seemingly half the world away, several hundred kilometres to the south.

Northern Kruger, which stretches all the way up to the Limpopo River, has always been elephant country and is home to some of the largest tuskers in Africa. It also does not go unnoticed by first-time visitors to the region that the elephants of the north are significantly less even-tempered than their southern counterparts; a fact not missed in two of the stories that follow.

Given the relative scarcity of visitors to the north, this section of the book was always going to be the leanest – but the handful of extraordinary stories from the north perhaps capture a few grains of the indefinable magic of this unblemished tract of Kruger.

93

REVERSING INTO CAMP
Issi Potgieter

EVERY TIME I PASS THROUGH the small eastern gate at Shingwedzi rest camp, I smile a little and remember our holiday to the Park back in 1969 when my late father set tongues wagging by making the most unconventional entry through those gates. 'That man liked reversing so much,' they said, 'he even reversed into camp!'

My father was a gentle man: quiet and reserved, a photographer of some note and a renowned handyman. He was a manager at the orange warehouse in Rustenburg, but really Kruger was his life, and every year in June, along with my mother and my four siblings, we would pile into his old 1960 Mercedes Benz and make our annual pilgrimage to the Park.

Kruger was a less cultivated beast back then, and visiting the Park was a mildly different experience. In those days there were no Park shops as we know them today – you had to bring everything with you. It was all carefully packed into the boot: the frying pan squeezed in behind the spare wheel, the gas cannister lodged into the corner, while rusks, bully beef, condensed milk, canned meatballs and loose vegetables all fought for space amongst the suitcases. In camp, all the bungalows came replete with an old basin and jug, and a freshly-lit paraffin lantern would welcome you back after a long day. Fresh bread and milk – real luxuries – were delivered just twice a week to reception.

The daily routine was not all that different from today. You would rise early, fetch hot water from the wood-fired kettle stove in the middle of the camp, which burned day and night, and enjoy coffee with condensed milk and rusks. Then you would take to the roads to look for game. Just before gate closing time, you'd be back in camp and there would be a rush to be first in the communal bathrooms before the water from the 'donkey' ran out. Then, around the communal campfire in the middle of the circle of huts, the adults would share their stories of the day's sightings.

The Park itself looked very much like it does today, except in those days all the roads were gravel and much narrower than they are now; you'd often have to give way to other cars coming in the opposite direction. There were no shoulders to the roads then, and the bush grew right up to the edges.

Every day we would drive around slowly, my father regularly stopping and reversing to inspect some ears he had glimpsed – far behind that branch, just left of the mopane tree. Stick-lions! For a car full of kids, it was, to say the least, boring, cramped and hot. In between game viewing, my mother would listen to snatches of Wimbledon tennis on the radio, the signal dropping now and again, crackling back on only to reveal that her favourite had just lost the point.

With five children, space in the back of the car was scarce and one of us had to sit on a piece of sponge wedged between the two front seats – the best seat in the house. The other four were strung out like sardines and left to bicker.

After a few days of hot weather and hotter tempers, my mother and father had had enough and decided as punishment to leave all of us in the camp one afternoon while they went out to enjoy a game drive in peace. For us, whether in the car or in camp, it was play time. We made roads in the red dust and pushed my brother's toy cars around them, while my older brother stole away to smoke a few forbidden cigarettes.

My parents took the road out of the east gate of the camp and followed the Shingwedzi River south towards where Engelhard Dam lies today – elephant country. As usual, they had to turn into each and every loop along that road that offered a closer view of the river. It was right about when they should have turned and headed back to camp that my father turned off into one of those loops and switched off the engine to enjoy a few minutes of late afternoon silence.

Soon it was time to go. He reversed a little and swung the car around, but as he shifted into first gear, there was a worrying clank and the car revved loudly. This was a problem. Something had snapped, and the car would no longer shift into first gear nor any of the other forward gears. If my older brother had been there he would have been able to make a plan, such was his skill with things like that. But he was back in camp smoking cigarettes – so my father made his own plan. He got out and pushed the car backwards, then jumped back in and let it roll forwards with the clutch in. Over and over again he repeated this, each time turning the car a little, until finally its rear end was facing the road out. From there he headed out of the turning and back onto the main road all the way to camp – in reverse!

It's a long way to drive with your head turned 180 degrees, and very soon my father was starting to feel it.

'*Ouvrou*, I just can't do it any more. My neck is killing me,' he groaned. 'You watch the road and I will just use the mirrors.'

And so they continued, in reverse, with my mother acting as his eyes, forgetting about elephants and not bothering to look for any other game – there was no time. The camp gates were about to close and their top speed was no more than if they had been driving the entire way in first gear. By some miracle, they didn't encounter any other cars nor a single elephant – which is just well, as nobody would want to confront an aggressive Shingwedzi bull head-on with no way of reversing backwards, given that they were already reversing *forwards*!

After what felt like miles and miles – which was in fact precisely 11 miles in total – they approached the final bend before the gate at Shingwedzi. Just before the gate, my mother jumped out of the car and took her chances walking. She was too embarrassed to be seen reversing into camp.

Meanwhile, us children were wondering why on earth our mother and father were out for so long. The biscuits in the hut had long since been polished off and the cooldrink bottle was empty. So with our hunger great and our tempers short, we walked to the gates to wait for their return. Our timing was impeccable. 'Look!' one of us yelled. 'There they are, reversing into camp!'

At reception, the khaki-clad staff fell about laughing. 'Did you just see that?' said one. 'That man just reversed into camp!'

'He must really like reversing!' quipped another, sagely.

My father parked up and asked if there was anyone who could help him. 'My car was stuck in reverse,' he told his tittering audience.

That evening, it seemed everyone was talking about the crazy man who reversed into camp. Everywhere we turned, comments and conjecture were flying: 'He liked reversing so much he drove into camp backwards,' was a favourite. Everyone had a different version of the story and a different theory for this bizarre behaviour.

And my father? He just sat quietly and listened.

With a piece of galvanised wire, the AA mechanic sorted out the problem the following day and it never caused a problem again. I am sure that if our old Mercedes – licence plate TRB 1949 – is still on the road today, and I like to imagine it is, there is a still a piece of wire from Shingwedzi inside it, holding the gears in place.

94

NOT OUR MORNING TO BE EATEN
John Muirhead

IT WAS NOT OUR MORNING TO BE EATEN. That's what my friend and columnist for an Eastern Cape newspaper wrote 10 days after our close encounter in Mopani rest camp. The piece was entitled 'Within a whisker of ending up as breakfast', and the writer was entitled to use such hyperbole – after all, he was with us on that trip and he was right: it truly was an awfully close shave.

Mopani is one of Kruger's newer camps and was only completed in 1993, just a year before our visit. It is set on a hillside overlooking an expansive dam, but what makes it unique for a large camp in the Park is that the stone-walled bungalows have been built sympathetically into the landscape and spread out amongst large swathes of natural bush, grass and trees. As such, it feels a lot wilder than its well-manicured and landscaped counterparts further south, like Satara or Skukuza.

We were only at Mopani for one night. So at first light the following day, I roused the group for an early morning walk along the in-camp trail that traverses the fence line between the dam and the bushy slopes leading up to the restaurant. We followed the trail from our bungalow, down past the swimming pool and on past the restaurant.

We hadn't gone too much further when we came across an unsettling sight. A couple of waterbuck, inside the camp and on the path in front of us, were hurling themselves repeatedly at the fence in a vain attempt to get out. How had they got in, we wondered? As they were clearly in a state of distress, we gave them a wide berth and did our best not to frighten them even more. With the camp so quiet, and with plenty of vegetation and cover around, we couldn't understand their panic. After all, the inside of a camp like Mopani must surely be one of the safest places in the Park for an antelope.

The answer came as we reached the area near the camp gate. A ranger came running down the road in a state of great agitation and told us to get back to our bungalow immediately. 'There are lions in the camp!' he puffed.

We dashed back via the shortest possible route and stood excitedly on the veranda peering around into the bush, wondering where the lions were. Just then, a giant of a man with a thick black beard and huge feet in open sandals came jogging past. He was armed with a large calibre rifle and was followed by a posse of 10 armed assistants in quickstep behind him. As they passed us, he shouted back to his men in Afrikaans: *'Kom manne, ons gaan hierdie leeus levendig uit die kamp kry.'* (Come on chaps, we're going to get these lions out of the camp alive).

It was soon revealed that the lions were holed up in the long grass immediately below the restaurant. This meant that if we walked down a little to a hillside vantage point not far in front of our bungalow, we would have ringside seats to the action. So we all filed down, then waited and watched.

After a while there was a loud crack as the ranger fired a round into the ground near the lions. Immediately, three lionesses jumped up and made a beeline for the service gate at the north of the camp. The group of rangers followed them and, we were later told, successfully chased them right out of the camp.

After the excitement had died down, we were all suddenly struck with a most chilling thought: not half an hour earlier we had walked in single file just three metres from where the lions were lying in the long grass below the restaurant.

It transpired that the service gate at the north of the camp had been left open overnight, and the lions had chased three waterbuck into the camp and followed them in. They had brought down one of the buck and were actually feeding on it when we ambled past them. Incredibly, we had neither heard nor seen a thing, as our eyes had been focussed on the dam to our right and the path in front of us – not the long grass on our left.

The camp officials removed the waterbuck carcass and placed it outside the fence, visible from various points in the camp. As night fell we decided to watch and see which predators and scavengers would turn up, as the area around the carcass was well lit. We sat for hours in the freezing cold, but disappointingly not a single animal visited the carcass.

So it was with great surprise when, the next morning, we visited the site to see what was left of the waterbuck and found that it had completely disappeared. Such is the way of the bush, I suppose.

As it fortunately wasn't us, just who had been the first to discover the lions in the camp that morning and raise the alarm? Apparently it had been the ranger's wife. She was in the kitchen of her house and happened to look up and see a lion walking past the window. What potential tragedy she had averted we'll never know. But for us, alive and happy, we were able to continue our holiday in the Park having avoided – for no reason other than blind luck – becoming breakfast for those three Mopani lions.

95

SCARS OF A CHARGE RUN DEEP
Dianne Henderson

IF THE SAYING 'ONCE BITTEN, TWICE SHY' is true, then I believe an appropriate modification to that idiom would be something like: 'once charged, forever terrified'.

Back in the mid-seventies, my mother and I had a booking at Shingwedzi rest camp up in the north of the Park, an area famed for its particularly large and often aggressive elephants. It was getting towards the end of the day, and on our way up to the camp we made what, in hindsight, turned out to be a very poor decision. We calculated that we could take the pleasant river road towards camp, and provided we motored along at just within the speed limit, we would make it to the camp gate right before it closes.

It was a peaceful drive, following the gravel road that skirts the contours of the river, until a big bull elephant came crashing out of the bush in front of us – evidently making a dash to the river for its evening drink. It got halfway across the road and stopped dead in its tracks, looked at the car – then charged.

This was no mock charge either. The elephant had lowered its enormous head, tucked its trunk up and suddenly five tonnes of trumpeting pachyderm was thundering towards us. There was little I could do but put the car in reverse and hope and pray that I could accelerate faster than the elephant's great big legs could run. With my head twisted rearwards trying to navigate backwards, and my foot flat on the accelerator, all I could hear was the enraged trumpeting of the elephant; the clatter of the stones, kicked up by its feet, hitting the windscreen; and the panicked shrieking of my mother yelling 'Go! Go! Go!'

My frenzied retreat eventually matched, and finally bettered, the speed of the elephant's charge. After what felt like an inordinate distance, it lumbered to a halt and just stood in the road, framed by billows of dust, watching and daring us to move an inch forward. We waited a while, but eventually, with the elephant going nowhere, we realised we had no option but to go all the way back the way we had come, join up with the main road again and continue on to camp in the dark.

When we finally reached the camp gates, I melted into a pool of fear and shock. Instead of getting a fine for being late, we had the camp staff calming us down with cups of sweet coffee and sympathetic back rubs. That night, I apparently screamed loud enough in my sleep to wake the entire camp. Any sight of an elephant for the rest of the trip caused me to shake so much I would stall the car, and I recall the end of that trip being the only time I was ever glad to leave the Park.

But the scars of the elephant charge near Shingwedzi ran deep, and my problems with elephants, I was soon to discover, were not yet over.

I worked in Wadeville on the East Rand of Johannesburg at the time. Every morning I would cut through the grounds of Boksburg Lake, as I enjoyed seeing the ducks paddling on the water or waddling around on the lawns. About a week or so after my return from the Park, I was on my way to work, peacefully driving past the lake and enjoying the ducks, when suddenly a great big grey form loomed in front of me. As true as the day is long, an elephant was walking down the middle of the road straight towards me.

I honestly cannot explain what went on in my head at that moment, but all I can remember is an overwhelming compulsion to get out of the car and save myself. I braked sharply, flung open the door and, with the engine running and my handbag still on the seat, started running – as fast and as far from that elephant as I could. Fortunately, driving behind me was a sane and sensible gentleman who quickly parked his car behind mine, before jumping out and giving chase.

Had I been hallucinating, you may ask? No, there really was an elephant in the road that morning. It was calmly explained to me by the man that the circus was in town, and they had set up camp at the lake. The elephant had apparently managed to break loose from its pen and gone for a stroll. It was all too late for me to laugh, though – by then I had had enough of elephants to last me a lifetime.

96

ZEBRA CROSSING
Raymond Hewson

IN THE WINTER OF 1978, my wife, Cynthia, and I took along our very good friend for her first ever visit to the Park. As is often the case when you have a first-time visitor in the car, Kruger delivered a most dramatic sighting – so dramatic, in fact, that it changed the way I feel about seeing such things.

Cynthia was the opposite of our first-timer in the back seat. She had been visiting Kruger from as far back as 1936, and her father – a keen amateur cinematographer – had, over the years, amassed piles and piles of cine film from the Park. So when he died in 1976 and Cynthia inherited his old Super 8 cine camera, we decided that with so much footage already in the bag we would only use the camera to film anything out of the ordinary. We placed it on the back seat alongside our friend and hoped the 'rule of the first-timer' would deliver some good sightings for us to capture.

On our first morning in Shingwedzi, I decided to take the back route out of the camp's smaller eastern gate, which had only been revealed to me by the petrol attendant whilst filling up at the camp's pumps the previous evening. We passed the old causeway on our left and followed the road along the south bank of the river, which, while not yet totally dry, was more a series of long, deep pools rather than a single channel of water.

We soon came across a small herd of zebra grazing on the side of the road. Amongst them was a tiny young foal which couldn't have been more than just a few weeks old. We hardly noticed the pool of water in the riverbed to our left, but this would soon be the stage for a most dramatic battle – and that zebra foal would prove to be the catalyst.

You would think a zebra makes a noise like a horse, but its call is not dissimilar to the yapping of a small dog – and it was this sound that we suddenly heard from the far side of the pool. A zebra mare had emerged from the bush on the opposite bank and appeared to be in some distress, yelping across the water to the herd alongside us. The foal seemed particularly agitated by the yelping, which led us to conclude that the mare must have been its mother, and they had somehow become separated in the night. Now the large pool, which stretched as far as we could see up and down river, was keeping them apart.

The mare shuffled to the water's edge and looked longingly across, before flicking around and running back into the bush, still yelping. A moment later she was back at the water's edge again, calling across to her baby, before once more turning on her hooves and disappearing back into the bush. But the motherly instinct was too great and she appeared again a third time. This time there was more determination in her gait, and when she got to the water's edge she didn't stop – she just waded right in. After about 10 metres the water got too deep and she began to swim.

I remarked to the ladies in the car that I had never seen a zebra swim a river before, so we waited and watched to see her get across to the foal. The water in the pool was still and calm, and with the mare swimming confidently, there was no reason to think she wouldn't be successful.

The zebra hadn't got far when suddenly she jerked her head to the side, and horror of horrors, we realised that a crocodile had latched onto her right shoulder from behind.

And so began a furious battle, as the croc lashed the water with its tail and the zebra reared up to dislodge the attacker. The water around the two animals at times looked as though it was boiling, and it was only when the crocodile rolled the zebra right around and exposed itself above the surface for a second that we saw just how big it was. In spite of its monstrous size, the croc could not get the better of its prey, and when it released its grip for a few seconds, the zebra paddled desperately back towards the shore.

The tenacious mare looked to be in the clear when suddenly there was an explosion in the water and the croc re-emerged – this time from below – and grabbed her by the throat. In her short moments of freedom, however, she had managed to swim close enough back to the far shore that she could just touch the bottom and brace herself against the crocodile's renewed onslaught.

Minutes passed, and after a while the croc appeared to tire, as it only occasionally lashed out violently. But if the croc was tired, the zebra was exhausted and beaten, and her muzzle was only barely breaking the surface. The end was in sight, and it was not nice to watch. I can assure you, if I had had a gun with me I would have taken a pot shot at the crocodile. Yes, I know that this was nature at work, but something I had always wanted see – a kill in front of my eyes – seemed abhorrent to me now.

Well, did the croc get its meal, you may ask? No, it did not. As the zebra's muzzle was about to sink below the surface, there was a swirl in the water a few metres to the right, and the croc, realising another crocodile was about to crash its party, released its grip to fend off the intruder. In a flash the zebra staggered out of the water. Inexplicably, though, instead of getting as far from danger as she could, she stood on the edge and shook herself. In one voice we shouted: 'Move! Move! The croc will catch you again if you stand there!'

Our mental willing must have worked, because, with that, the zebra took off and disappeared into the bush beyond the far bank.

And the foal? We too often wonder what happened to it because I doubt it would have survived without its mother. Through my binoculars I had seen a huge gash on the zebra's right shoulder and a lot of blood on her neck.

On our return to camp, we told a ranger and all he said was: 'If the animal does not survive its injuries then it will become food for another predator.'

Fair enough. But since that day, on all subsequent trips to Kruger and other game reserves, I find I only get pleasure from watching a predator enjoying its meal, never from it 'doing the shopping', so to speak.

The cine camera? Oh yes, the cine camera – it stayed on the back seat, and nobody thought of putting it to use. The whole traumatic affair had numbed our senses. But that footage – had we shot it – would have been unique, as we were the only car on the scene.

97

A RECORD CASE OF FOOLISHNESS
FOR A RECORD PAIR OF HORNS
Buks Oberholzer

WHEN I WAS STILL A STUDENT back in the late eighties, my mother took my brother and I to the Park, where we stayed for a few nights at Shingwedzi rest camp. Now students, they say, are neither humans nor animals but rather something roughly in between. So whether or not that amounts to a defence for what my brother and I got up to, I don't know. But given how blindingly foolish we were – not to mention criminal – that's the best defence I have. Oh, and the Scotch didn't help much either.

Late one afternoon just before gate closing time, we were driving slowly along the mostly-dry Shingwedzi River when, about two kilometres before camp, we spotted a majestic set of buffalo horns lying undisturbed in the riverbed. Casting a long shadow across the sand, the horns looked gigantic, and I remarked to my brother how nice they would look mounted and displayed on a wall. A stern glance and a few sharp words from my mother made it clear that my only half-joking suggestion to quickly hop out of the old Volkswagen Passat and scramble down to the riverbed to retrieve them was, under no circumstances, going to be entertained.

Much later that night back at camp, with a couple of 'Scotland's finest' beneath the belt and our mother long since retired to her bed, fireside conversation turned to those remarkable buffalo horns lying just a few kilometres from where we sat. With the stupidity of adolescence that passes for bravery, we determined that we were indomitable enough to face any animal outside the camp and that those horns *must* be retrieved.

Ensuring our mother was sound asleep, and armed only with a pocket knife, a *knobkierie* and the light of the moon, we set off on a mission so very foolish, it still makes me shudder to think of it now.

It had gone midnight as we walked along the camp's perimeter looking for the best place to hop the fence. We decided that the section next to the swimming pool looked most promising. But knowing the trouble we'd get into if caught, we first wandered nonchalantly over to the main camp gate to see if anybody was moving around there. It was all quiet; the break-out could proceed.

Back at the swimming pool, we stood in silence just to make sure nobody was watching us and that no hungry hyaena – or something worse – was waiting for us on the other side. Then, as quietly as we could, we scaled the fence (which was not electrified in those days) and walked through the bush for about 100 paces, stopping every now and then to listen for any signs of detection by the Park authorities.

With no obvious indications that we'd been spotted absconding, we marched on quietly through the bush and, again, waited for a couple of minutes before breaking cover and walking along the main gravel road.

By then it was almost pitch black, and doubts about whether it was in fact terribly wise to walk unarmed through the African bush at night began to set in. The bravado gifted to us by the whisky had started to fade, and the sobering realisation that we were in Big Five country began to make our rudimentary choice of weaponry feel more like a butter knife and a dowel stick. But we were on a mission and we had resolved to retrieve those horns no matter what, so we pressed on.

Just as we broke our way through the thick bush from the road down to the river bed, we froze as the sliver of moon revealed a flash of fur and a frenzied rustling in the bushes right next us. We had startled a scrub hare, which fled the scene in a panic. Ironically, despite its frenetic leaps off into the darkness, I can confidently say that it was not as frightened as we were.

As we approached the horns, we imagined that the very moment we reached them, every available spotlight in the Kruger National Park would be focused on us; an arrest would follow and we would be carted off to Skukuza's holding cells where a trial, and perhaps capital sentence, would await us.

We sat beside the horns for a couple of minutes, listening for any signs of the authorities, but nothing disturbed the gentle night sounds of the bush.

With spirits high, we marched back along roughly the same route, taking it in turns to lug the giant trophy back to the safety of Shingwedzi. But, as we approached the fence, we were in for a surprise: illuminated by the few lights still left on in the camp was the clear silhouette of a lone hyaena, all ruffled fur and gnarly teeth, patrolling the fence. It was standing exactly where we had hoped to climb back over into the camp. But we were trophy hunters now and felt invincible; we had survived a four-kilometre trek through Africa's wildest terrain, and a scavenger at the finish post was not going to stop us. I picked up a thick stick and threw it at the hyaena, which turned and sloped off into the bush.

It proved to be a quite a task getting those big horns over the fence, but with a bit of huff-and-puff and a little teamwork, we eventually hauled them over. Using shadows as cover, we smuggled the prize back to our hut.

The following morning, having discovered the contraband, my mother was extremely upset and wanted us to leave the horns behind. But I was adamant that they were going back to the Free State with us. Those horns took up almost all the space in the boot, and there was only room left for a couple of loose items. The result was that I had to carry most of the luggage on my lap through the rest of the trip and all the way back home, which I suppose amounted to a punishment of sorts.

Some 20-odd years later, the horns are now mounted and displayed on a wall in my office and look as magnificent as I had suggested they would when we first drove past them.

There is an interesting footnote to this story. Many years later I used the horns as a prop for a Round Table melodrama where I played the part of Adam, in a number called *Tarzadam*, and used the horns as a seat. A member of the audience was a taxidermist, and as soon as the curtains closed, he rushed up to me excitedly and told me whatever I do I *must* bring the horns to him the following Monday so that he could measure them – which I duly did. A few days later he confirmed some astonishing news. The horns were so big, he said, that they qualify for *Rowland Ward's Records of Big Game* – a kind of *Guinness Book of Records* for hunters, and the universally accepted source for establishing what constitutes a record-sized trophy animal.

98

BEETLE EXPRESS
Julius Kunzmann

I WAS EIGHT YEARS OLD when I first visited the Kruger National Park with my grandparents and my great-uncle Bee. Since then, I have been back to the Park countless times, but the memories of that first trip still remain so vivid in my mind: the slow pace everyone drove on the dirt roads, the communal *braais* with red hot coals regularly topped up by the shovel-load from a central fire, the thick smell of the thatch inside the rondavels, and above all, the bizarre incident of the conjoined cars and the rapidly reversing vw Beetle.

My grandfather drove a Studebaker Lark, and Uncle Bee had a gloriously rangy Ford Galaxie 500. Both cars had big v8 engines, but as the roads in those days were un-tarred through most of the Park, particularly in the north, everybody drove slowly so as not to kick up dust.

On the first day we drove the northern loop from Punda Milia (as the camp was called back then; it was only later changed to Punda Maria) up to Crooks Corner. On the second morning, we left for Shingwedzi rest camp further south, where we would spend the next night. The area around Punda Milia was known for its big herds of elephants, and being a sub-tropical region the vegetation can be very dense; many a tourist has been startled by an elephant appearing suddenly out of the bush, as if from nowhere.

Uncle Bee was driving in front of us. Through his open window, he pointed to the left where some elephants were standing in a clearing about 50 metres ahead of us. With everybody's attention on the elephants to the left, my grandfather did not see the elephant that stepped out of the bush on the right, just metres from the front of Uncle Bee's Ford Galaxie. Uncle Bee hit the brakes and came to a halt. But for my grandfather it was too late; despite braking hard, his heavy Studebaker Lark slid along the dirt road and, with a nasty crunch, bumped straight into the back of the Galaxie.

As I said, people drove slowly in those days. Yet while this all happened at little more than a walking pace, the outcome was bizarre. The Studebaker was always distinguishable by the two vertical bump stoppers on its chrome front bumper, and in the collision one of these had slid under the massive rear bumper of the Galaxie, effectively locking the two cars together.

The two men got out to inspect the damage, while the women and child had to stay in the car. The damage report delivered by my grandfather to us was that, apart from a rubber smear on the Galaxy's bumper, there was no damage – except, of course, for the rather complicated issue of the two cars now being locked together.

My grandfather and Uncle Bee tried standing and then jumping on the Lark's bumper to dislodge it, but to no avail. Next, the women were asked to sit on the Lark's bonnet while the men again jumped on the bumper. The added weight of the women brought some positive results, but it was still not enough to separate them. The cars remained tightly intertwined.

This being sweaty work, and on a hot day in December, it was decided that a rest break was in order, and indeed if we waited long enough, someone else might even turn up to lend a helping hand. So we got some food and drinks out of the well-stocked picnic baskets and sat relaxing in the cars.

Silence settled over the bush. And it was then that we heard an approaching engine roaring furiously from beyond the bend in the road. The rear end of a blue Volkswagen Beetle appeared and screamed towards us as fast as its reverse gear would allow, its driver hooting like a madman. It narrowly missed us and disappeared backwards up the road in a cloud of dust.

Before the dust settled, we could make out the rough shapes of the elephants that were chasing it – and which were now rapidly closing the distance between us. Sandwiches and coffee went flying in all directions; luckily, the coffee missed me but I distinctly recall that one of the sandwiches didn't. Both cars were started, and a confused mêlée developed where we didn't know whether the Galaxie pushed or the Lark pulled, but joined at the bumpers we reversed out of there *post-haste*.

A short time later and a long way up the road, the two cars became separated when we hit a furrow in the road and normality returned at last. After an excited inquest, we drove straight to Shingwedzi (although slowly and very carefully past the spot where the elephants had given up the chase and broken off into the bush) to have the car cleaned of the remains of our hastily abandoned picnic.

I will never forget the sight of hundreds of electric blue-black starlings glittering in the sun as we drove into Shingwedzi camp. We never found out what happened to the Beetle, nor did we see him again – but two V8's at full throttle could not catch him in reverse!

99

BLACK MAMBA AND THE CROCODILES
Kerstin Stöwahse

I STILL DREAM ABOUT THAT BLACK MAMBA. It haunts me in my sleep – I find myself egging it on, willing it to escape the furrow on the riverbank before the crocodile reaches it. I want there to be a different ending, because I saw how it really ended and the savagery of it still numbs me. No matter what you may think of snakes, no creature – not least one as beautiful and brave as this – should have to die like that.

It was a sighting like nothing else I have ever seen – and, it turns out, nothing anybody else has ever seen either. But like most great sightings in Kruger, it was down to blind luck: a simple matter of being in exactly the right place at precisely the right time.

The landscapes and rivers in Kruger's north fascinate me and draw me back every time I visit South Africa. So, on a trip in May 2012 with a friend, we stationed ourselves at the red-soiled Shingwedzi rest camp, up in the sub-tropical reaches of the Park, far away from the bustle of the southern rest camps.

Our first morning we slept right through the sunrise. Normally, we'd have been up and out of the gates as soon as they opened, but that day the sun was already very high when we finally got into the car. We drove out of the camp through the small east gate and meandered along the loops that lead towards the Kanniedood hide along the banks of the Shingwedzi River.

In the car it was boiling hot, and in the bush most animals were hiding in the shadows. We were just about to write off the morning for game viewing when we decided to take one last loop and stopped at the river bank. The river was almost dry. The few ponds and puddles on the riverbed looked to be getting smaller by the day as winter approached. There was still one relatively large body of slow-moving water directly in front of us, though, and it was besieged by a number of enormous crocodiles. They lay motionless on the mud and in the shallows of the far bank. I wondered how so many large crocodiles survive when the river dries up. Even at the very start of winter, the available water seemed too sparse to support them all.

Just then, my friend pointed at the water and chimed, 'Look at the crocodile there!' In front of me, about halfway across the water, a crocodile rose ominously from the depths and glided along the surface. My friend lifted his camera and began filming. He didn't know it, but he was about to capture something that would go on to astound even veteran wildlife experts – some of whom would venture to say that this may well be the most extraordinary footage ever captured on camera in Kruger.

Just at that moment, I noticed movement on the near bank. It took a few seconds before I realised what it was and blurted out, 'The snake! The snake!' Slithering across the mud straight towards the water was an enormous grey snake, three-and-a-half metres long at least, and easily as thick as my wrist. Its length, along with its coffin-shaped head and its pale olive-grey colour with distinct white belly, pointed to it being a black mamba – Africa's most feared and most aggressive snake.

Before the snake even reached the water's edge, the croc had clocked it and began drifting straight towards it. I didn't believe that the crocodile would actually attack it. But as the snake entered the pool, the cumbersome crocodile gathered pace and splashed through the water. For the final few metres, it broke all speed records and shot like an arrow towards the mamba. Quite how my friend held the camera still I do not know, but I could feel the adrenaline surging through my body as I watched this all unfold.

As the crocodile torpedoed forward through the shallows, the snake took swift evasive action and cut sideways along the waterline, lifting the front third of its body clean off the ground, and slithering along in a series of nimble hops to dodge the advancing missile. Its movements were like a wild dance, and they worked; the crocodile thrashed around and snapped confusedly at its own muddy splashes and ripples rather than at the body of the snake. In its frenzy to snatch it, the crocodile found itself facing the wrong way and the mamba slithered off in the opposite direction.

But rather than cut its losses and abandon its quest to cross the river, the mamba headed straight back in and began furiously sailing across the surface of the water towards the far bank. For a creature without legs or paddles, the speed with which it swam was remarkable. However, it was still no match for the speed of the crocodile, which had flipped itself around and was again steaming through the water towards the mamba. It opened its mouth and, with a flick of its head, grabbed the back of the snake. Despite our elevated position, the waves thrown up by the advancement of the crocodile obscured what happened next.

Had the crocodile caught the mamba? After its desperate dance on the banks a few seconds earlier, I was fiercely hoping that the snake could perform the same feat again – despite the advantage being clearly in favour of its aquatic opponent. The splashing and thrashing continued all the way across to the far side of the water where, incredibly, the snake eventually emerged onto the bank. Exhausted, the crocodile sank back into the shallows, a gush of water pouring from its mouth. It had missed the mamba. But the snake was not unscathed – a small section of its tail had been lost in the fight. It slithered from the water a fraction shorter than when it had gone in.

The lightning attack had seen the crocodile expend a huge amount of energy with nothing to show for it. I felt sorry about that, because even for crocodiles the struggle for survival is tough. Nevertheless, I was thrilled for the tenacious black mamba. With its elegant, dance-like movements, it had twice escaped the jaws of a crocodile in the croc's own habitat. It was indeed a marvel of nature.

Unfortunately, the far shoreline where the snake emerged was very muddy and was gouged with deep grooves and gullies where larger animals had come down to drink. Its flight had robbed it of much strength, and now, without a portion of its tail to help propel it forward, it battled to push itself through a muddy furrow.

The mamba's laboured efforts had not gone unnoticed. Another large crocodile, lying on the bank some distance away, had been watching quietly from afar and suddenly rose from its belly in slow motion. Its feet sank into the mud as it took a few slow steps forward. Then, like its motor had suddenly started, it began scuttling towards the mamba, accelerating with each step. About fifteen metres from the snake, it stopped and crouched again. Having seen how fast the snake had moved on the near bank earlier, I was confident that it still had enough time to extricate itself from the quagmire and cover the stretch of dry riverbed between the water and the bush before the croc reached it. But instead of slithering away, its writhing became more lethargic and it didn't move from the furrow. Why was it not trying to escape?

The crocodile set itself in motion again, starting slowly at first, getting faster and faster until its short legs became blurs, and its tail swung wildly from one side to the other as it rocketed forward. It was all too late now for the mamba.

The crocodile bit down and caught the snake just above its midsection. The snake recoiled violently, but the croc's grip was firm and it gave the mamba a good couple of shakes. Then, exploding into a frenzy, the crocodile began shaking it with such brutal ferocity it is painful to describe. The crocodile had pushed its entire body up off the mud, and with its thick tail flicking violently back and forth as a counterweight, it shook the snake like a pitbull tearing into a rabbit. Back and forth the crocodile swung its head, so fast it was just a blur and the mamba's limp body whipped around like a loose fire hose. The snake had danced its last dance. Nothing on earth could have survived more than a few seconds of such staggering violence.

Despite the ferocity of the shaking, what happened next still seems unbelievable: the crocodile shook the snake so violently that the snake's head and a short section of its neck detached cleanly from its body and flew through the air, landing on the dry mud three or four metres to its left. Remarkably, it had not broken apart at the point where the crocodile's jaws were crushing down on its midsection – it detached some distance up the length of the body, singularly through the force and velocity of the thrashing. We simply could not believe our eyes.

This being Kruger, little goes unnoticed and nothing goes to waste. A shadow hovered over the crocodile, and a large fish eagle swooped down and landed about a metre to the left of the severed head. Curious, the eagle eyed the snake's head, but with the crocodile just a few metres away, it didn't dare make a grab for it. Meanwhile, the crocodile was eyeing the bird cautiously; it wasn't about to lose its lunch to a scavenging eagle. For a few moments there was a paused standoff, and it was unclear just which animal was more worried about the other.

Taking no chances, the crocodile heaved itself up and, with the snake in its mouth, turned around and trudged down towards the water. With the thick body of the snake dragging beneath its front legs, and its feet sinking into the mud, it stumbled clumsily a few times on the way.

The fish eagle's eyes remained locked on the crocodile. As soon as it saw the croc enter the water, it pounced onto the snake head. But the eagle wasn't the only one with its eyes on a prize. The first crocodile that had earlier tried its luck on the mamba in the water had slithered onto the bank behind the eagle and began edging forward. Catching sight of this, the fish eagle spread its wings and took off with the snake's head in its claws.

And with that, it was all over. In just three minutes, a dead morning's game drive had ballooned into the sighting of our lives. We had been the only car to see this all happen, and it was only when we returned to camp and I registered the wonder on the faces of our bush-hardened neighbours when we played them the footage that I started to get an inkling of the rarity of this incident. An old man who had visited the Park regularly for more than 30 years was so taken aback by the footage that he seemed quite overwhelmed. Over time, I shared the sighting with employees of the Kruger National Park, with hunters and with conservationists who have spent many years in the bush, and each time their faces reflected the same look of fascinated amazement. To a person, not a single one of them had ever seen nor heard of a crocodile killing and eating a black mamba – never mind anyone having caught it all on film, too.

100

TEENAGE RUNAWAYS TREK THROUGH THE PARK
Keith Griffiths

IN THE LATE AUGUST OF 1965, the nation was gripped by the story of two matric schoolboys missing for weeks in the Kruger National Park. Those two boys happened to be my classmates at boarding school in Pietersburg – now Polokwane – and their story is so remarkable it is still worth retelling all these years later.

Their names were Terence and Johan, and their escapade began with the looming onset of our mock exams, which is always a high-pressure time in the life of any matriculant. Neither of them felt that they had done enough studying to pass, so in the time-honoured tradition of boys that age who know little and fear even less, they hatched a plan to skip the country and find a job in neighbouring Rhodesia, as it was called then. Johan, who hailed from the town of Phalaborwa, suggested that they could leave from his home, on the next 'out weekend' from boarding school.

Arriving in Phalaborwa on a Friday afternoon, they began secretly packing for their adventure, being careful not to alert Johan's family of their plans. The following morning they visited the general dealer in Phalaborwa and stocked up on provisions for their journey. They'd need to carry all the food and drink for the entire journey, as the route they would be taking to Rhodesia didn't include any shops: Terence and Johan were planning to steal straight up through the 'game reserve', as Kruger was generally called then, and wade across the Limpopo River into Rhodesia. It was a monumentally foolhardy plan. Johan, living in close proximity to Kruger, knew which direction to head and believed he had a good feel for the 180 kilometres of lion and elephant country that they would need to cross.

Only when Johan's mother had summoned the family to Sunday lunch was it realised that something was amiss. Terence and Johan, with their bundles of food and clothing, had tiptoed out of the house in the early hours of the morning and headed east through the town, which lies just a kilometre from the edge of the Park. They entered the game reserve by crawling through a hole in the game fence, and then set off through the thick mopane *veld* in the direction of Crooks' Corner, way up in Kruger's far north-eastern corner.

That evening, back at school, we were very surprised by a rare appearance of our headmaster at supper. He informed us about the boys' disappearance and asked if any one of us could shed any light on their whereabouts. One of the boys who shared their dormitory raised his hand and explained that he had overheard Terence and Johan planning to run away, and he thought that they may be heading for Rhodesia by the way of the game reserve. For a few moments the dining hall fell into a hushed silence at this revelation. Then, as if on cue, the hall erupted with guffaws of laughter from all the boys, who fell about themselves at the thought of Terence and Johan bushwhacking through the Park on foot. Quieting us, the headmaster then announced that if anyone else was planning on running away, they should have the courtesy to inform him and he would gladly facilitate their departure.

Johan's father, on receiving the information from the school, contacted the Park authorities for assistance locating the missing boys. They were only too willing to oblige, and soon every ranger in the northern section of Kruger was on the lookout for our classmates. Tourists entering the Park were also asked to keep their eyes open for them. It wasn't too long before the media got to hear about the missing lads, much to our headmaster's displeasure. At school, we were all agog at our friends' daring escapade, and this being back in the days when corporal punishment was dished out with unbridled enthusiasm, we knew that if found alive, Terence and Johan would find it rather uncomfortable being back behind their school desks.

The exposé by a big Sunday newspaper a week later was to grip the nation's attention. There had not been any sighting of the missing schoolboys, and the air force had deployed a plane to assist with the search. The border authorities were also on high alert, but after almost a fortnight there was still no trace of them and we were beginning to expect the worst. You certainly wouldn't have bet on anyone surviving for that long, on foot, with no firearm, in the middle of the Kruger National Park.

Miraculously, though, news broke several days later that Johan's father, with the aid of an experienced tracker, had found the boys just a few kilometres short of their target, at the Thulamela archaeological site, right up in the far north of the Park, not far from the Pafuri picnic spot.

Looking somewhat worse for wear, they returned to school the following Monday to face the music. After a severe dressing down by the principal, the chastened matriculants returned to their classroom.

When the dust had settled, Terence explained to me that it had not been as easy as they thought it would be to walk such a huge distance through the Park. They had had a problem finding clean water for much of their trek, and by the time they were eventually discovered, they had almost depleted their food supply. The worst part of it all was coping with very little sleep, he said, as they had spent the nights sheltering in trees to escape the attention of predators.

Terence and Johan endured much ribbing from their peer group for the remainder of their matric year, but happily for them their fears of poor study preparation proved unfounded – they both passed their matric exams without a hitch.

101

THE RAREST KRUGER PREDATOR
Ron van Rooyen

I HAVE TOLD THIS STORY countless times since it happened back in the eighties, but with no photographs to prove it, I am met almost universally with snorts of incredulity. It is true, though, down to the last word – and as unlikely as it may seem, it really did happen.

It was a hot February in 1985 and I was camping with a girlfriend at Punda Maria up in the north of the Park. One day we decided to drive up to Crook's Corner on Kruger's north-eastern boundary where the Luvuvhu River meets the Limpopo, and where the corners of Zimbabwe, Mozambique and South Africa all converge in a single point.

The gravel road between the Pafuri picnic spot and Crook's Corner follows the course of the Luvuvhu and is punctuated with various spots where you can pull up under a shady tree and watch the river flow by, or, if you're lucky, maybe catch a glimpse of a nyala coming down to drink. It was at one of these spots, just as the sun was reaching its peak that afternoon, where it all happened.

With an excellent view of the river and in the shade of some big trees, we sat chatting in my car, periodically scanning the riverbank with binoculars for any sign of animals.

We had been there about 20 minutes when my girlfriend suddenly gasped. Unable to find any words, she shook my arm frantically and gesticulated with her other arm towards the far bank of the river.

I quickly began focussing my binoculars in that direction and as the blurry image sharpened, my jaw slackened. There was surely no way it could be – not in the landlocked Kruger National Park? We were 400 kilometres upriver from the Indian Ocean, for goodness' sake.

My girlfriend had seen a splashing and thrashing about on the surface of the water, about two metres from the far bank. With my binoculars trained on the spot, I could see exactly what it was. The hairs on my arms stood rigid. A large river eel was coiling and uncoiling desperately, its belly glistening in the sun. But clamped around its midsection were the jaws of Kruger's most unlikely predator: a shark!

The shark – which I now understand would have been a Zambezi shark – had attacked and bitten into the eel, which was whipping about trying to flee. Not many things escape the jaws of a shark, not even a great big slippery eel, and with a thrash and a lunge the shark bit completely through it. From where we were positioned, we could clearly see the shark's dorsal fin and the unmistakable shape of the its body, as it chomped away on its catch.

Then, as fast as it had appeared, the shark slid out of sight and disappeared into the depths of the Luvuvhu. We were stupefied; who on earth was going to believe that we'd just seen a shark attack in the middle of Kruger? We could barely believe it ourselves. Decades later I am still lamenting the fact that I didn't take any photographs – at the very least so that I could have something to show the sceptics – but the whole thing had happened so quickly, and was all so astonishing, that I'd been glued to my binoculars and hadn't even thought of the camera.

Despite my doubters – and there is no shortage of those – I feel vindicated by my recent discovery that Kruger's history books reveal this story is not as far-fetched as it may seem. In the 1950s, an official stationed at Pafuri actually hooked and landed a Zambezi shark while fishing at Crook's Corner – barely a stone's throw from where we had been sitting. His catch officially weighed 21.8 kilograms and measured 1.47 metres. Wisely, he kept the skull of the shark as proof. I imagine from time to time he would unveil it triumphantly in front of any doubting Thomases – but, heartbreakingly for him, the hard evidence was later stolen by a hyaena and never seen again.

AND THE ONES THAT DIDN'T QUITE MAKE IT

DURING THE PROCESS of collating this book, I received countless wonderful stories and anecdotes that really stood out but, unfortunately, couldn't all be included in the final line-up. Many of these unused stories were so captivating, however, it would be a pity not to share a digested version of just a few of them.

Dana Atkinson discovered why it's never a good idea to smile at a monkey, when she ended up being attacked by one in Letaba. Only through the actions of a brave ranger sitting nearby, who sacrificed his lunch and got between her and the monkey, was she saved from any serious injury. To this day, she still harbours a fear of primates.

Ajay Bhowandas shared a bit of toilet humour as he described how his 'bathroom break' on the Olifants River Backpack Trail was rudely disturbed by a panicked waterbuck that crashed through the bush and leapt right over him, forcing him to abandon his activity and scuttle trousers-down back to the group.

Gavin Black was worried that a plastic wheel rim that he had spotted resting against a cluster of rocks on the Rabelais Road near Orpen could cause a curious animal an injury, so urged his wife to quickly hop out of the car and retrieve it. Not 15 minutes later they drove back past the spot and, to their horror, a lioness lay spread out on those very rocks, while three other lionesses lingered in the background. His wife was not best impressed.

Craig Blend watched for an hour as a young leopard just south of Lower Sabie tried to get the better of a porcupine – and lost.

Derek Boshard showed how rich Kruger can be for cat sightings. He first spotted a leopard in a marula tree not far from Afsaal picnic spot. Then, just a few hundred metres down the road, he came across a lion and lioness in the grass. Turning his head, a cheetah strolled along in the distance on the other side of the road. A few kilometres down the road he added to the tally by spotting one of Kruger's least-often seen cats: a caracal. In total, four species of cat in the space of

10 kilometres. No stranger to lucky sightings, on another occasion he saw three Cape clawless otters in a standoff with a male lion on the banks of the N'wanetsi River. The otters won, and the lion eventually retreated and went to find a more peaceful spot along the river to have a drink.

Richard Browne was in Satara when he discovered a large puffadder up against the cooler box in his tent. A brave ranger caught the snake with his bare hands before driving one-handed out of the camp to release it back into the bush. Unfortunately, it later transpired that the ranger had been bitten by the snake and had to be rushed to hospital in Phalaborwa. He survived the ordeal and was back at work within a week.

Sharon Bothma was in Mopani rest camp when she discovered a large female leopard had found its way into the camp and was hiding out in the thick bush just beyond her family's bungalow. The story has a happy ending: the leopard was successfully chased out of the camp, unharmed, by a skilled helicopter pilot, who later described it as one of the largest and most beautiful specimens he had ever seen.

Fred de Groot recounted the horrific tale of how his young daughter was bitten on the foot by a night adder as they walked along a pathway in Pretoriouskop early one evening. After rushing her to hospital in a town outside the Park, they were greeted by a nursing strike and had to perform all nursing duties themselves. There was a happy ending, though, as she was discharged the next day and they were able to continue their Kruger holiday.

George & Nan de Jager were witness to a remarkable event at a very dry Gudzani Dam. A leopard appeared below the weir with a buck in its mouth, but before long two crocodiles emerged at speed from the pool below and executed a brazen snatch-and-grab. The leopard fought valiantly, but the crocs eventually managed to wrestle the prey from its jaws. The thieves even had the tenacity to eat the spoils on dry land – only later dragging the carcass into the water – while the poor leopard watched forlornly.

Ken & Pearl English had a most extraordinary encounter near Balule 25 years ago that left them wondering whether they were the unsuspecting foils in a Leon Schuster movie. They were flagged down by a group of exhausted-looking men wandering along a dirt road, who politely asked in Afrikaans whether there was any work available. On being told they were in the middle of a game reserve, the men chatted amongst themselves then tutted and walked off most upset.

Keith Griffiths and his family were watching a troop of baboons on the side of the road not far from Skukuza when an hysterical bleating caught their attention; one of the baboons had caught a young steenbok by the leg. They watched in horror as the baboon drew the steenbok to its mouth and began eating it alive, while its bleating mother looked on helplessly.

Linda Groenewald got the surprise of her life when she stepped out of car near Berg-en-Dal to relieve herself in the long grass. She'd barely dropped her trousers when a rustling in the bushes, some loud trumpeting and the alarmed cries of her daughters alerted her to the enraged elephant charging her.

Doreen Hansen and her family had a close shave with a rather menacing leopard near Punda Maria when their passenger-side window would not close because the engine was switched off. Frantically turning the key, they only managed to close window just as the leopard's head drew level with it.

Ingrid Harrison watched a pride of lions swarm and kill a wildebeest that had slipped over in the Gudzani waterhole near Satara. After three-and-a-half hours of feasting, an outraged young bull elephant stormed in and sent the lions scattering.

Matt Hayward was finding it hard to keep his young daughter amused on an uneventful drive from Punda Maria to Pafuri when suddenly, cresting a rise, he was gifted with the rare and remarkable sight of a pack of wild dogs chasing down, killing and devouring an impala ram right in front of the car. As the action ended, he looked across to his daughter, only to find she had missed much of it – she had fallen asleep!

Candace King played a role in saving the life of a young rhino that appeared to be caught in a snare not far from the Timbavati picnic spot. Ignoring a lion sighting that was causing a traffic jam en route, she hurried on to Satara where she alerted the section ranger. She later discovered that the poor rhino had not been snared but had rather got its leg caught between the branches of a tree. Park staff freed the rhino by cutting down the tree. They reported, with a smile, that the little guy was so flustered that it launched a mini-attack on its rescuers as soon as its leg was free.

Marie Knock and her husband found themselves caught in the middle of a terrifying 10-minute long buffalo stampede that thundered around their tiny red hire-car on a gravel road somewhere between Olifants and Satara.

Michael Koch thought the leopard he had just seen near Letaba was gone, when it suddenly burst out of the bush and snatched a guinea fowl in mid-air right alongside his car.

Trevor Lagerwall shared a wonderful leopard-spotting anecdote that happened in the shade of a river view-point near Olifants. His son had asked his friend, sitting alongside them in another car, whether he had ever seen a leopard before. His friend replied through the open window that when he was young, his parents took him to Kruger and they spotted a leopard 'about the distance away from where that fish eagle is over there. It then walked towards us, then crossed over the road,' he continued, tracing its path with a pointed finger, 'and sat down next to the car, about where that leopard is over th… bloody hell!' he shouted, 'There's a leopard!' Lo and behold, sitting next to his car was a leopard.

Henk Maree came close to being trampled by a charging elephant on foot as he stared down the viewfinder of his camera, trying to capture a one-in-a-million photo. It was only when he lowered the camera that he realised it was just him and the shouting ranger still standing there – his Nyalaland Trail companions had all scattered behind some mopani saplings 10 metres away. Did he get the special photo? Unfortunately not – he was shaking too much.

Richard McKibbin recounts what must amount to one of the most successful night drives ever undertaken in the Park. The sightings encountered on the drive, which set out from Letaba, read like a tick-list from a month's worth of National Geographic programming: a 100-strong elephant herd, a 500-strong buffalo herd, a lion attack on a young buffalo, a white lion cub, a spitting cobra with its hood raised and a den of bat-eared foxes.

Jacolene Meyer struck a cautionary note in the tale of how her friend – as blind as a bat without her contact lenses in – almost trod on a big puffadder on the concrete floor of the communal ablutions at Lower Sabie while they were brushing their teeth one hot evening.

Bradley Muir had just called his daughters to come and see a baby squirrel that was scurrying about under their chairs as they sat around their *braai* at Mopani, when a spotted genet emerged from nowhere and snatched the squirrel, then devoured it just a few metres from where they sat.

Sloane Munro shared his remarkable account of how a suddenly-startled impala ran straight for his family's car and launched itself clean over the roof. Incredibly, they we weren't in any ordinary low-slung sedan; their car was a big Chevrolet Captiva SUV which stood over 1.7 metres high and was almost a full two metres wide. The impala cleared it with ease – and with barely any run up at all.

Deborah Myburg recounted the tale of how she evacuated the passenger seat of her car and bundled into the back with some alacrity – incredibly not spilling a drop from the glass of wine she had in her hand – as a baboon hopped through the window and helped itself to some of the *padkos* at her feet. Amusingly, the baboon shunned all the junk food and opted instead for a healthy crispbread snack.

Christa Niederer was on a walking trail in the Park when her group came across the sickening sight of slaughtered white rhino with a gaping hole where its horn once was, lying alongside its dead calf. As they inspected the corpse, her guides spotted another rhino – very much alive – and as they all scattered to hide behind bushes, Christa tripped and fell to the ground just as the rhino thundered narrowly past her.

Grant Pearson was sceptical when his cousin and her friend frantically announced that they had just seen a leopard wander right past their Letaba bungalow as they smoked cigarettes on the veranda one night. Despite alerting the camp officials, no obvious trace of the leopard could be found. However, some months later he spotted a news snippet in a travel magazine reporting that a leopard had been shot in Letaba camp. Some quick calendar cross-referencing connected the date in the magazine story with the date they'd been there. The girls had almost certainly been correct – a leopard had slunk right past them through the camp.

Sharmla Pillay was driving with her husband near Punda Maria following some heavy rains when they came across a distressed and traumatised elderly couple who had become stranded in mud the previous day and had been forced to spend the night in their car.

Hungry and thirsty, the couple were given provisions by the Pillays, before a rescue was hastily arranged.

Belinda Pitt tells a white-knuckle tale of how her husband, in the quest for a good photograph, subjected her and her son to a terrifyingly close encounter with a bull elephant in musth near Duke waterhole. They survived the ordeal – just – only to discover a short while later that the hair-raising encounter had been in vain: her husband had forgotten to put any film in the camera.

Louw Pretorius submitted a wealth of amusing tales, including how he and a bunch of others all watched with amusement as a troop of baboons on the road between Skukuza and Lower Sabie devoured a big bunch of bananas from the roofrack of one poor couple before leaving them a 'thank you present'. He also told of the time he rescued some foolish German tourists who had walked right up to an elephant that was browsing alongside Tshokwane picnic spot. Not a few hours later he stumbled upon the hapless party again – this time stranded on the road to Satara with a flat tyre. And no wheel spanner!

Sharmeli Ramchander demonstrated sheer beginner's luck when she spotted the Big Five – leopard, lion, elephant, rhino and buffalo – within the first three hours of her very first visit to the Park. Incredibly, the first of the five to be ticked was a leopard stalking a wildebeest immediately as they entered the gate. This was followed by a pride of lions feasting on a kill just around the very next bend. Further down the road, another lion dragged the remains of a giraffe carcass through the bush. The elephants they spotted a short while later were a herd of 30, stampeding through the bush. The rhino sighting included a display of territory-marking right next to the road. Only the buffalo sighting was ordinary – they just lay in the grass and stared back lazily.

Jessica Renssen, just 10 years old when she submitted her story, recounts how she watched two clever lionesses ambush a herd of impala, then how one of those impala became dinner, while another ended up with a broken ankle (and a terrible concussion) after it slipped, skidded and smashed head-first into a parked car.

Beth Restrick was 12 years old when she and her sister were alarmed one night by a low, growling sound from the bushes near the ablutions at the camping area in Skukuza. Early the following morning she passed the bushes and heard the same growling and so tip-toed around the bushes – only to discover a snoring man in a small one-man tent. Amusingly, the rest of his party were pitched in a tent on the other side of their car, as far away as they could possibly get from the snorer.

Trevor Riddin perhaps set a Kruger record when, squinting into the sun, he came across a leopard in a tree just north of Tshokwane picnic spot. Stopping to view it, someone in the car whispered, 'There's another one!' And then, 'And another one!' And again, 'One more!' Four leopards in total, all in the same tree – with an impala kill in the lower fork.

Sharon Smith was on a rainy game drive in an open safari vehicle in the far north of the Park when an angry elephant charged the vehicle, pushed it a short distance from behind and then lifted its rear wheels right off the ground, as the driver struggled to start to the engine. She is still afraid of elephants to this day – but the German tourists in the group seemed to quite enjoy the experience.

Tony van der Helm recounted the uproarious night-time tale of how, torch in hand, he got such a fright after unexpectedly illuminating an elephant browsing right up against the fence at Balule that he hurtled – *smack-bang!* – into the wall of a rondavel (smashing his spectacles) as he tried to flee.

Ronel van Rooy tells the wonderful story of how a baboon found itself with its hand stuck in a big bag of oranges on the back of her father's *bakkie*. Too stubborn to let go of the fruit in its fist, the baboon was trapped. But, not to be outdone, it simply picked up the whole bag, tucked it under its other arm, leapt from the *bakkie* and disappeared into the bush – with its hand still firmly clasping the orange inside the bag!

Ruth Van Zyl got a surprise in her safari tent at Lower Sabie when she discovered a cute little *nagapie* (bushbaby) running along a section of rope in the bathroom. Rushing out to call her husband to come and see, they returned to discover the *nagapie* gone – and in its place, a deadly boomslang.

Amanda Wheeler shared a most peculiar incident that occurred after they took a wrong turning down a narrow disused track near Mopani. A braying zebra – a striped guardian angel of sorts – rushed past them before skidding to a halt in front of the car, braying some more and rearing up on its hind legs. They followed it for some time as it seemed to beckon them along the track. Eventually, when the road widened and they were able to turn around, it disappeared into the bush. Further back down the road, it reappeared and performed the same routine. Eventually, as they approached the junction where they'd taken the wrong turn, a blur of black and white flashed past, screeched to a halt, curled its lips in a smile, brayed one last time as if to bid them farewell, and headed off into the bush.

Jerry White shared a thrilling but tragic tale of the night a leopard was discovered lying in the grass just beyond one of the huts inside the Wolhuter Trail bush camp. The trailists were instructed to return to their huts and remain there while the rangers patiently set a trap and eventually lured the leopard into a cage. It was then darted by a vet and safely driven away to Skukuza for examination. Sadly, the battle-scarred leopard, which was estimated to be about 13 years old, was found to be diseased – which probably explained its unusual and unnatural behaviour – and had to be put down.

While there is no room in this book for every great story received, mention should also go to the following people whose Kruger tales and anecdotes stood out:

Dave Allan, Gillian Armstrong, Asma Bava, Erica-Ann Becker, Sanet Bezuidenhout, Ben Botha, Samantha Bradley, Gail Brierley, Claire Cahill, Sue Caithness, Daniel Carter, Justin Cohen, Mavis Crundwell, Ryan Davis, Mary de Jager, Jean de Villiers, Fanie Du Plessis, Pixie Emslie, Sara Essop, Eugene & Lesna, Freddie Fox, Yvette Guerra, Joss Haddeman, Morne Hamlyn, Wendy Harbottle, Sheila Harris, Buks Henning, Lawrence Hughes, Peter Hunt, Ryan James, Cheryl Jennings, Mohammed Jinnah, Gareth Jones, Aadila Kadwa, Birgit Kaiser, Lenny Koboyankwe, Kurt Krause, Ronald Krieger, Rayne Layfield, Glenda Lewis, Carla Lyle, Hanlie Marais, Nafisa Moolla, Muriel Moreau, Joy Morrison, Albie Morkel, Lyn Morty, Di Muller, Johannes Nel, Penny & Rory Nel, Grant Nicol, Kimberley O'Sullivan, Robin Owen-Morley, Dimitri Paizis, Michael Peirce, Ilona Petzer, Andy Raouna, Audrey Raubenheimer, Marcelle Robbins, Rika Roos, Shelley Seiderer, Robert Shepardson, Susan Skirving, Ronell Smedley, Alan Smith, Rosemarie Stols, Candyce Thompson, Wendy Utermark, Liza van der Merwe, Xylon van Eyck, NJ Vermaak, Johan Vermeulen, Fred & Christa von Fintel, Johann Vorster, Roy Wakefield and Diane Wales Baillie.

GLOSSARY

Afrikaans – A prominent South African language, derived predominantly from Dutch but with words also adopted from, amongst others, Malay, Portuguese and indigenous African languages. The first language of around seven million people, including more than half of the country's white population, it is also widely spoken and understood as a second, or third, language by most South Africans. Of the South African visitors to Kruger, as many as 70 per cent are Afrikaans-speaking.

Bakkie – A popular type of vehicle with an open (or sometimes canopied) rear cargo area. Beloved by South Africans, bakkies are as ubiquitous on the Park's roads as impala are in the bush. They come in all shapes and sizes, the most common these days being the four-wheel drive, double-cab variety. Americans will know them as 'pickups', and Australians as 'utility vehicles' or 'utes'.

Boet – The Afrikaans word for brother. Also sometimes used colloquially in the same way one would use 'buddy' or 'mate' when addressing someone.

Bokkie – The Afrikaans word for a small, or juvenile, antelope.

Boerewors – Traditional South African spiced sausage made of coarsely ground beef and pork. Usually cooked in long coils then cut into portions just before eating. A *braai* in Kruger would be incomplete without it, and its distinctive coriander seed and clove aroma provides a pleasant olfactory backdrop to early evenings in the rest camps.

Boertjie – Literally a 'young farmer', but more generally used to describe a young, typically-Afrikaans man.

Biltong – Traditional South African delicacy of salted and spiced, dried meat (mostly beef, but game such as kudu and springbok are common too) usually sliced into thin strips. Not dissimilar from American jerky.

Braai – The South African word for barbecue, derived from the Afrikaans word *braaivleis*, meaning literally 'grilled meat'. Used as a noun and a verb, a braai is an essential part of Kruger tradition, providing a focal point for reflecting on the day's sightings as night-time draws in at the rest camps. Coals are prepared by burning either hard wood (for the patient and reflective) or charcoal (for those after a quick meal and an early night) and the meat of choice is generally boerewors, lamb chops or steak. Each accommodation unit in the Park has its own braai, with the exception of the old bungalows at Punda Maria, where a communal braaï area is still used. In the early years of the Park, all braaing was done communally, but sadly this has died out – along with the new friendships and shared stories it engendered.

Braaivleis – See *Braai*, above.

Bundu-bashing – Cutting through the bush or *veld*, on foot or in a vehicle, off any established trail, track or road. With the exception of the guided walking trails, where no set routes are followed, the practice is strictly prohibited in the Park, particularly for vehicles. However, game drive vehicles operated by Kruger guides may, at discretion and in certain places, drive up to two metres from the edge of the road to get a better view of a sighting.

Bush Telegraph – The rapid spread of information, usually gossip, by word of mouth.

Bushveld – Popularised by Sir Percy Fitzpatrick's *Jock of the Bushveld*, the term 'bushveld' is generally used as shorthand for wildlife-rich, acacia-studded savannah. Strictly speaking, the Kruger National Park falls just outside of the true bushveld ecoregion, which covers much of north-eastern South Africa.

Bungalow – A single-storey building with a shaded veranda. In the context of Kruger, bungalows are the square, thatched (or sometimes tile-roofed) accommodation units which usually contain their own kitchenette and bathroom. Sometimes referred to as chalets or cottages.

Catty – A hand-held catapult or slingshot, usually fashioned from a sturdy, Y-shaped stick, with tyre rubber acting as the sling. Also spelled *kettie*.

Causeway – A raised road across a riverbed or river. In the context of Kruger, a causeway is often a low concrete bridge, and is sometimes referred to a low-level bridge or a low water bridge. It may also refer to the point where a gravel road or track dips down into, and crosses, a mostly-dry riverbed.

Cooler box – A portable insulated box, usually made of plastic with a polystyrene core, used for keeping food and drink cool.

Cooldrink – Commonly used South African word for a soft drink, fizzy drink or soda.

Donkey – A large drum of water mounted above a fire. Short for 'donkey boiler'.

Free State – A province in the very middle of South Africa, known for its endless grassy plains and miles and miles of cultivated *mielie* (corn) and wheat fields.

Groot Krokodil – Afrikaans for 'Big Crocodile', the nickname for former apartheid-era state president P.W. Botha, who was known for his hard-line and dogged approach to politics.

Guano – The excrement of bats. From the Spanish *huano*, meaning 'dung'.

Hide – A wooden shelter, usually alongside a waterhole, used to observe animals and birds at close quarters. Americans will know it as a 'blind' or 'bird blind'.

Highveld – The high-level plateau, reaching over 2000 metres above sea level in parts, that forms much of South Africa's interior. With its grass plains, harsh winters and generally milder summer temperatures, it is geologically, botanically and meteorologically distinct from the Lowveld, where the Kruger National Park is nestled. See also *Lowveld*.

Jersey – A knitted, long-sleeved garment. Called a 'jumper' in Britain, or a 'sweater' in North America.

Jislaaik – An Afrikaans expression of surprise or astonishment. Not dissimilar to the English 'Goodness'. Pronounced 'Yis-like'.

Kettie – See Catty above.

Knobkierie – An African wooden club comprising a thin shaft with a bulbous knob on one end.

Koppie – A small hill. Originally an Afrikaans word (in turn derived from the Dutch *kopje*), it is used universally by all South Africans.

Kopje – See *Koppie* above.

Matric – The final year of high school in South Africa, culminating in a set of standardised exams. A matric student is known as a matriculant.

Laager – Historically, a defensive circle or fortification of wagons.

Lowveld – The narrow, low-lying plateau to the east and north-east of the Drakensberg escarpment, characterised by blazingly hot summers, mild winters and an abundance of big game. The Kruger National Park lies along the Lowveld's eastern boundary.

Mik-en-druk – A simple, point-and-click compact camera.

Mopane veld – A term used to loosely describe the ecozones dominated by the distinctive butterfly-leafed mopane trees. Much beloved by elephants, mopane veld comprises a large portion of the Park's northern ecozones, from the Olifants River upwards.

Musth – A hormonal state of dramatically heightened testosterone (reportedly by as much as 60 times the regular level) that occurs periodically in male elephants. Characterised by leaky tear ducts, continuously dripping urine, and significant aggression. Derived from the Persian word *mast*, meaning 'intoxicated'.

Naartjie – The South African word for a satsuma, mandarin or tangerine. Originally derived from the Tamil word *nartei*, which means citrus. The Lowveld's agricultural area to the west of Kruger is one of the largest citrus producing areas in South Africa, and in winter the roads are often lined with informal traders selling the fruit.

Oom – The Afrikaans word for uncle, but also used more generally as a title of respect towards any older man. The female equivalent is *tannie*.

Ouvrou – An Afrikaans term of endearment between (usually long-married) husband and wife, meaning literally 'old lady'.

Padkos – An Afrikaans word, used widely by many South Africans, meaning snacks and provisions for a journey. Its literal translation is 'road food'.

Pan – A shallow, flat-bottomed depression in the land, usually bone dry and covered in hard, cracked mud. In the rainy season it can become covered with water to form a shallow lake.

Rand – The South African currency. Represented by the symbol R.

Rondavel – A circular, thatched hut. The majority of accommodation units in Kruger are rondavels, continuing a tradition from the very first overnight huts built in the Park. Over time they have evolved – in most camps – to include a shady veranda, kitchenette and bathroom. Sometimes spelled *rondawel* (Afrikaans).

Rusks – A rock-hard, semi-sweet biscuit and traditional South African breakfast snack. Best dunked in coffee or tea, they're often the cornerstone of any Kruger breakfast, particularly before setting out on an early morning drive – or enjoyed from a quiet spot, like a waterhole or hide, as the sun rises.

Rut – The once-a-year period of heightened hormonal activity in male antelope, particularly noticeable in impala, where access to the ewes is gained or lost through pitched, horn-clattering battles between the rams. In Kruger, rutting season falls around April and May each year.

Safari tent – Safari tents are semi-permanent accommodation units found in many of the Park's rest camps. Set on a wooden deck, usually on stilts, the canvas structures provide the romance of camping with the comfort of a more permanent unit. While some safari tents contain just a couple of beds, a cupboard and a fridge freezer, more luxurious safari tents are available which include en-suite bathrooms, sliding glass doors and a kitchenette on the veranda.

Shangaan – A dialect of Tsonga, and the dominant indigenous African language spoken in the Park. Many of the rivers and other geographical features, particularly in the north, bear Shangaan names, and guides of all language groups will often be heard to use Shangaan words when sharing animal sightings with one another, so as not to let on what may, or may not, lie ahead for their guests.

Skottel – A gas-fired griddle used as an alternative to a wood or coal *braai*. A skottel *braai* unit consists of the shallow, concave griddle plate, which stands at waist height, connected to a gas cannister via a thin stem. In Kruger, skottels are available to hire for a small fee at all picnic spots, where elaborate fried breakfasts are prepared on their sizzling surfaces.

Skottelbraai – See *skottel* above.

Slip-slops – The South African term for 'flip-flops' or open thong sandals.

Spoor – The track or trail of an animal, usually as footprints in the sand. Strictly speaking, spoor refers to all traces left by animals, including their tracks, trails, scents, droppings and other indications like broken branches or crushed grass.

Stoep – The Afrikaans word for a front porch or stoop.

Suurveld – The grassland, characterised by long, coarse grass, found in the western reaches of Kruger's southern bulge, particularly around Pretoriuskop. 'Suur' is the Afrikaans word for sour, and refers to the unpalatable nature of the grass after flowering. As a consequence, grazing animals tend to shun the area for the sweeter grasses of the basaltic plains further east, particularly in the dry season.

Torch – Flashlight

Veld – Open rural land, usually flat, covered predominantly in grass or low scrub. From the Afrikaans word for 'field' – although not in the agricultural sense. See also *Bushveld*.

Venter trailer – The small, near-ubiquitous luggage trailers favoured by many South Africans, not least those from the interior of the country.

While other companies make trailers too, the Venter brand has long had a monopoly on the market, and their white trailers with the distinctive yellow and red stripes are a common site on the roads, both in the Park and around the country, particularly in holiday season.

Veranda – A covered front porch. Found on almost all of Kruger's rondavels, bungalows and safari tents (with the exception of the basic huts in some of the older camps like Pretoriuskop, Balule and the old clover-leaf units at Lower Sabie).

Voetsak – The Afrikaans word, universally understood by all animals, meaning 'go away' or 'get lost'. Always spat, never said, and usually accompanied with a loud hand-clap. Also spelled *voetsek*.

Weskus – The Afrikaans word for South Africa's windswept west coast, famous for its fish *braais* and lobster.

GOT A KRUGER TALE OF YOUR OWN?

DO YOU HAVE your own Kruger story worth sharing? This is an invitation for you to jot it down and submit it for consideration for the next volume of tales.

Whether your own Kruger tale is extraordinary, intriguing, jaw-dropping, unusual, tragic, hair-raising or hilarious, it could land up being immortalised in black and white, just like the stories in this volume. Just remember the following important guidelines:

- Stories must have taken place in the Kruger National Park itself (not in Greater Kruger or the adjoining reserves).
- Stories must have happened on a tourist road, picnic site, rest camp or walking trail while you were in the Park as a regular visitor (no stories involving privileged or behind-the-scenes access, stories from guides, game rangers etc.).
- Stories do not have to be great works of literary genius; in fact, novel-style writing is discouraged. Simply write them exactly as they happened – like you were telling it to friends around the *braai*.
- Stories should preferably be submitted in English, but if you are more confident writing in your mother tongue, alternative language submissions are warmly welcomed and will be translated.
- Stories do not need to be accompanied by photographs, but if you do have pictures, please consider submitting them too.
- Stories should avoid overt or gratuitous references to politics and religion, and should not be used as a platform for axe-grinding or agenda-setting.
- Stories should be in the region of 300–1200 words, but shorter and longer stories will always be considered.

You can submit your stories at *www.krugertales.co.za*.

CONTRIBUTORS

BEHIND EACH STORY in this book lies a personal biography just as interesting as the stories themselves. I have included a little bit more about each of the kind Kruger-loving people who have so generously made this book come alive with their tales.

Wendy Abadi (*Impala in the Mud*) moved from the UK to South Africa in 2007 and, when not in Kruger, lives in Pretoria. She used to be a beach-lover but since discovering all that Kruger has to offer, now spends her holiday time in the bush. Every trip to Kruger includes at least one visit to Ntandanyathi hide.

Nigel Aitken (*The Shocking Death of a Leopard*) developed a love for the bush whilst growing up in Kenya. He has visited the Park regularly over the past 48 years and seen many changes – tarred roads, electricity etc. as well as some incredible sightings. It remains his favourite spot on earth. Semi-retired, he lives in St Francis Bay, Eastern Cape.

John Anslow (*Local Butcher Gored By Elephant*) runs a butchery in Stafford, England, where he does a fine line in *boerewors*. He got a taste for Africa with his first visit to Kenya in 1998 and since then feels that the continent has got under his skin. Along with his wife, Angie, they've returned to both Kenya and South Africa (though not to Kruger) and regularly visit Gambia, where they sponsor a local family.

Sauda Omarjee Amojee (*An Extra Night in the Park*) lives in Durban, Kwazulu-Natal where she studies nutrition. She began visiting Kruger at an early age, as it was her family's holiday destination of choice – and it still is (although in 20 subsequent visits, her parents have never driven the Bume road again!) She has a husband and two young children who are as fanatical about Kruger as she is.

Marijke Arends (*Lioness Joins the Picnic*) was born and raised in South Africa but now lives in the Netherlands with her Dutch husband and two children, where she runs a small sphynx cat cattery. As a child she visited Kruger often. Now she returns annually along with her family, who have all fallen in love with the bush, too. Their subsequent picnics have remained predator-free.

Johan Armstrong (*The Hyaena, the Fence and my Little Boy's Hand*) lives in Pretoria where he is an airworthiness inspector at the Civil Aviation Authority. Together with his wife, Riki, and their two boys, they love outdoor life and camping. Despite little Johan's brush with the hyaena, he harbours no fear of dogs or other animals, and greatly enjoyed his second trip to Kruger.

Elfie Barker (*An Accidental Translocation*) grew up on a farm and has always been an avid nature lover. She first visited Kruger when just three years old, spent her honeymoon there and still returns with her husband, Harry, at least once a year. She lives in Johannesburg, where she works as a financial secretary at a primary school. When she retires, she intends to become an honorary ranger.

Arshad Bhamjee (*An Unusual Sighting Downstream*) was introduced to Kruger by his parents when he was five years old. For the last 16 years he has visited the Park every year, usually at Easter. He lives in Lenasia, Johannesburg with his wife and daughter and is the importer of hand tool brand TOPTUL. You can email him at info@toptulsa.co.za.

Gavin Black (*Leopard in the Torchlight*) lives in Hillcrest, KwaZulu-Natal but is currently based in Angola as a medical advisor for International SOS. He first visited Kruger in 1969 as a five-year-old and still returns at least three times a year. His passion for nature has rubbed off on his daughters, who prefer a trip to the Park than a trip to the beach.

Anrie Botha (*A Short Stroll Through Lion Country*) first visited Kruger when she was still in the womb, and continues her family's 60-year tradition of visiting the Park at least once a year. She lives in George, Western Cape and is pleased to report that her current car is proving far more reliable than her old red Corolla.

Kevin Bouwer (*Breaking Down the Door* & *How My Sports Car Got Its Scars*) is retired and lives in Phalaborwa, Limpopo with his wife Christine. As nephew of the original owner of Riley's Hotel in Maun, Botswana, his passion for the bush was kindled at an early age, but his first visit to the Park was only in 1976 – on his honeymoon. The sound of a dustbin lid falling over at night still gives him flashbacks.

Kerri Bowie (*Battle Before the Gates of Skukuza*) first visited Kruger in 2010, which started her family's addiction to game viewing. Prior to that, her closest brush with the wild was being bitten by a secretary bird as a baby. She returns to the Park annually and continues to be luckier than most, enjoying cat sightings aplenty. She is a conference and events co-ordinator and, together with her fiancé, lives between Cape Town and Colorado, USA. The video of the buffalo kill can be seen at *www.bit.ly/kerribowie*

Hal Brindley (*Leopard Versus Crocodile*) is a wildlife photographer, filmmaker and writer in the United States. He travels the world extensively to photograph creatures but keeps returning to Southern Africa – four times so far. He and his wife are now promoting responsible wildlife tourism destinations through their website, Travel For Wildlife (*www. travelforwildlife.com*).

Richard Browne (*The Great Ones Do Have Feelings*) has been visiting Kruger for over 45 years and tries to visit at least once a year. His trips to the Park, which he feels are the best antidote to stress, also allow him to exercise his uncanny ability to mimic bird calls – often to the bemusement of nearby birdwatchers. He lives in Kloof, Kwazulu-Natal, where he is the regional director of a listed IT company.

David 'Buzz,' & Cheryl Budzinski (*Battle at Kruger*) are both retired and live in rural Virginia, USA. They first visited Kruger in 2004 – when they captured the famous footage – but have returned twice, each time with memorable videos to show their grandchildren. Africa has changed their lives and they plan on returning for years to come. Their famous video can be seen at *www.bit.ly/battleatkruger*

Andrew Clark (*Hijack on the Bridge*) regularly visited Kruger as a child with his family. He continued the tradition throughout his adulthood, visiting the Park at least twice a year and becoming a competent wildlife photographer with many a good story to tell. Sadly, he suffered a heart attack and passed away during his last visit to his beloved Kruger in July 2013. He was 55.

Pieter Colyn (*Rocking the Car to Escape the Rhino*) lives in Pretoria and works for the Government. He grew up visiting Kruger every year with his parents and two siblings, and now, with his own family, he continues that tradition. On his next visit he intends to locate the exact spot where he rocked the Corolla. His story is dedicated to the loving memory of his father, Piet Colyn (07 July 1933 – 05 November 2013), who so dearly loved Kruger.

Derek Conradie (*Lion Roar Uproar*) grew up on a sheep farm in the Richmond district of the Great Karoo. A keen nature lover and hiker, he's done many trails, including Kilimanjaro, Fish River, Otter, and Amatola but hopes to do a trail in Kruger one day. He works as an accountant in local government, resides in St Helena Bay on the West Coast – and still enjoys a good prank.

Andy Crighton (*Not an Eagle or a Birdie – But a Wild Dog*) is a high school teacher from Johannesburg. Growing up, his family visited the Park every July for a week. Now, with 40 years of visits under the belt, he continues that tradition with his wife and two children, who all love the bush. He is passionate about sport, wildlife and photography.

Mariana de Klerk (*The Elephant and the Drowning Calf*) lives in Phalaborwa and tries to visit the Park at least once a week. She loves camping and has travelled to many African countries, but Kruger is her favorite wildlife destination. A keen wildlife photographer, with the patience of a saint, you can see pictures at *www.marianadeklerk.blogspot.com*. Her famous video of the elephant rescuing its calf can be seen at *www.bit.ly/marianadeklerk*

Romey Doubell (*Monkey Man and the Skukuza Offensive*) resides in Mwanza, Tanzania, where he is general manager for a construction company called Group Five. He often visits the Serengeti National Park, which he describes as 'awesome', however Kruger – which he has visited many, many times – is still his favourite. Thus far he's escaped any further animal attacks.

Riël du Toit (*Herding Warthogs* & *Pulling a Baboon's Tail*) is a retired South African Air Force lieutenant colonel with strong ties to Kruger. He became an honorary ranger in 1972 and performs all manner of voluntary duties around the Park. An accomplished writer, he has published a number of books of short stories. He lives with his wife, Susan, on the banks of the Crocodile River, just outside the Park.

Lourens Durand (*Tidal Wave of Elephants*) is a food scientist and part-time artist, writer and wildlife photographer. Passionate about the bush, he has visited Kruger more times than he can remember but has yet to see such a large herd of elephants again. You can view and purchase his artwork and photos at *www.bit.ly/lourensdurand*

Ewoud Duvenage (*Leaving my Child to the Lions*) lives in Witbank, Mpumalanga and works for one of the major banks. He was introduced to Kruger at a young age in the mid 1970s and continues to visit as often as possible. It remains his favourite place in the world. He recently introduced friends from New Zealand to the Park and reports that he did not accidentally leave any of them to the lions.

Caroline Evans (*Between a Lioness and her Cubs*) grew up on a farm in the heart of the Eastern Cape, where she spent most of her time outdoors, exploring her surroundings and being inspired by the complexity of the creatures she encountered daily. Family holidays were spent in Kruger where her love for nature became even more ingrained. She is now an environmental scientist.

Johann Fankhauser (*The Nhlanganini Baby Snatcher*) grew up in Phalaborwa, on Kruger's front doorstep, where he enjoyed frequent hot and dusty day visits into the Park crammed into the back of the family sedan. Although he now lives in Switzerland, he still returns to the Park regularly to live his passion for wildlife photography.

Steve Farrell (*Bumbling Lions in the Jackalberry Tree*) is a born and bred Capetonian with a penchant for both the bush and the sea. He tries to get to Kruger once a year, despite the long trek up from Cape Town. He's yet to see any more tree-climbing lions, but he and his wife have twice returned to the scene of the proposal: tent number 40 at Tamboti.

Mario Fazekas (*A Kill From Our Veranda*) is a wildlife photographer and author of the *Photographer's Guide* series of eBooks. He and his wife, Jenny, have spent over 750 days travelling on self-drive and guided photo safaris through African national parks, but Kruger remains their favourite due to its size and diversity – plus the case of spotting leopards! You can read more about their eBooks at *www.bit.ly/k2k-ebooks*

Winston Floquet (*Yes, All Cars Have Coils*) lives in Cape Town, far from the bush, but he and his bush-mad wife visit game parks all over Africa at least twice a year. They have yet to meet another python as accommodating as their friend in the Kruger.

Pieter & Patricia Fourie (*A Matter of Knife and Death*) live in Pretoria where Pieter is a semi-retired vet, having worked both privately and for the State (including some time on the Park's northern borders). He first visited Kruger in 1963 for his 21st birthday but only began returning regularly with his family in the 1980s. Their love for nature has taken them on trips throughout Southern and East Africa.

Brian Gardiner (*The Leopard that Killed the Cheetah that Killed the Impala*) was born in Zimbabwe, where he developed a deep love for the bush. Working in the safari and hospitality industries, together with his family he has lived and worked in virtually every East and Southern African country, spanning continents and oceans too, with managerial positions in far-flung places like the Belize rainforest and the atolls of Maldives. Based at Victoria Falls, he is now a senior figure at Zimbabwe's leading tourism company.

Beukes Geldenhuys (*The Newly Deputised Officials*) comes from a family whose visits to Kruger stretch back to the 1940s. Based in Hoedspruit, Limpopo, he now works as a freelance manager and guide (beukes@ lifeskillprogrammes.co.za). Using his hat as a weapon, he once fended off a pride of lions that had sneaked up on a guest in a private reserve. The only mortality was the hat.

Melissa Grib (*Perils of the Call of Nature*) lives in Piet Retief, Mpumalanga, just three hours from Kruger. She first visited the Park as a one-year-old and continues to make regular trips, despite an inexplicable phobia of elephants. As a youngster, she and her two brothers made a brief appearance in a Kruger documentary – something they only discovered years later.

Keith Griffiths (*Teenage Runaways Trek Through the Park* & *Walking Towards the Lions*) lives below Table Mountain in Cape Town and works as Tour and Wildlife Club administrator at Bishops Prep, where he has taught since 1987. He first visited Kruger in 1950 (when lions killed a kudu outside his rondavel at Pretoriuskop) and has returned numerous times since.

Piet Grobler (*The Crocodile that Stood Up*) lives in Phalaborwa, just outside the Park. A retired water scientist, he also worked as a game ranger in Etosha, as well as in Kruger for a short time. His main interests are indigenous trees and snakes, and he loves nature photography (*www.flickr.com/oom_piet*). He has yet to sell his crocodile-scratched Mercedes.

Diederik Harmse (*A Bite at Berg-en-Dal*) is an architectural technician from Pretoria. Introduced to Kruger at a young age by his father, he also recalls his mother giving him his first driving lesson in the Park. A part-time photographer, he visits up to five times a year. After Mecyla's bite, a very informative identification brochure of all the Kruger snakes, scorpions and spiders can be found at most camps' receptions.

Dianne Henderson (*Lions are Faster than Lawn Mowers* & *Scars of a Charge Run Deep*) is retired and lives in Benoni, Gauteng. Thanks to her father, who started visiting Kruger soon after it opened, she has returned every year for the last 60 years. She even worked in the Park for three years as restaurant manager at Skukuza, as well as acting camp manager at Skukuza, Letaba and Olifants. She eventually overcame her fear of elephants after doing an elephant-back safari in Zambia.

Lesley Henderson (*A Cry in the Night*) lives in Pretoria and is a botanist specialising in invasive alien plants. Her love of the African bush was instilled at an early age by annual family holidays to Kruger. She has visited the Park almost every year since a baby, mainly as a tourist but also in a professional capacity as part of an invasive alien plant advisory group.

Raymond Hewson (*Skukuza Leopard Kills* & *Slapping a Hyaena in the Face* & *Zebra Crossing*) and his wife Cynthia were married in 1953 and have recently celebrated their 60-year diamond wedding anniversary. Kruger is their favourite of all the national parks they have visited, and they should know: Cynthia first visited in 1935 and Raymond in 1948. Retired and in good health, they live on a smallholding on the Gonubie River near East London, Eastern Cape.

Sander Hofman (*Angry Elephant's Road Rage Rampage*) is the curator of two major Belgian zoos, overseeing more than 120 mammal species, including elephants (Asian, though – not African). He first visited Kruger whilst doing a trainceship at a reserve in Kwazulu-Natal and has returned to the Park another three times, preferring the quieter summer months. He is married, with two young daughters, and lives in the Netherlands.

Gabi Hotz (*Dragging a Carcass*) has visited reserves throughout Africa (with the exception of the Serengeti, which is still on her bucket list) but feels that nothing, as yet, compares to Kruger. She loves the unpredictability of the Park and visits between five and seven times a year. She is a psychology honours student at University of Johannesburg but hopes to pursue a career in conservation.

Theuns & Elzet Hurter (*The Lioness that Opened the Door*) live in Pretoria. Theuns' late father was a senior State Vet whose areas included the Kruger National Park, which gave Theuns a taste for the excitement of the bush. He first introduced Elzet to Kruger in the mid-1980s and then later their daughter too when she was just one year old. They now keep their car doors firmly locked at lion sightings. You can watch the video of the incident at *www.bit.ly/theunshurter*

Glenda Keys (*New Year's Eve Birthday Suit*) has been visiting Kruger with her husband, Rod, for almost 40 years. Along with their two daughters, who are now grown up with kids of their own, their Park trips have often been family affairs, and over the years they've racked up countless experiences, both animal and human. Both retired, they live in Gauteng but can't get enough of Kruger.

Ursela Klitzke (*Bouncing Off the Fence*) lives in Johannesburg. She was introduced to Kruger by her father, who would even take her out of school for clandestine trips. She has since got her fiancé hooked on the Park and hopes her young son will develop a love for it too. Since the kill at the fence, her brother has never returned and probably never will. It is still a touchy subject.

Klaus Kreft (*The King Cheetah*) first visited Kruger in a vw Beetle many years ago as a student and still remembers the outcry when it was announced that some of the Park's roads were to be tarred. His whole family, including children and grandchildren, are crazy about the bush. Retired and living in Fourways, Gauteng, he's never seen a king cheetah again.

Anton Kruger (*And the Leopard Will Lie Down With the Kid*) lives in Pretoria and works in his family's property development and investment business. He and his wife, Renate (who, rather fittingly, is a midwife and delivers babies for a living) both have a passion for wildlife. Keen birders, they're tantalisingly close to reaching the 700 bird mark for Southern Africa. He's seen another two animal births since, but fortunately no leopard showed up for either.

Julius Kunzmann (*Beetle Express* & *Reversing a Caravan*) lives in Johannesburg and still visits Kruger occasionally. He is an animal transport specialist with his own company, Pets Exclusive Travel Services (*www.pets2000.co.za*). He also brews beer as a hobby (*www.tradeger.co.za*) and welcomes you to try some craft beers on tap at the Walkerville Farmers' Market every Saturday. His recommendation? The Walkerville SpringBock.

Colin Lagerwall (*There's a Lion Outside our Tent*) lives in Newcastle, Kwazulu-Natal where he and his wife, Fay, run a church and two church schools. They have been visiting Kruger annually since the 1980s – when their eldest son was just nine months old – and spent a full 25 days there for their 25th wedding anniversary. Their longest ever trip was in 2007 when they stayed for 38 days.

Trevor Lagerwall (*Water!*) was introduced to Kruger as a child by his uncle, who worked alongside Nick Steele and Ian Player in Operation Rhino at Umfolozi. Now retired, he has two great passions in his life: tennis and Kruger. So heaven is to watch Wimbledon followed by a trip to the Park – which he does every year in July.

Jacky Le Roux (*The Strange Tale of the Dog in the Night*) first visited Kruger in 1947. She returns every couple of years and still gets that special feeling upon passing through the gates. The spare bedroom in her home is dubbed the 'Kruger Park room' and is full of her favourite photographs from the Park. She lives with her husband in Port Elizabeth, Eastern Cape.

Penny & Bob Legg (*Barely in the Park* & *One Wild Morning in Lower Sabie*) are both conservation activists and firm supporters of anti rhino-poaching pressure group OSCAP (*www.oscap.co.za*). Their children, who have always preferred the bush to the beach, are conservation-minded too, and their ex-game ranger son now runs the project, Brands for Change (*www. brandsforchange.com*). They live in a 110-year-old listed property in Durban, Kwazulu-Natal, where a resident genet lives in the ceiling above their bed.

André Liénard (*Dog Day Morning*) is retired and lives in Antwerp, Belgium with his wife, Helen. They first visited South Africa in 1997 and so fell in love with Kruger that they return every year – usually for three weeks at a time, covering the entire length of the Park. They are possibly the first people to ever photograph a confrontation between wild dogs and a domestic dog.

Geoff Lockwood (*Boomslang Bite and a Long Drive Home*) became hooked on Kruger at the age of five following a close encounter with a bull elephant near Punda Maria. Working in the environmental field, he is based at the Delta Environment Centre in Johannesburg. He also leads tours to various southern African countries for a US-based natural history tour company, where he gets to share his love of wildlife – particularly birds – with mostly American visitors.

Andy Maclaurin (*Don't Panic, I'm a Kingfisher* & *The Waterbuck and the Laager*) came to Southern Africa from England in 1948. Married to Angie, they instilled in their three daughters a love of the bush from a very young age. No surprise therefore that dotted around the globe, his daughters – now married, with offspring of their own – choose Kruger as the family's venue of choice for their periodic 'gatherings of the clan'.

Leon Maré (*Lion Charge Miracle*) has a closer connection to Kruger than most: he is the great, great grandson of President Paul Kruger. An alumnus of the University of Pretoria (and ex Student Council chairman) he is a regular visitor to the Park and has so far avoided any further lion charges. Still a practising attorney at the age of 76, he is married to Antoinette and lives in Pretoria.

Henk Maree (*A Small Knife and a Big Dilemma*) is a semi-retired businessman from Johannesburg. Married for 43 years, he has two daughters and three grandsons. Despite multiple trips by vehicle to many of Africa's great reserves, including the Serengeti, Ngorongoro, South Luangwa, Mana Pools and the Okavango, he still returns time and again to Kruger for the natural diversity it offers.

Bertus Meiring (*Good Morning, Groot Krokodil* & *Good Turn Turns Bad*) has been visiting the Park since he was a baby and has early memories of being chased around Skukuza by warthogs after getting too close. He has spent most of his adult life working in Africa and the Middle East and is currently the sales executive for a well-known mushroom grower. Passionate about the bush, he lives in Johannesburg but visits Kruger as often as possible.

Nicole Meiring (*A Kill Under Spotlights*) lives in Melkbosstrand, Cape Town. An avid Stormers supporter, she has a background in travel and tourism, but is currently a stay-at-home mother. She first visited the Park when just five years old, and it remains a passion she shares with her husband – and now her kids too. They've recently discovered the wonder of Kruger's wilderness trails and considers them the ultimate Kruger experience.

Lorraine Mollentze (*Crouching Leopard, Silly Fool*) has a long history of visits to Kruger with her children and grandchildren. Many of them now pursue careers inspired by the bush: one manages a game farm, while another majors in wildlife photography. She lives in Barkly East, Eastern Cape and works at the family business, *The Reporter*, a country newspaper and printing works.

Sylvester Motaln (*The Hippo, the Impala and the Natural Order of Things*) was raised in Bedfordshire, England but moved to South Africa in 1984 – the same year he first visited Kruger. He now lives in Gauteng, where he is managing director for an IT printing and network distribution company (*www.bigs.co.za*) and a committee member of sports charity EXPRO (*www. expro.co.za*). A qualified pilot and yacht skipper, he returns to the Park three or four times a year.

John Muirhead (*Not Our Morning to be Eaten*) often says of Kruger that 'it is like it must have been at the beginning'. Incredibly, he has seen all of the Big Five from *inside* the camps, with a lion kill close to the restaurant at Letaba and a leopard near the dam at Berg-en-Dal. Eastern Cape born and bred, he is semi-retired and lives in Port Alfred.

Darran Myers (*A Fine Place to Bath*) first visited Kruger with his primary school, which cemented his love for the bush. He now lives in Nelspruit and visits the Park at least six times a year. His company, Africa Tracks & Trails (*www.africa-tnt.com*) focusses mainly on walking safaris in private reserves, but he still keeps his eyes open for naked bathers. He admits it is possible he was actually the guide in his story.

Petro Nel (*Almost Leopard Breakfast*) is a retired businessman and current councillor in Jan Kempdorp, Northern Cape. A devoted nature lover, he has visited Kruger since 1970, where in addition to his close encounter with the leopard, he once also lost a tyre to some over-eager lions near Lower Sabie. He has just completed the first commercially available 3D Blu-ray DVD of the Namakwaland flowers (email namakwa3d@gmail. com for details).

Christa Niederer (*Spat on from Above*) is a South African translator and interpreter based near Lake Constance in Switzerland. A passionate wildlife photographer, she needs a regular dose of Kruger – which she receives courtesy of her three children who work in the airline industry. She is dismissive of people's irrational fear of snakes and has happily returned to stay in the safari tents at Lower Sabie.

Buks Oberholzer (*A Record Case of Foolishness for a Record Pair of Horns*) grew up on a farm near Bothaville where his love for nature began. His parents visited Kruger every year and first took him along in 1966. It was during that trip that he shot a francolin with a *kettie* and got the hiding of his life from his father. He is a practising attorney in Welkom, Free State.

Johan Opperman (*How the Elephant got its Trunk*) grew up visiting Kruger annually but has only returned twice as an adult – the last trip being the time he snapped the famous elephant and croc photo. Since then his interest in photography has ballooned, and he recently turned professional, setting up Pretoria-based event photography company Aes Sídhe Photography (*www.aessidhe.co.za*) with his photographer wife, Marietjie.

Gordon Parratt (*The Biyamiti Stowaway*) was born in Southern Rhodesia (now Zimbabwe) and grew up amongst abundant game and birds of Kafue and Broken Hill in Northern Rhodesia (now Zambia), cycling everywhere with his camping gear, fishing rods and inevitable 'catty'. He first visited Kruger in 2002 and now returns twice a year. A retired serviceman of both the Rhodesian Army and South African Defence Force, he lives in Pretoria with his wife, Ilda.

Issi Potgieter (*Reversing into Camp*) was born in White River; half-raised in Rustenburg; and brought up in Strand, Western Cape, where she now lives. Her late father played a big role in who she is today and, like him, she loves Kruger, loves photography, loves children – and even loves reversing. For the past 40 years she has visited the Park annually to cure what she calls 'Kruger fever'.

Samantha Pittendrigh (*Blessed Impala's Flying Leap of Faith*) grew up in Nelspruit – where she had a pet ostrich – and has visited the Park more often than she can remember. She is currently completing a BCom at Tuks, where her new-found fame has led to her being known as 'Impala Girl'. You can watch her remarkable video at *www.bit.ly/samanthapittendrigh*

Angie Shackleford (*Wrong Place, Wrong Time, on a Rhino's Turf*) married a game ranger and lived in Kruger for over a year before heading a number of international companies. She and her husband now live in the Southern Drakensberg Mountains and run a small rural business, which allows her to spend any free time painting, with wildlife her favourite subject.

Gavin Selfe (*Empty Spool Heartbreak*) grew up visiting the Kruger twice a year with family and is crazy about wildlife. He has a house on a game reserve adjoining Kruger, from where he consults as a geophysicist. He loves camping in the bush and once had a pride of lions play trampoline on his pup tent while he and his wife lay whimpering inside.

Ian & Melanie Smith (*Spotting a Different Kind of Mammal*) first visited Kruger after the floods in March 2000 and soon began spending all their annual leave in the Park. Having passed through the gate at Phalaborwa a few times, they decided to retire there. Now qualified honorary rangers, they do their bit to preserve the Park's heritage, undertaking voluntary tasks like litter patrols, tree surveys and public awareness projects.

Alma Sparrius (*Too Busy Fiddling to Notice*) has led a colourful life. The great, great granddaughter of the Baroness van Rheede, she was at Queen Elizabeth's 21st birthday party in Cape Town, is a pilot, an accomplished horse rider and a crack shot. She resides in Sedgefield, Western Cape – and has yet to buy a new video camera.

Philippa Spruyt (*Safari Tent Spitting Games*) is a Pretoria girl, born and bred. Having studied interior design, she now manages a tenant installation department for a local property management and development company.

Growing up she visited the Park every year – and continues that family tradition today. She is pleased to report that she has had no further dangerous loo encounters in Kruger.

Kathleen Stevens (*Hiding Under the Hide*) is well travelled, having spent 18 years in France and three years in North Yemen, where scuba diving in the Red Sea became a passion. She first visited Kruger on a school trip when she was just eight years old and has returned at least 20 times since. Based in Bela-Bela, Limpopo, she works as an estate agent, helping people find their dream *bushveld* home.

Keegan Lloyd Steward (*A Close Scrape with Poachers*) was born and bred in Cape Town but spent most of his family holidays in Kruger, which nurtured his passion for the bush. Still living in Cape Town, he hopes to one day manage a game reserve, while his wife, Meghan, strives to become one of the great wildlife photographers.

Stella Stewart (*Paddling Cubs and the Croc*) is an international aerobic gymnastics judge and lives in Umhlanga, Kwazulu-Natal. A board member of the KZN Gymnastics Union and the aerobic gymnastics administrator for the SA Gymnastics Federation, she also has a burning passion for wildlife and is actively involved in the quest to save the rhino. She visits Kruger at least twice a year and always makes the most of it – her longest single trip lasted 23 days.

Kerstin Stöwahse (*Black Mamba and the Crocodiles*) is a German author living on the Spanish island of Mallorca. For many years she ran a diving centre there, where as an instructor she introduced people to the underwater world. She first visited Kruger in 1997 and has since completed a course as a field guide. Unable to resist the call of the African bush, she returns to the Park often. You can watch the extraordinary video of the sighting at *www.bit.ly/kerstinstowahse*

Neil Taylor (*Black Mamba Hitches a Ride*) lives in Dubai where he 'earns a crust' as a scaffolding manager. He continues to 'treat' his wife, Marie, to exotic wildlife-watching holidays: steamy rainforests in Borneo, Malaysia and Central America; Etosha in mid summer; and the sewers of India tracking the elusive Indian pitta. They try not go anywhere twice, but Kruger is different – they've returned many times and will continue to do so.

Sheenaugh-Lee Thompson (*Granny and the White Lions*) grew up on a farm in Tzaneen, Limpopo just an hour from Kruger's Phalaborwa Gate. No stranger to wild animals, she once stared down an angry black mamba whilst seven months pregnant – and sitting on the loo. Married, with two young daughters, she lives in Ermelo, Mpumalanga. She has still never seen another white lion.

Johan van der Merwe (*Baboon Bullies and the Leopard Cub*) is a professional hunter and snake handler. He knows Kruger like the back of his hand, having grown up visiting the Park with his father most school holidays and long weekends. He now lives in the Waterberg in Limpopo, where he has the displeasure of seeing baboons on an almost daily basis – and they still irritate him.

Hennie van Deventer (*An Astonishing Confluence of Killers*) is a retired newspaper editor and author of 17 books – mostly about the world of newspapers, unforgettable characters, and the bush. He splits his time between Melkbosstrand, Western Cape and the Lowveld, where he has a cottage on the leafy banks of the Sabie River. A keen photographer and energetic blogger, his website is *www.hennievandeventer.com/hvdblog*

Gretha van Huyssteen (*Leopard Raids the Braai*) lives in Nelspruit, Mpumalanga and visits the Park regularly during her school holidays – and sometimes in term time too. She has seen a few leopards since her encounter at Afsaal but definitely not while outside the car. She is currently in high school and hopes to one day become a pastor in the NG Church.

Ron van Rooyen (*The Rarest Kruger Predator*) had only visited Kruger a few times prior to spotting the shark in the Luvuvhu, and it was his first time to the north of the Park. No stranger to unusual wildlife incidents, he once discovered a fully intact egg from the long-extinct 'Elephant Bird' while on a diving holiday in Madagascar – which he managed to secure and then sell on a Christie's auction in London. A third extraordinary incident still eludes him.

Tyla Jade Veenendaal (*Bull Elephant and the Mini*) works as a primary school teaching assistant on Johannesburg's East Rand while also studying for a degree in education. She considers Kruger her home away from home and maintains the family tradition of visiting the Park every year. Funnily enough, she currently drives an old 1982 Mini – but has no plans to emulate her great grandmother by driving it in the Park.

Marion Vlaming (*At the Mercy of the Rising Timbavati*) lives in Springs, Gauteng and runs a gifting and decor company (*www.sirium.co.za*) with her daughter, Shireen. She has been visiting the Park regularly since she was five years old and now, at the tender age of 63, has recently qualified as an honorary ranger. Still traumatised by her 30-hour ordeal, she feels it has left her with a greater appreciation of life.

Louis von Broembsen (*The Other Kruger Millions*) lives in Cape Town but visits the bushveld every year with wife, Penny, and family. His interest in Kruger was cultivated by his close association, via the citrus industry, with Patrick Niven, grandson of *Jock of the Bushveld* author Percy Fitzpatrick. His nephew, Mark, is a thoroughly outdoorsy fellow and loves fishing – but has yet to catch a fish with R1 000 in its mouth.

Helene von Wielligh (*Mauling on the Hillside*) lives in Pretoria, where she works as a civil engineer. She has a passion for the arts and enjoys ballroom dancing but admits that her piano and church organ skills need a little work. She is still edgy around lions (even photos and video clips spark a reaction) but feels she learned a lot about herself from the incident, not least the practical benefits of her compassionate side.

Janet Wills (*The Calculating Leopard*) and her husband, John, run the historic Porcupine Ridge Guest House (*www.porcupineridge.co.za*) in the quaint escarpment town of Sabie, just 40 minutes from Phabeni Gate. She has visited Kruger countless times but still gets envious of her guests heading into the Park, and never tires of talking about it. Despite her close encounter, she can't imagine driving around Kruger with the windows closed.

PERMISSIONS

I WOULD LIKE TO ACKNOWLEDGE the following individuals for granting permission to edit and publish their extraordinary stories. This constitutes an extension of the copyright page.

A Bite at Berg-en-Dal. Published by permission of Diederik Harmse. Copyright © 2011 Diederik Harmse.

A Close Scrape with Poachers. Published by permission of Keegan Lloyd Steward. Copyright © 2013 Keegan Lloyd Steward.

A Cry in the Night. Published by permission of Lesley Henderson. Copyright © 2013 Lesley Henderson.

A Fine Place to Bath. Published by permission of Darran Myers. Copyright © 2012 Darran Myers.

A Hissing in the Engine. Published by permission of Marlene Swart. Copyright © 2012 Marlene Swart.

A Kill From Our Veranda. Published by permission of Mario Fazekas. Copyright © 2011 Mario Fazekas.

A Kill Under Spotlights. Published by permission of Nicole Meiring. Copyright © 2011 Nicole Meiring.

A Matter of Knife and Death. Published by permission of Pieter & Patricia Fourie. Copyright © 2013 Pieter & Patricia Fourie.

A Record Case of Foolishness for a Record Pair of Horns. Published by permission of Buks Oberholzer. Copyright © 2010 Buks Oberholzer.

A Short Stroll Through Lion Country. Published by permission of Anrie Botha. Copyright © 2011 Anrie Botha.

A Small Knife and a Big Dilemma. Published by permission of Henk Maree. Copyright © 2011 Henk Maree.

Almost Leopard Breakfast. Published by permission of Petro Nel. Copyright © 2011 Petro Nel. Translated from the Afrikaans by Jeff Gordon.

An Accidental Translocation. Published by permission of Elfie Barker. Copyright © 2011 Elfie Barker.

An Astonishing Confluence of Killers. Published by permission of Hennie van Deventer. Copyright © 2011 Hennie van Deventer. Translated from the Afrikaans by Jeff Gordon.

An Extra Night in the Park. Published by permission of Sauda Omarjee Amojee. Copyright © 2011 Sauda Omarjee Amojee.

An Unusual Sighting Downstream. Published by permission of Arshad Bhamjee. Copyright © 2011 Arshad Bhamjee.

And the Leopard Will Lie Down With the Kid. Published by permission of Anton Kruger. Copyright © 2011 Anton Kruger.

Angry Elephant's Road Rage Rampage. Published by permission of Sander Hofman. Copyright © 2012 Sander Hofman.

At the Mercy of the Rising Timbavati. Published by permission of Marion Vlaming. Copyright © 2013 Marion Vlaming.

Baboon Bullies and the Leopard Cub. Published by permission of Johan van der Merwe. Copyright © 2011 Johan van der Merwe.

Barely in the Park & *One Wild Morning in Lower Sabie.* Published by permission of Penny & Bob Legg. Copyright © 2010 Penny & Bob Legg.

Battle at Kruger. Published by permission of David 'Buzz' & Cheryl Budzinski. Copyright © 2013 David 'Buzz' & Cheryl Budzinski.

Battle Before the Gates of Skukuza. Published by permission of Kerri Bowie. Copyright © 2011 Kerri Bowie.

Beetle Express & *Reversing a Caravan.* Published by permission of Julius Kunzmann. Copyright © 2011 Julius Kunzmann.

Between a Lioness and her Cubs. Published by permission of Caroline Evans. Copyright © 2012 Caroline Evans.

Black Mamba and the Crocodiles. Published by permission of Kerstin Stöwahse. Copyright © 2013 Kerstin Stöwahse. Translated from the German by Jeff Gordon.

Black Mamba Hitches a Ride. Published by permission of Neil Taylor. Copyright © 2011 Neil Taylor.

Blessed Impala's Flying Leap of Faith. Published by permission of Samantha Pittendrigh. Copyright © 2013 Samantha Pittendrigh.

Boomslang Bite and a Long Drive Home. Published by permission of Geoff Lockwood. Copyright © 2011 Geoff Lockwood.

Bouncing Off the Fence. Published by permission of Ursela Klitzke. Copyright © 2012 Ursela Klitzke.

Breaking Down the Door & *How My Sports Car Got Its Scars*. Published by permission of Kevin Bouwer. Copyright © 2011 Kevin Bouwer.

Bull Elephant and the Mini. Published by permission of Tyla Jade Veenendaal. Copyright © 2010 Tyla Jade Veenendaal.

Bumbling Lions in the Jackalberry Tree. Published by permission of Steve Farrell. Copyright © 2013 Steve Farrell.

Crouching Leopard, Silly Fool. Published by permission of Lorraine Mollentze. Copyright © 2010 Lorraine Mollentze.

Dog Day Morning. Published by permission of André Liénard. Copyright © 2013 André Liénard.

Don't Panic, I'm a Kingfisher & *The Waterbuck and the Laager*. Published by permission of Andy Maclaurin. Copyright © 2011 Andy Maclaurin.

Dragging a Carcass. Published by permission of Gabi Hotz. Copyright © 2011 Gabi Hotz.

Empty Spool Heartbreak. Published by permission of Gavin Selfe. Copyright © 2011 Gavin Selfe.

Good Morning, Groot Krokodil & *Good Turn Turns Bad*. Published by permission of Bertus Meiring. Copyright © 2011 Bertus Meiring.

Granny and the White Lions. Published by permission of Sheenaugh-Lee Thompson. Copyright © 2013 Sheenaugh-Lee Thompson.

Herding Warthogs & *Pulling a Baboon's Tail*. Published by permission of Riël du Toit. Copyright © 2011 Riël du Toit. Translated from the Afrikaans by Jeff Gordon.

Hiding Under the Hide. Published by permission of Kathleen Stevens. Copyright © 2012 Kathleen Stevens.

Hijack on the Bridge. Published by permission of the Clark family. Copyright © 2011 Andrew Clark.

How the Elephant got its Trunk. Published by permission of Johan Opperman. Copyright © 2011 Johan Opperman.

Impala in the Mud. Published by permission of Wendy Abadi. Copyright © 2012 Wendy Abadi.

Leaving my Child to the Lions. Published by permission of Ewoud Duvenage. Copyright © 2012 Ewoud Duvenage.

Leopard in the Torchlight. Published by permission of Gavin Black. Copyright © 2012 Gavin Black.

Leopard Raids the Braai. Published by permission of Gretha van Huyssteen. Copyright © 2013 Gretha van Huyssteen.

Leopard Versus Crocodile. Published by permission of Hal Brindley. Copyright © 2011 Hal Brindley.

Lion Charge Miracle. Published by permission of Leon Maré. Copyright © 2012 Leon Maré.

Lion Roar Uproar. Published by permission of Derek Conradie. Copyright © 2011 Derek Conradie. Translated from the Afrikaans by Jeff Gordon.

Lioness Joins the Picnic. Published by permission of Marijke Arends. Copyright © 2011 Marijke Arends.

Lions are Faster than Lawn Mowers & *Scars of a Charge Run Deep*. Published by permission of Dianne Henderson. Copyright © 2012 Dianne Henderson.

Local Butcher Gored By Elephant. Published by permission of John Anslow. Copyright © 2011 John Anslow.

Mauling on the Hillside. Published by permission of Helene von Wielligh. Copyright © 2012 Helene von Wielligh.

Monkey Man and the Skukuza Offensive. Published by permission of Romey Doubell. Copyright © 2011 Romey Doubell.

New Year's Eve Birthday Suit. Published by permission of Glenda Keys. Copyright © 2012 Glenda Keys & Grant Pearson.

Not an Eagle or a Birdie – But a Wild Dog. Published by permission of Andy Crighton. Copyright © 2013 Andy Crighton.

Not Our Morning to be Eaten. Published by permission of John Muirhead. Copyright © 2012 John Muirhead.

Paddling Cubs and the Croc. Published by permission of Stella Stewart. Copyright © 2013 Stella Stewart.

Perils of the Call of Nature. Published by permission of Melissa Grib. Copyright © 2011 Melissa Grib. Translated from the Afrikaans by Jeff Gordon.

Reversing into Camp. Published by permission of Issi Potgieter. Copyright © 2012 Issi Potgieter. Translated from the Afrikaans by Jeff Gordon.

Rocking the Car to Escape the Rhino. Published by permission of Pieter Colyn. Copyright © 2013 Pieter Colyn.

Safari Tent Spitting Games. Published by permission of Philippa Spruyt. Copyright © 2011 Philippa Spruyt.

Skukuza Leopard Kills & *Slapping a Hyaena in the Face* & *Zebra Crossing*. Published by permission of Raymond Hewson. Copyright © 2011 Raymond Hewson.

Spat on from Above. Published by permission of Christa Niederer. Copyright © 2013 Christa Niederer.

Spotting a Different Kind of Mammal. Published by permission of Ian & Melanie Smith. Copyright © 2012 Ian & Melanie Smith.

Teenage Runaways Trek Through the Park & Walking Towards the Lions. Published by permission of Keith Griffiths. Copyright © 2011 Keith Griffiths.

The Biyamiti Stowaway. Published by permission of Gordon Parratt. Copyright © 2011 Gordon Parratt.

The Calculating Leopard. Published by permission of Janet Wills. Copyright © 2011 Janet Wills.

The Crocodile that Stood Up. Published by permission of Piet Grobler. Copyright © 2012 Piet Grobler.

The Elephant and the Drowning Calf. Published by permission of Mariana de Klerk. Copyright © 2013 Mariana de Klerk.

The Giraffe that Committed Suicide. Published by permission of Jeff Gordon. Copyright © 2009 Jeff Gordon.

The Great Ones Do Have Feelings. Published by permission of Richard Browne. Copyright © 2011 Richard Browne.

The Hippo, the Impala and the Natural Order of Things. Published by permission of Sylvester Motaln. Copyright © 2013 Sylvester Motaln.

The Hyaena, the Fence and my Little Boy's Hand. Published by permission of Johan Armstrong. Copyright © 2011 Johan Armstrong.

The King Cheetah. Published by permission of Klaus Kreft. Copyright © 2012 Klaus Kreft.

The Leopard that Killed the Cheetah that Killed the Impala. Published by permission of Brian Gardiner. Copyright © 2011 Brian Gardiner.

The Lioness that Opened the Door. Published by permission of Theuns & Elzet Hurter. Copyright © 2011 Theuns & Elzet Hurter.

The Newly Deputised Officials. Published by permission of Beukes Geldenhuys. Copyright © 2011 Beukes Geldenhuys.

The Nhlanganini Baby Snatcher. Published by permission of Johann Fankhauser. Copyright © 2011 Johann Fankhauser.

The Other Kruger Millions. Published by permission of Louis von Broembsen. Copyright © 2011 Louis von Broembsen.

The Rarest Kruger Predator. Published by permission of Ron van Rooyen. Copyright © 2011 Ron van Rooyen.

The Shocking Death of a Leopard. Published by permission Nigel Aitken. Copyright © 2008 Nigel Aitken.

The Strange Tale of the Dog in the Night. Published by permission of Jacky Le Roux. Copyright © 2011 Jacky Le Roux.

There's a Lion Outside our Tent. Published by permission of Colin Lagerwall. Copyright © 2012 Colin & Fay Lagerwall.

Tidal Wave of Elephants. Published by permission of Lourens Durand. Copyright © 2013 Lourens Durand.

Too Busy Fiddling to Notice. Published by permission of Alma Sparrius. Copyright © 2012 Alma Sparrius.

Water! Published by permission of Trevor Lagerwall. Copyright © 2012 Trevor Lagerwall.

Wrong Place, Wrong Time, on a Rhino's Turf. Published by permission of Angie Shackleford. Copyright © 2013 Angie Shackleford.

Yes, All Cars Have Coils. Published by permission of Winston Floquet. Copyright © 2012 Winston Floquet.

PICTURE CREDITS

I AM GRATEFUL to the following individuals for providing photographs and video stills (including video for the purpose of stills) to accompany the stories, as well as to the publications that kindly granted permission for the newspaper clippings to be used. While every effort has been made to trace and acknowledge all copyright holders, I would like to apologise for any errors or omissions and would be grateful to be notified of any corrections.

A Bite at Berg-en-Dal. Photographs copyright © Rene Wolfaardt & Monique Harmse.

A Hissing in the Engine. Photographs copyright © Marlene Swart. Video stills by kind permission of John Baldwin. Video copyright © John Baldwin.

A Kill From Our Veranda. Photographs of kill copyright © Mario Fazekas. Photograph of rondavel copyright © Marijke Arends.

A Short Stroll Through Lion Country. Photograph by kind permission of Esther Erasmus. Photograph copyright © Esther Erasmus.

A Small Knife and a Big Dilemma. Photograph copyright © Henk Maree. Photograph of impalas copyright © Jeff Gordon.

An Unusual Sighting Downstream. Photographs copyright © Arshad Bhamjee.

And the Leopard Will Lie Down With the Kid. Photographs copyright © Anton Kruger.

Angry Elephant's Road Rage Rampage. Photograph copyright © Sander Hofman. Video stills by kind permission of Sander Hofman. Video copyright © Sander Hofman.

At the Mercy of the Rising Timbavati. Photographs copyright © Shireen Anne Vlaming & Marion Vlaming.

Battle at Kruger. Video stills by kind permission of David & Cheryl Budzinski. Video copyright © David Budzinski.

Battle Before the Gates of Skukuza. Photographs copyright © Kerri Bowie. Photograph of Skukuza gate by User:Ataileopard/Wikimedia Commons/ Public Domain.

Black Mamba and the Crocodiles. Video stills by kind permission of Giosue Spinosa & Kerstin Stöwahse/Image and Sound. Video copyright © Giosue Spinosa & Kerstin Stöwahse/Image and Sound.

Black Mamba Hitches a Ride. Photographs copyright © Neil Taylor.

Bumbling Lions in the Jackalberry Tree. Photographs copyright © Steve Farrell.

Dog Day Morning. Photographs copyright © André Liénard.

How the Elephant got its Trunk. Photograph copyright © Johan Opperman.

Impala in the Mud. Photographs copyright © Wendy Abadi.

Leopard Raids the Braai. Newspaper clipping reproduced with kind permission of Lowveld Media. Original photograph copyright © Susan van Huyssteen. Photograph of Afsaal by kind permission of Grant Nicol. Photograph of Afsaal copyright © Grant Nicol.

Leopard Versus Crocodile. Photographs copyright © Hal Brindley (www. halbrindley.com)

Lion Charge Miracle. Photographs & video stills copyright © Leon Maré.

Mauling on the Hillside. Photograph of lion on hillside copyright © Helene von Wiclligh. Photographs of injured guide and his wounds by kind permission of Rudi Lorist and thanks to www.krugerpark.co.za and Siyabona Africa. Photographer unknown.

One Wild Morning in Lower Sabie. Video stills by kind permission of Penny Legg. Video copyright © Penny Legg. Photograph of Lower Sabie gate copyright © Jeff Gordon.

Paddling Cubs and the Croc. Photographs copyright © Stella Stewart.

The Biyamiti Stowaway. Photograph copyright © Gordon Parratt. Newspaper clipping reproduced with kind permission of Pretoria News.

The Calculating Leopard. Photographs copyright © Chris Wills.

The Crocodile that Stood Up. Photographs copyright © Piet Grobler.

The Elephant and the Drowning Calf. Video stills by kind permission of Mariana de Klerk. Video copyright © Mariana de Klerk.

The Hippo, the Impala and the Natural Order of Things. Photographs copyright © Sylvester Motaln.

The Hyaena, the Fence and my Little Boy's Hand. Photographs copyright © Riki Armstrong. Photograph of father holding son reproduced with kind permission of Phalaborwa Herald. Photographs of hyaena and Balule fence copyright © Jeff Gordon.

The King Cheetah. Video stills copyright © Klaus Kreft.

The Leopard that Killed the Cheetah that Killed the Impala. Photograph by kind permission of John Griffin. Photograph copyright © John Griffin.

The Lioness that Opened the Door. Video stills copyright © Theuns Hurter.

The Shocking Death of a Leopard. Photographs of leopard thanks to www.krugerpark.co.za and Siyabona Africa. Photographs copyright © Nigel Aitken. Photograph of Lower Sabie gate copyright © Jeff Gordon.

Wrong Place, Wrong Time, on a Rhino's Turf. Newspaper clipping reproduced with kind permission of The Star.

Yes, All Cars Have Coils. Photographs copyright © Winston Floquet.